IMAGES
of America

SEAFORD
DELAWARE

IMAGES
of America

SEAFORD
DELAWARE

Shannon Willey

ARCADIA
PUBLISHING

ISBN 978-0-7385-0207-6

Published by Arcadia Publishing
Charleston, South Carolina

Printed in the United States of America

Library of Congress Catalog Card Number: 99-64821

For all general information contact Arcadia Publishing at:
Telephone 843-853-2070
Fax 843-853-0044
E-Mail sales@arcadiapublishing.com
For customer service and orders:
Toll-Free 1-888-313-2665

Visit us on the Internet at www.arcadiapublishing.com

This book contains information based on the memories of local historian Wright Robinson, and was produced by a partnership of Seaford Main Street, the City of Seaford, and the Seaford Museum under the direction of Shannon Willey.

Contents

Acknowledgments

Without the help of many individuals, organizations, and companies, the making of this book would not have been possible. I would like to thank all of the following for their contributions and assistance (and patience): Charles Allen, John Allen, Karen Bongard, the City of Seaford, Dick Collison, DuPont, the Greater Seaford Chamber of Commerce, Jack Knowles, Mike Lambert, Chip Lank, Joe Lynch, Joel Marvel, Ron Marvel, Diane McDonnell & the Seaford Library, Claudia Melson, Bob Palmer, the Portrait Shoppe, Wright Robinson, Will Rogers, Bill Royal, George H. Sapna II, Judy Schwartz, Robert J. Scott, Seaford Main Street, the Seaford Museum, Ross Smith, Sally Stewart, Cecil Tull, Earle Tull, and Dave Webb.

I would like to single out two of the individuals listed above that were absolutely critical to the production of this book: Bob Palmer and Wright Robinson. To both of them, I owe a huge thank you, and to Wright Robinson, the man who brought many of the pictures to life, I dedicate this book.

—Shannon Willey

Introduction

The Leni-Lenape Indians called the future Seaford area home in the 1600s, hunting and fishing a land rich in resources and eventually introducing the first European settlers to the bountiful region. According to Captain John Smith's report from 1607, the new settlers found the native people to be quite civilized and adept at trading. The area was vacated by the Nanticokes in 1698, when a reservation was established for them in Vienna, Maryland.

The first legal document referencing Seaford dates to 1726 and was recorded in the county seat of Georgetown. The land was deeded to one Thomas Hooper, and was probably owned by the Hooper family some 20 years prior to that documentation of ownership, but Thomas Hooper is often called the "first citizen of Seaford." His seven children also settled here, beginning the growth that would result in an established town by 1835.

There were other notable figures who molded the little town that grew. William Neal, an immigrant from Seaford's possible namesake in England, plotted several lots for a Mr. William Conwell in the year of 1815, and also settled in town. Meanwhile, Mr. Henry Adams opened the first successful store on the corner of Front and Water Streets, which was run by Levin Cannon after Adams's death. Captain Solomon Boston spent much of the year sailing the Atlantic coast and conducted extensive trade in the coastal towns. Sailing up the Nanticoke to winter inland, Solomon discovered Seaford and soon purchased several properties in the area. By 1809, he purchased 16 additional lots, adding another block to the growing town. The town began to attract stores, hotels, and medical practices, in addition to businesses ranging from leather tanning to the manufacturing of pig iron, and from shoemaking to carriage building. It also attracted people of faith.

The earliest reference to a church occurred in 1633 as a chapel branch of St. Luke's Episcopal Church, which moved to Seaford in 1818. St. John's Methodist Episcopal Church, originally called the Bochim Meeting House, was organized about 1780. In 1818, a deed was signed and a structure erected for worship. Mount Olivet Methodist Church was established later in 1830, and in 1850, the first church was built on present Olivet land. Today there are well over 20 churches within the Seaford school district, which includes the incorporated town limits and the outlying areas not yet annexed by the City.

In 1826, Seaford got its first post office, which was run by its first postmaster, Jeremiah McNeely. In 1832, the Seaford Bridge Company, owned by Captain Hugh Martin, built a wooden toll bridge that became public property in 1865.

In 1840, Seaford became home to William Henry Harrison Ross, a future Delaware governor whose family had settled here by 1730. His Italianate home, built in 1859 and maintained today by the Seaford Historical Society, was at the center of a huge agricultural plantation, and Ross introduced many of the cutting edge farming techniques of that time. Competitors shipping fresh produce to metropolitan areas like Philadelphia caused Ross to fight for a railroad station and line he could use to beat the competition to market. In 1856, the Delaware Railroad, operated by the Pennsylvania Railroad, completed the line from Wilmington to Seaford and was nicknamed the "Ole Dorchester Line." With rail and river transportation readily available, both the seafood packing and produce businesses exploded, and launched Seaford as a primary shipping center for the Eastern Shore.

In 1860, the Civil War came to Seaford, and the town, like the state of Delaware itself, was split over the slavery issue. The war necessitated the first bank in town, which assisted businesses on a short term basis until it was incorporated as the Seaford Bank early in 1861. The act was repealed almost one year later, and the First National Bank of Seaford was organized in February of 1865. Two months later, the town became incorporated and a general survey taken by James Stuart. A Councilman/Alderman form of government was adopted at that time, with Alfred Cottingham, Alfred Williams, Benjamin Stockly, Henry S. Hopkins, John Conaway, and John K. Brown acting as the first city council. Their first action taken was to levy a property tax, which provided money for the grading of High Street and the erection of the Seaford Town Hall in 1873. Taxes also supplied the financing of brick sidewalks, as well as 24 oil lamps lit nightly by the town bailiff.

In 1894, a $20,000 bond issue provided the installation of a water pumping system, and the following year Seaford received electric service. By 1901, electricity was provided by the town power plant, but the Sussex Power & Light Company received the franchise for Seaford electric service the following year, at which time electric street lamps were installed. West Seaford was annexed to the city. In 1902, the Acorn Club started a public library. By this time, Seaford was a town of 2,000 people, and, in the next decade, the poultry industry became a rising star in the firmament of economic growth as new housing and feeding techniques were introduced. Crops shifted from truck produce to grains and corn used for chicken feed.

Seaford's first volunteer fire department was organized in 1901, and a Seagrave fire engine and other equipment were purchased by 1921. In 1923, Samuel Stein recognized the need for a road from Seaford running west to Reliance. He obtained a free right of way for the road, and the State built Stein Highway, named in honor or Mr. Stein. By 1932, Seaford had more paved roads than any other town in Sussex County.

In 1939, the "Town of Seaford" became the "City of Seaford" and was governed by a city manager, with a mayor and council.

Of even greater economic and growth impact than the railroad was the decision by E.I. duPont de Nemours & Co. Inc. to purchase 340 acres of land for a textile plant in 1939. It was the first nylon plant in the world. Seaford experienced another population explosion, and set to building new housing, while expanding town limits.

DuPont produced a great deal of nylon for use by the allied forces during World War II and introduced a new product called Dacron in the 1950s. The plant directly and indirectly influenced town growth, wealth, and convenience. Seaford today is the largest city in Sussex County, with a population of just more than 6,000, and is a major shopping destination for the area. It continues to grow in the areas of industry, recreation, tourism, and historic preservation while retaining small town intimacy and charm. It is a community reaffirming its past along with its abundant resources, while it commits to an equally bright future. Explore the spirit of what was and is the community of Seaford, Delaware.

—Karen Bongard

One

Industry & Agriculture

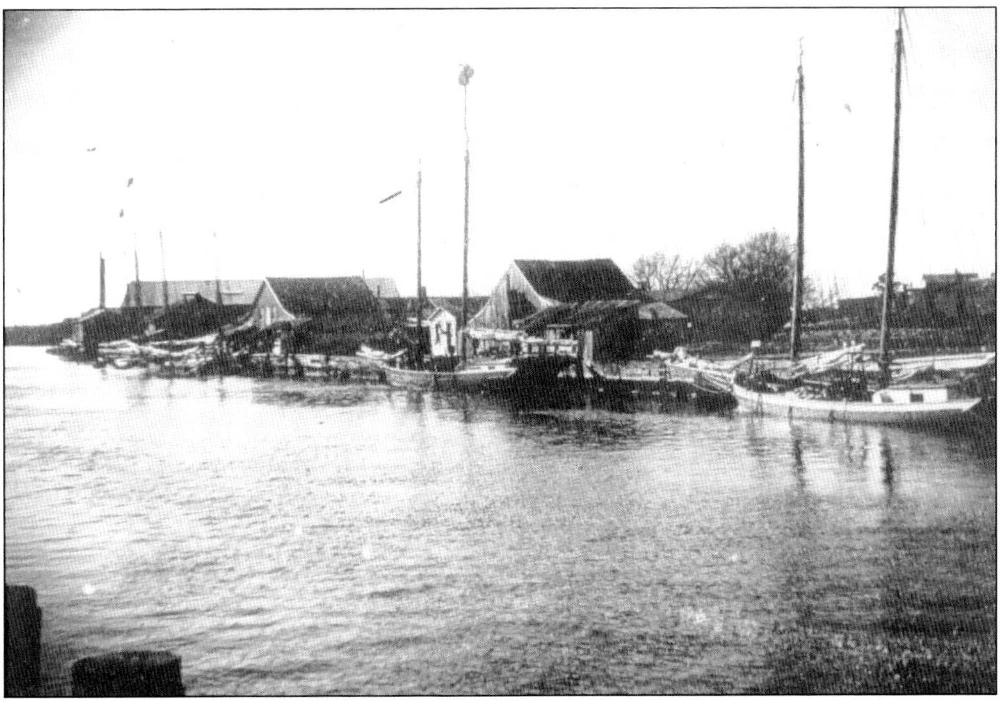

The Nanticoke River enabled a number of businesses to flourish in Seaford. Among them were oyster houses, canneries, and boat yards. This picture, taken from the railroad bridge looking west, shows the oyster houses that dotted the shores of the river in the late years of the nineteenth century and early years of the twentieth.

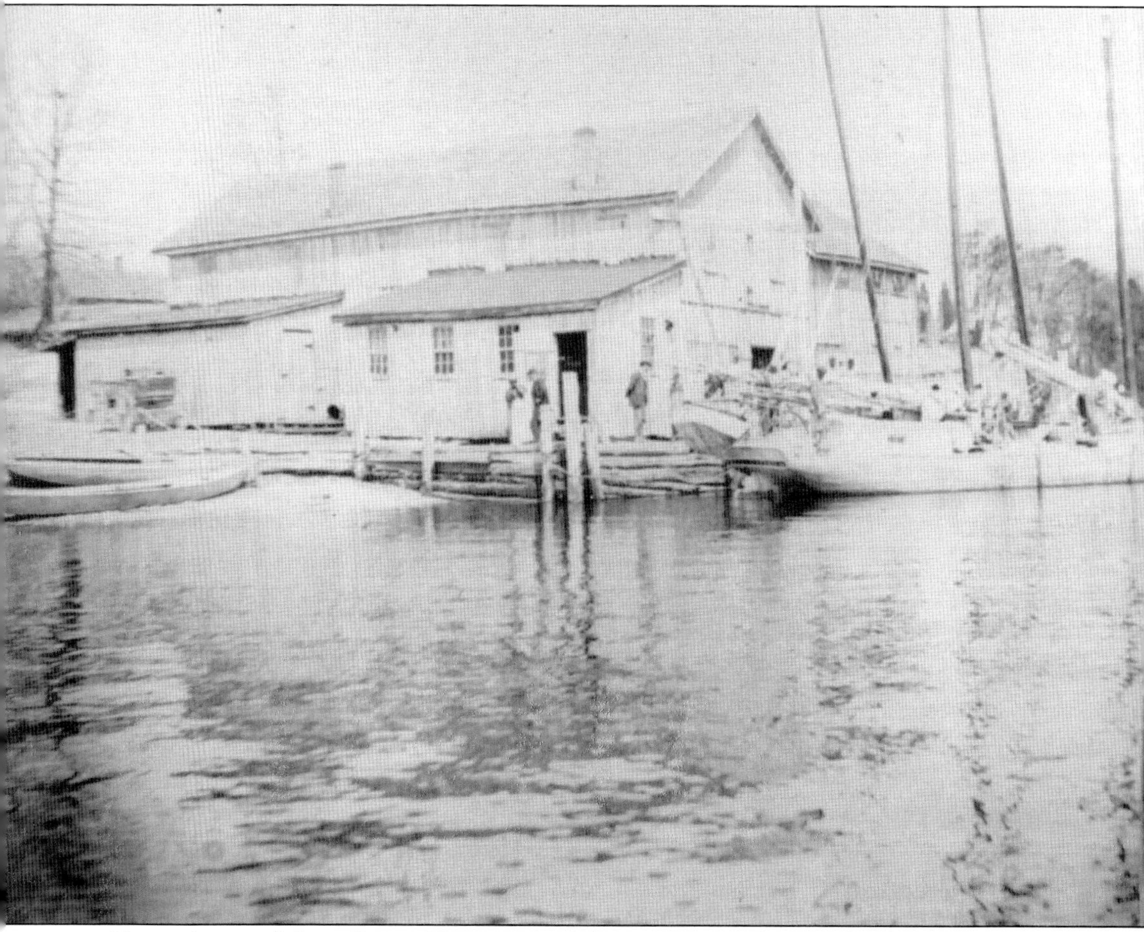

Shown here is Adams Oyster House, one of the many oyster houses that lined the Nanticoke River in the late nineteenth century. Typically, boats like the one in the picture would bring up oysters from the Chesapeake Bay. The oysters were then hauled into the Oyster House where they were opened. Afterwards, the shelled oysters were sent by freight to Metropolitan markets in the east.

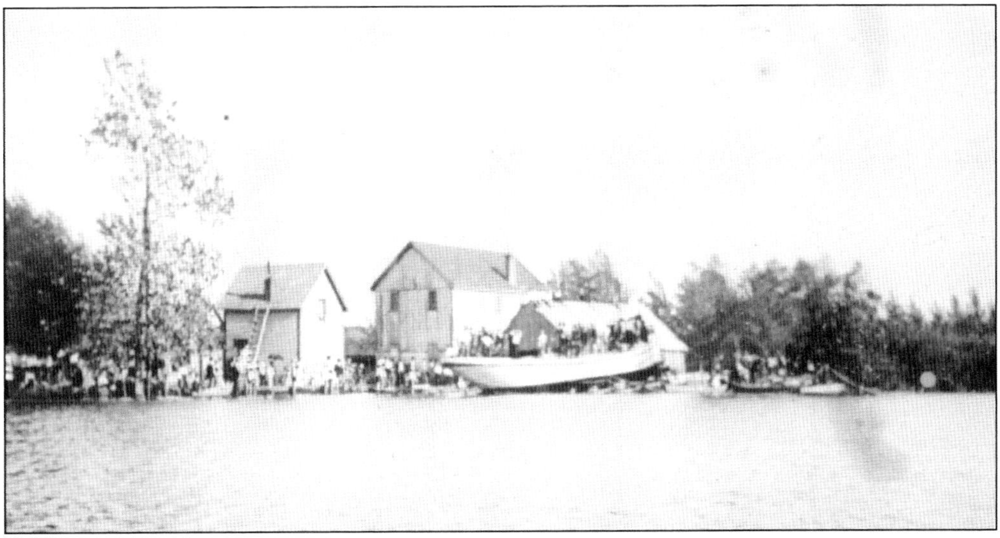

This picture shows the launching of the Riggin from an old boat yard that stood at the foot of South Cannon Street. The boat yard, although not very big, repaired and even built small motor craft.

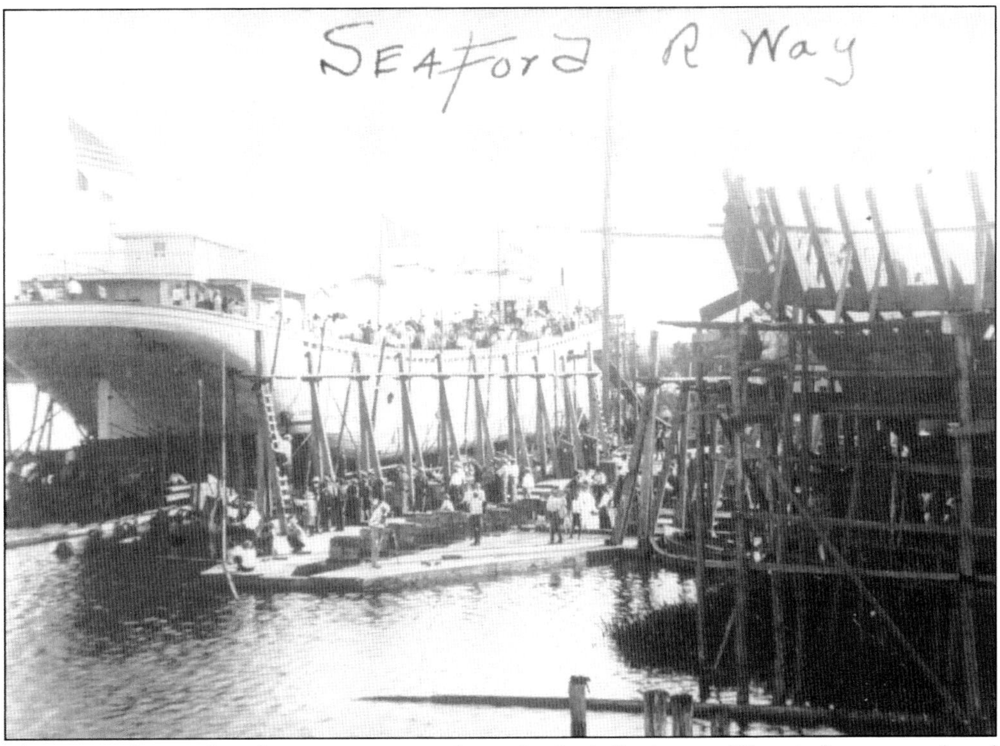

This is a large ship being constructed at Seaford Railways. The industry employed approximately 30 to 40 men and created three masted vessels that sailed all over the world. The shipyard was operated by Captain A.P. Vane during WW II, when it revived itself under the ownership of Captain John Smith. During the War, craft for the navy were built here, and after the war ended, so did the shipyard. By 1939, what had been one of Seaford's biggest industries was dead.

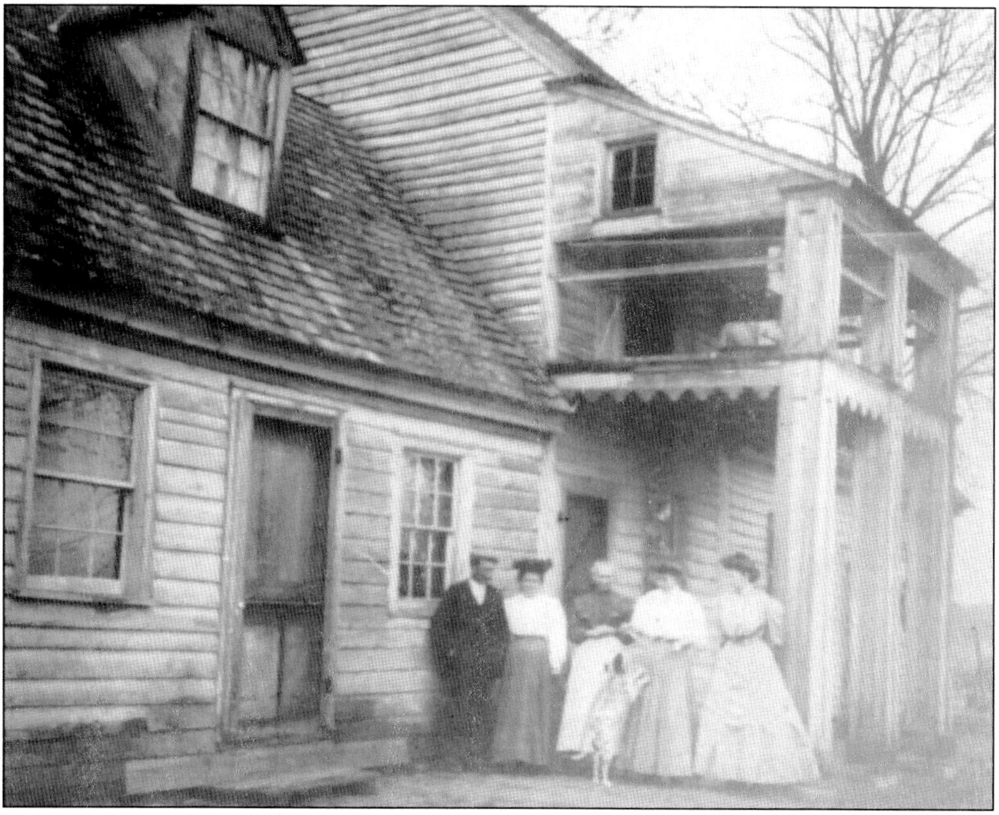

Seaford was a community that relied heavily on farming. Shown in this picture is a typical farm house that stood over one hundred years ago.

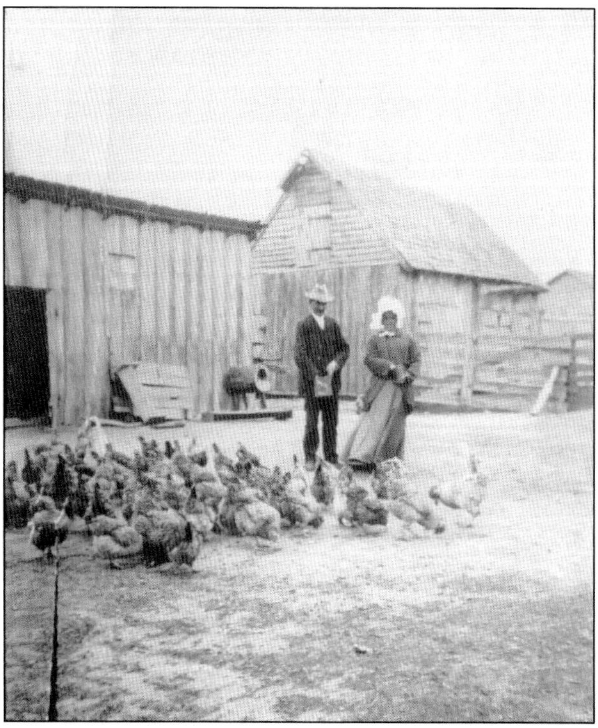

This picture was taken on one of Seaford's early farms. The people shown are feeding a flock of chickens.

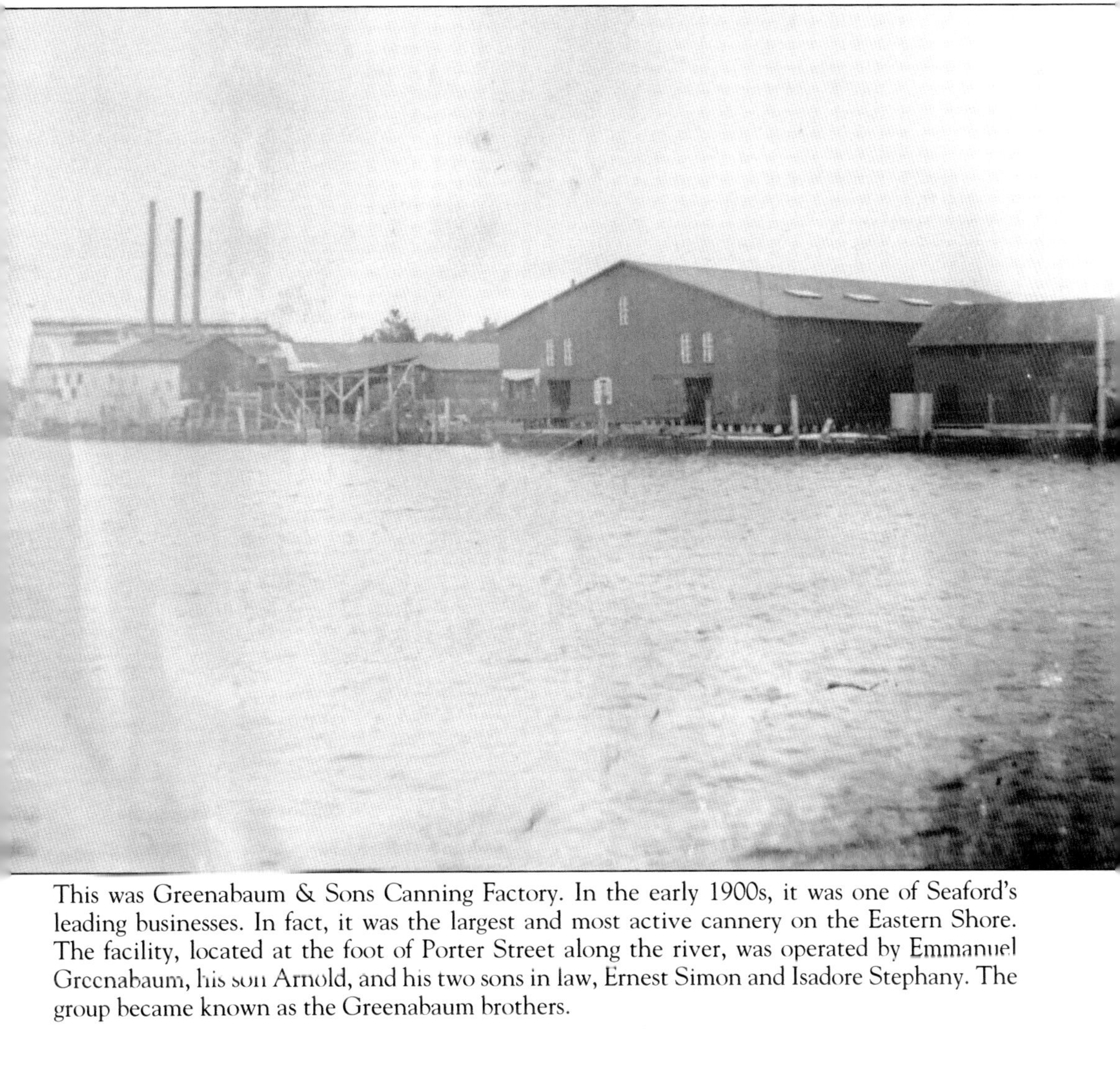

This was Greenabaum & Sons Canning Factory. In the early 1900s, it was one of Seaford's leading businesses. In fact, it was the largest and most active cannery on the Eastern Shore. The facility, located at the foot of Porter Street along the river, was operated by Emmanuel Greenabaum, his son Arnold, and his two sons in law, Ernest Simon and Isadore Stephany. The group became known as the Greenabaum brothers.

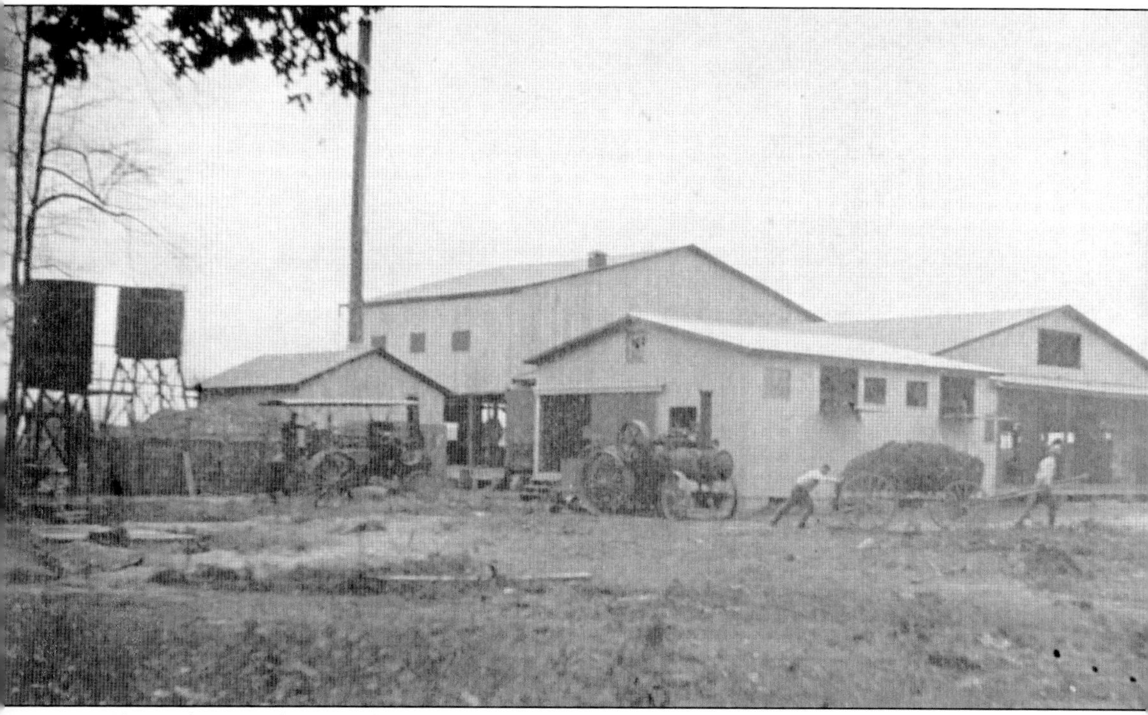

Shown here is what was the Ross Cannery. It was just west of the Greenabaum Cannery. It was not quite as big as the Greenabaum operation, but it employed many people year round and did quite a business during the canning seasons in the summer in the late nineteenth century.

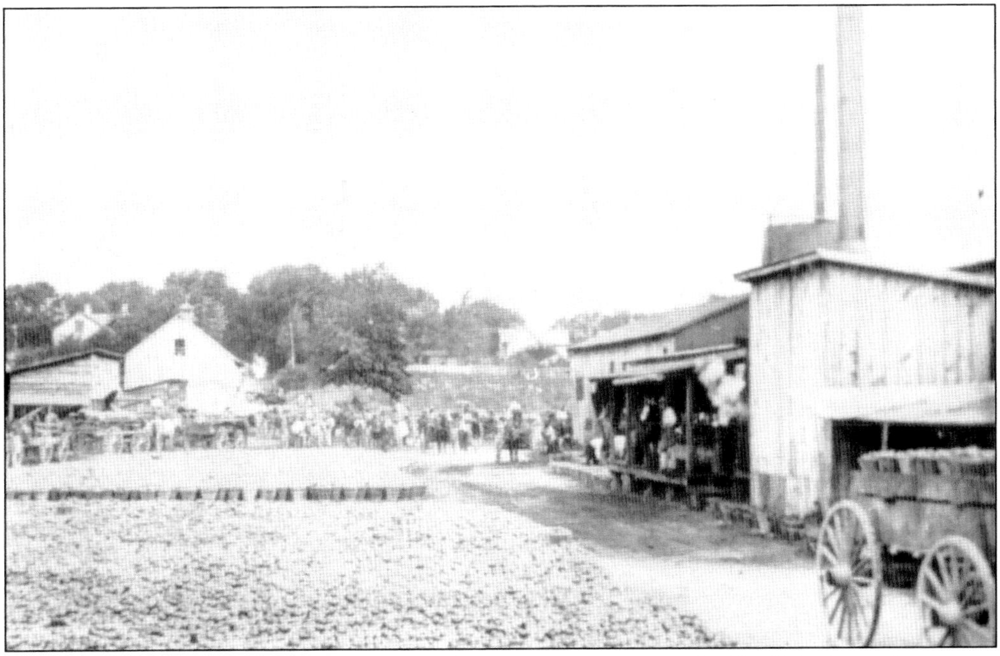

This photo shows Greenabaum's Cannery during tomato season. The 7,000 baskets of tomatoes on the yard of the factory (not an uncommon sight) were waiting to be processed into Sundale (the brand name) Ketchup and Chili sauce.

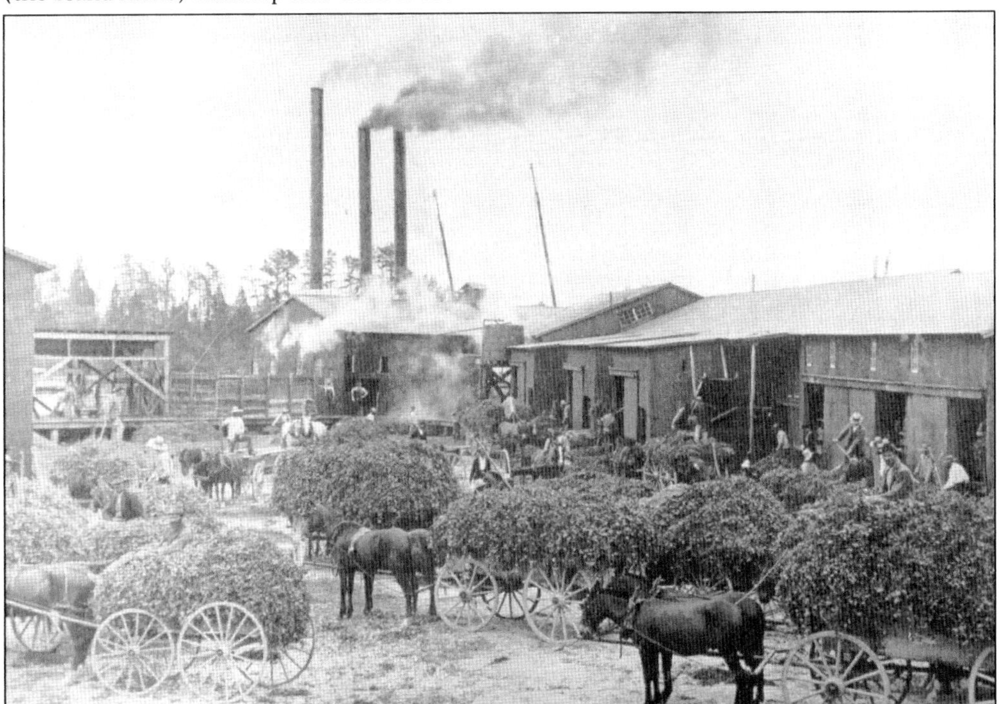

This is another photograph taken at Greenabaum's Cannery. This one was taken during the pea canning season. The many cartloads of peas were waiting to be taken in and canned. At one time, Greenabaum's was the largest pea cannery in the United States.

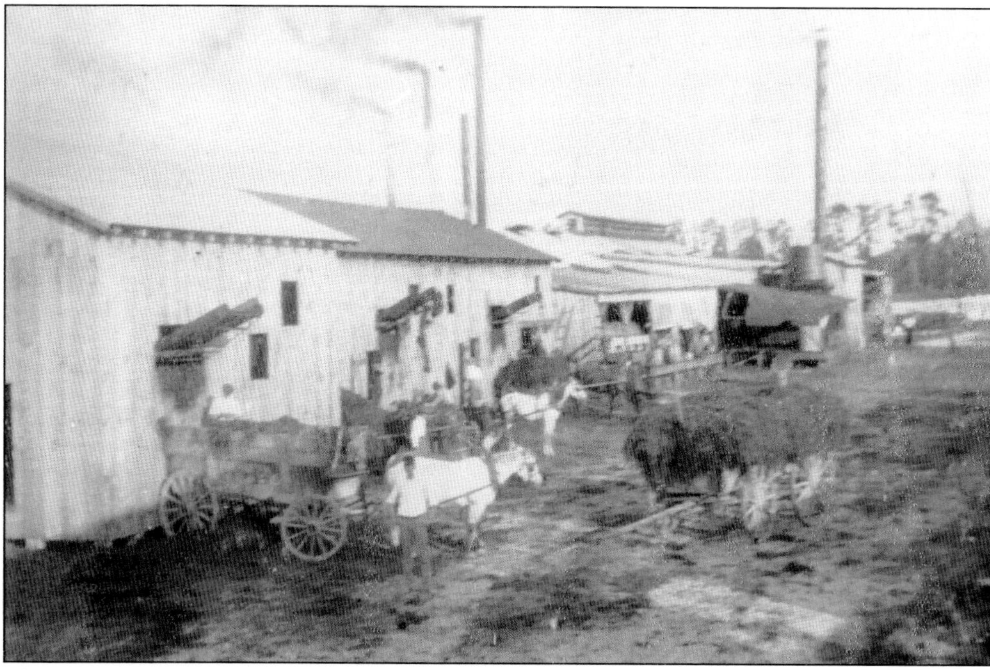

These cartloads of produce are being hauled by farmers to Ross's Cannery (a common sight in Seaford during this time).

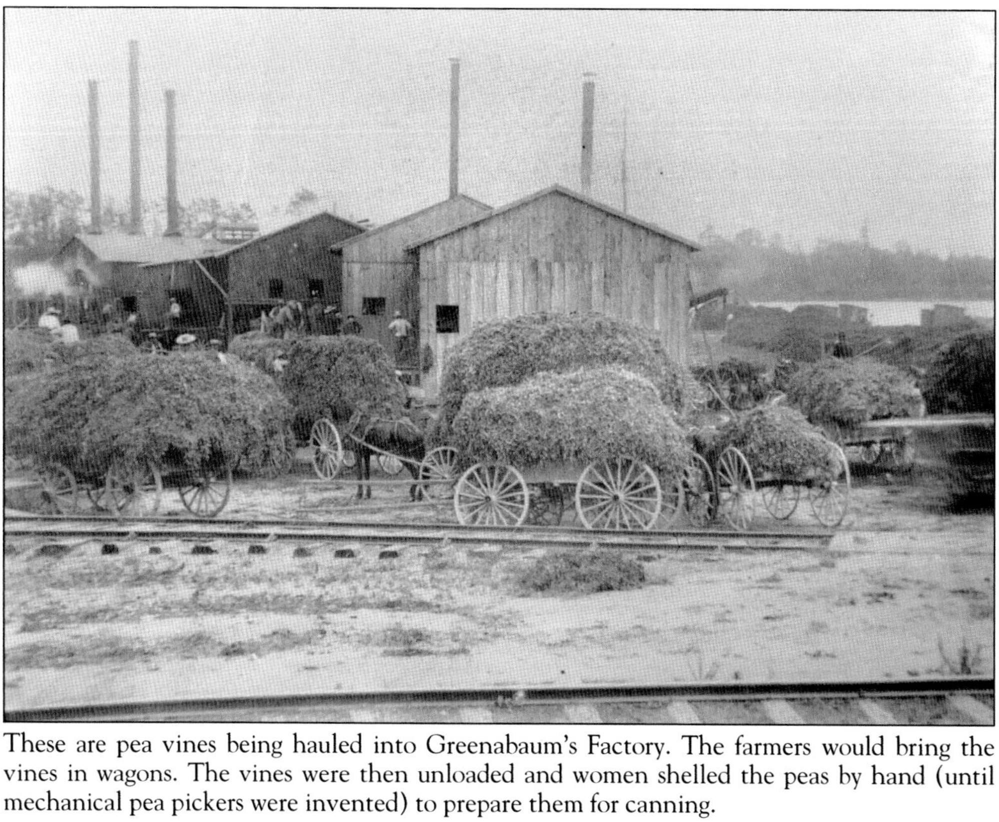

These are pea vines being hauled into Greenabaum's Factory. The farmers would bring the vines in wagons. The vines were then unloaded and women shelled the peas by hand (until mechanical pea pickers were invented) to prepare them for canning.

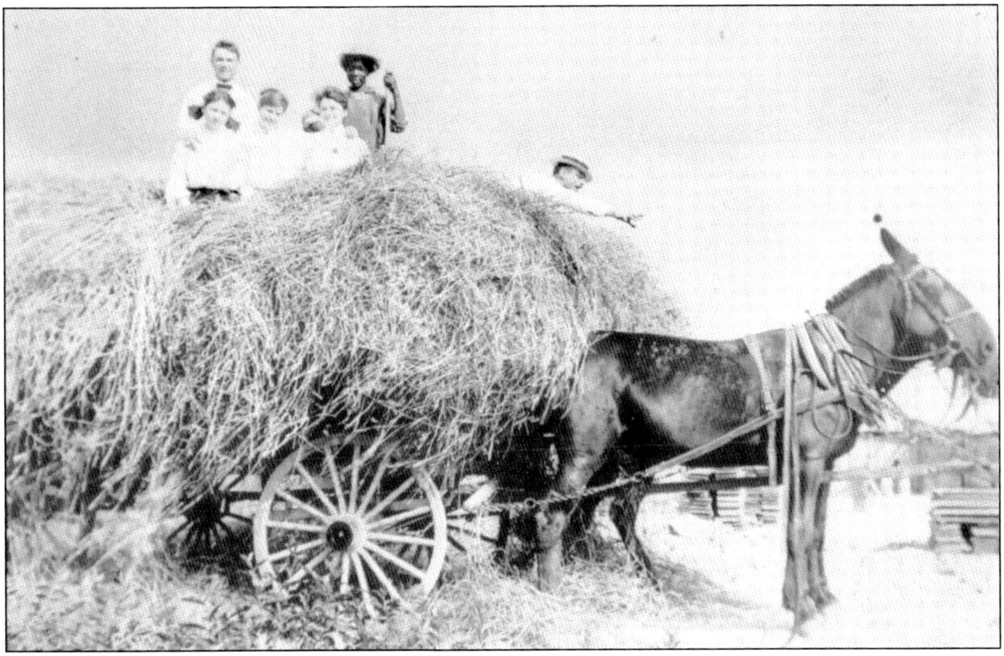

This is a close-up view of one of the wagons bringing pea vines into town. The wagons would bring produce not only to the canneries, but to the railroad station for sale. Notice the entire family riding on the wagon for the trip into town.

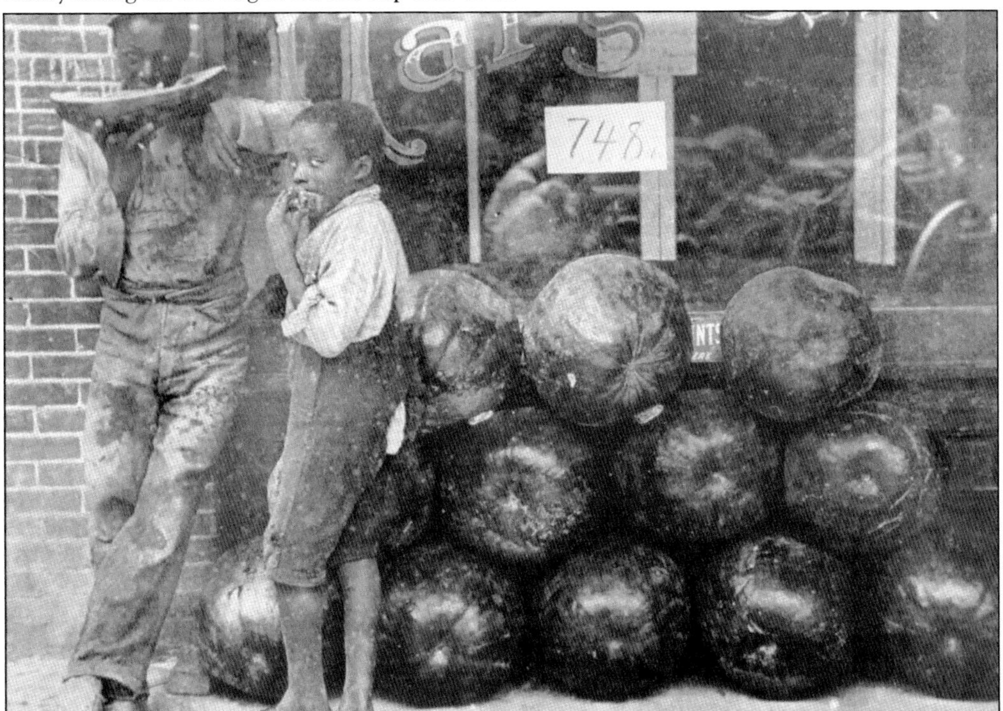

Peas were not the only popular crop in Seaford. Shown here are two gentlemen enjoying fresh watermelons.

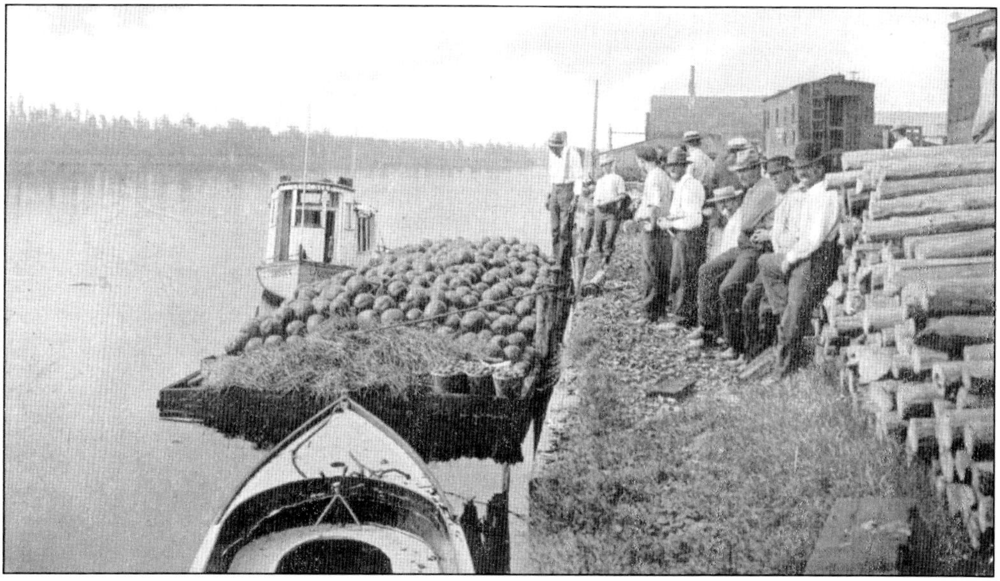

This picture shows watermelons that have been floated up the Nanticoke River to be sold to fruit brokers that assembled at the railroad station. Here, farmers' commodities would be purchased for reshipment to larger cities. Watermelons were actually an unusual crop to be coming up by water, as most farmers brought the produce by wagons and, later, by trucks.

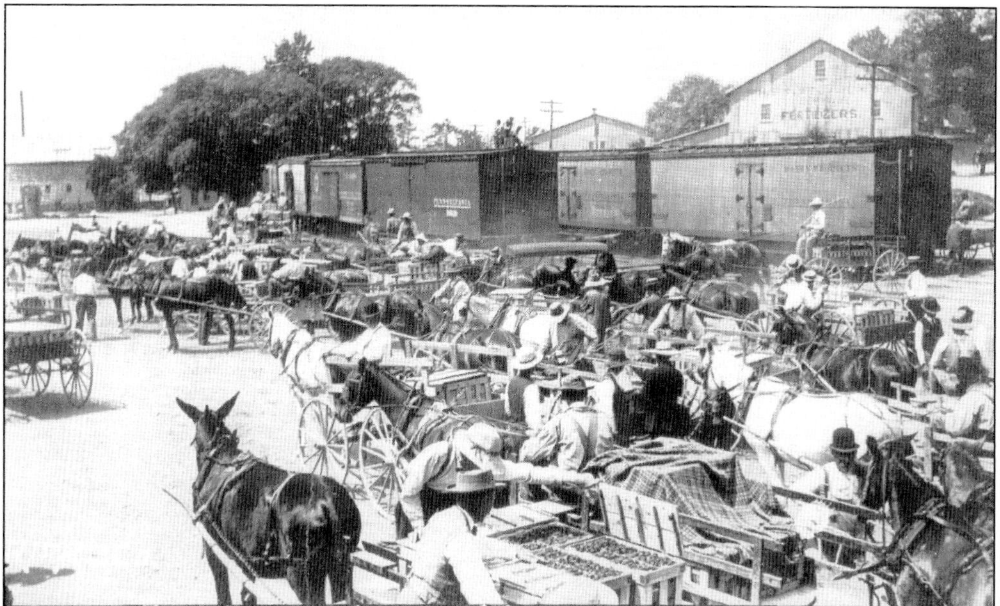

This picture, taken between 1905 and 1915, shows the farmers bringing their produce into town. They would pull cartloads of asparagus, cantaloupe, watermelons, cucumbers, and strawberries into town and place them on view for produce brokers. Once sold, the produce would be placed in refrigerated freight cars, like the ones shown, and shipped to the New York and New England markets. The building in the background of the picture was a fertilizer company owned by Houston Culver and Company, whose partners also served as produce brokers.

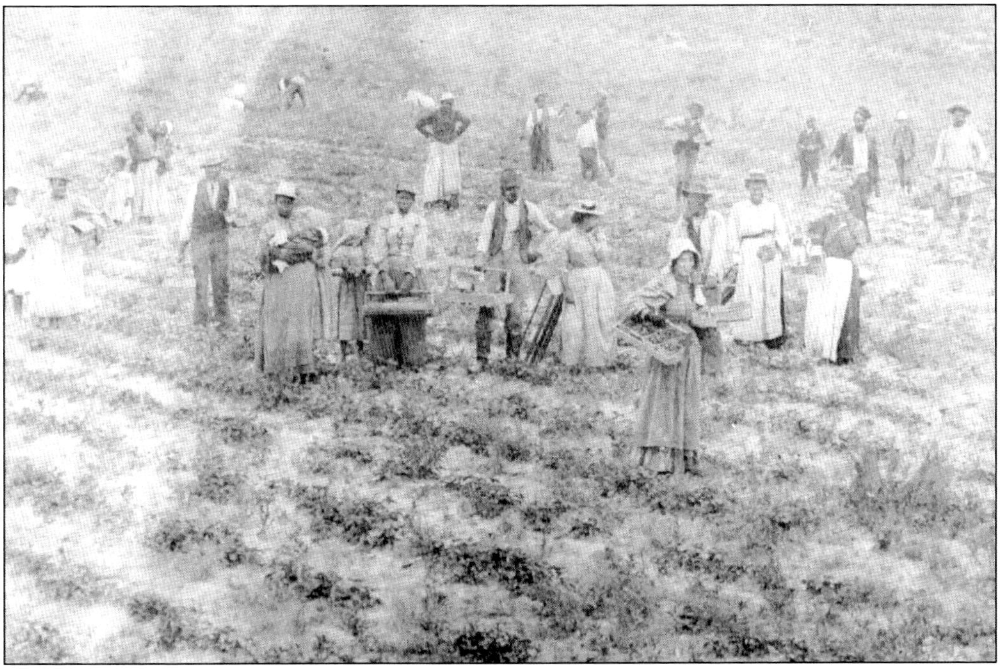

Strawberry pickers can be seen in this picture. This was a big thing in Seaford. Children would pick strawberries before school, get strawberry checks for what they had picked, and on Saturday, they would turn the checks in and get paid. The strawberries, like most of the crops in Seaford, were then sent into town for shipment to other markets.

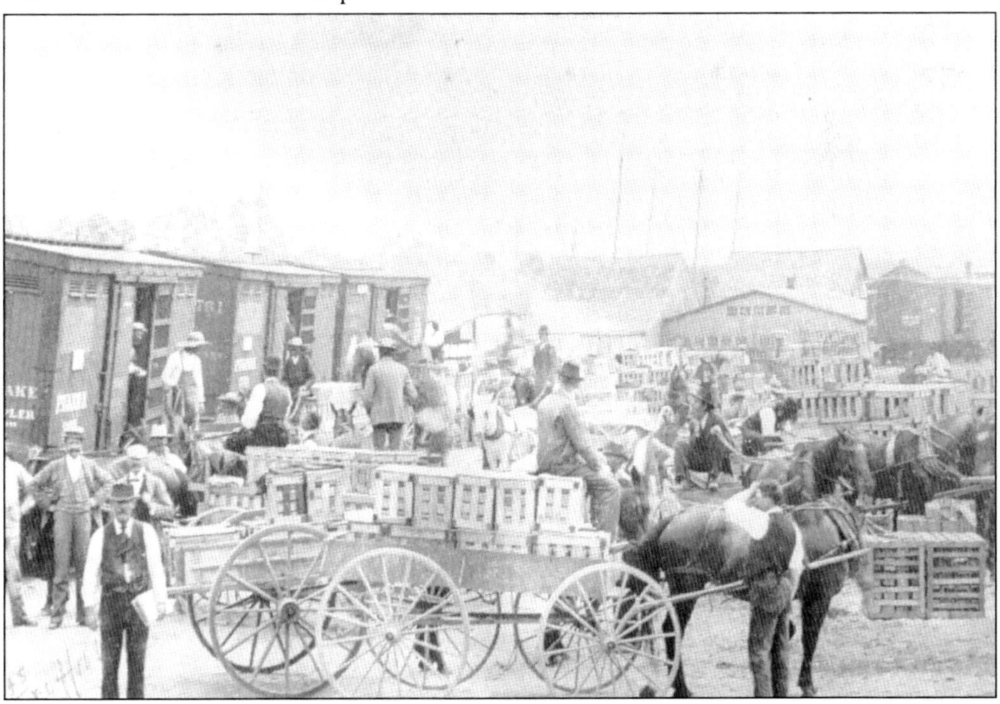

This view is of strawberries loaded in carts at the railroad yard. They are being loaded onto refrigerated cars for shipment to Metropolitan markets.

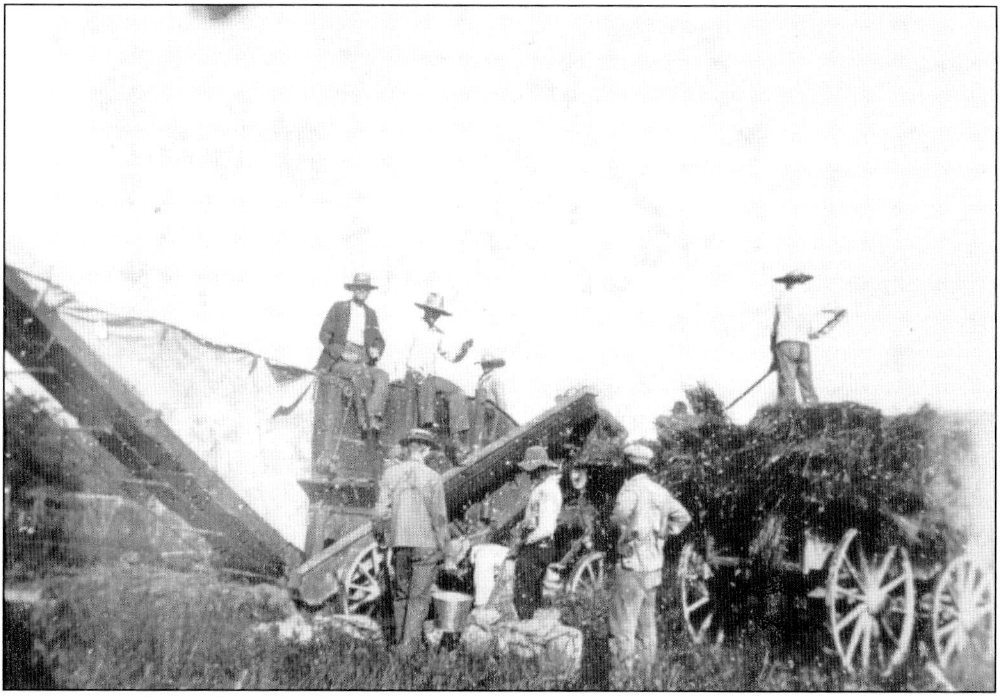

This picture shows wheat threshing. The threshing was both a big social and work event in the late summer and early fall in Seaford.

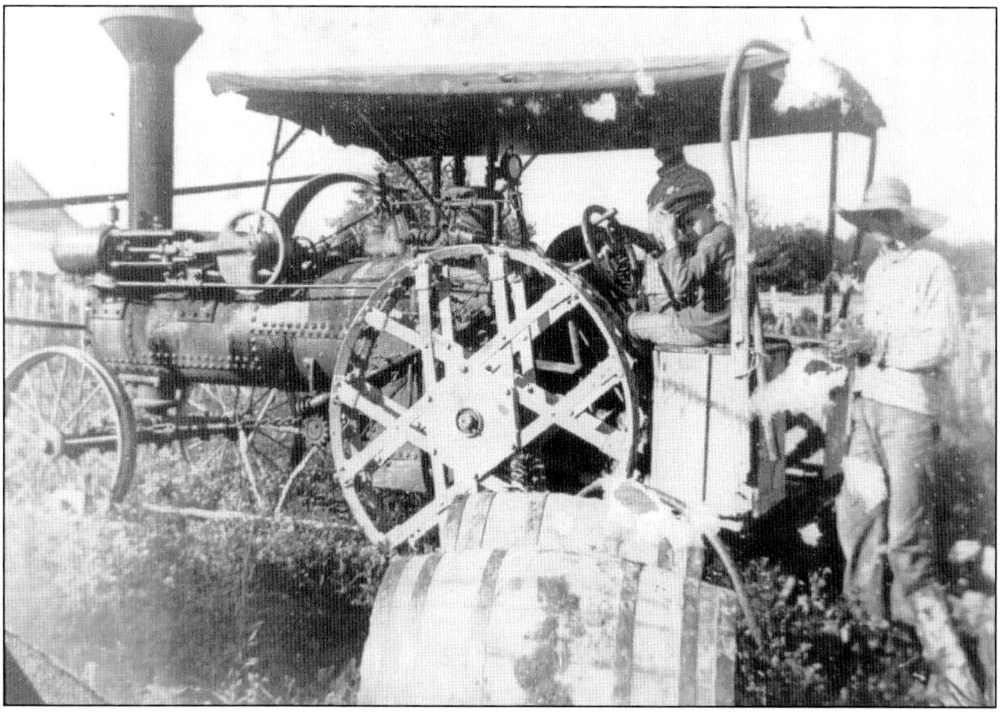

This is one of the old steam engines that was used in the wheat threshing operation in Seaford. This particular engine would move from farm to farm.

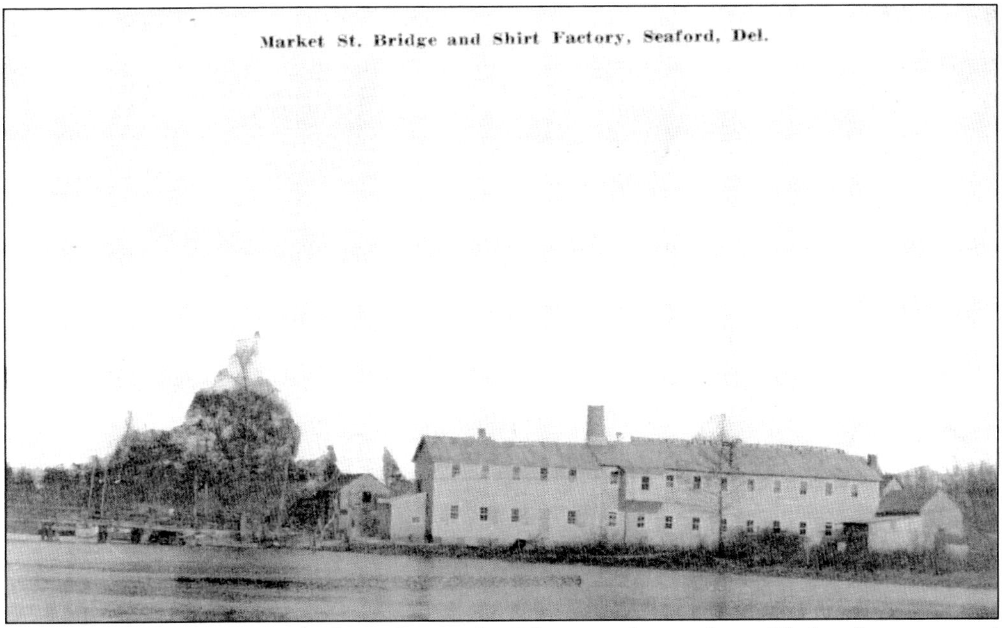

This old shirt factory stood where Peninsula Oil currently stands in Blades. It was owned by L.C. Longfellow. Lightning struck the building around 1914, however, and it burned to the ground. Mr. Longfellow later built a shirt factory on Water Street that was eventually converted into a cash only store, which became one of the county's largest retail operations. After Mr. Longfellow's death, Mr. Wright Robinson bought the building and ran his editorial offices out of it.

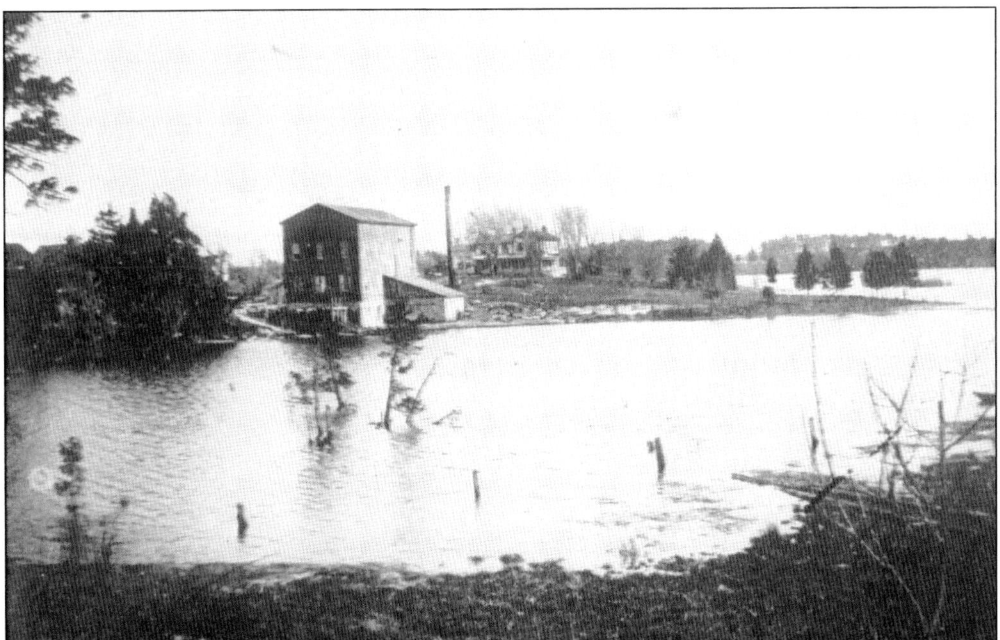

This old mill stood where the Nanticoke Memorial Hospital's parking lot stands currently. Spencer Decates owned the pond rights to the mill. It went out of business, however, before the hospital was built.

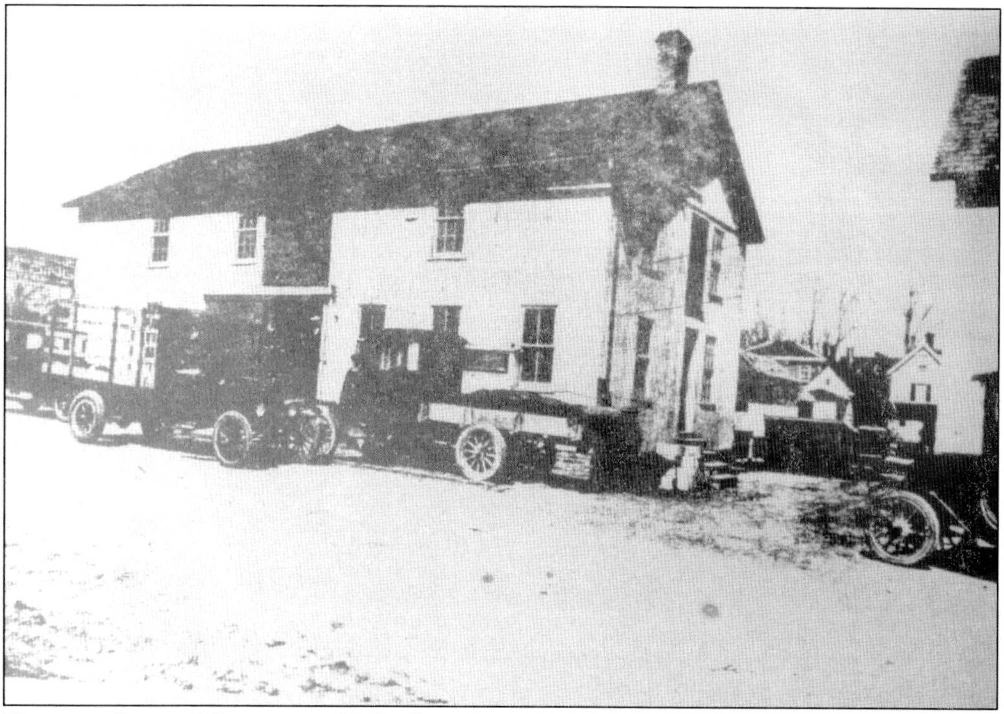

This is a photo of Hastings and Eskridge Company, a prominent business in Seaford at one time. This lumber yard was located where the Seaford Museum now stands on New Street. The building shown in this picture burned in the late 1930s, and was replaced with a new building.

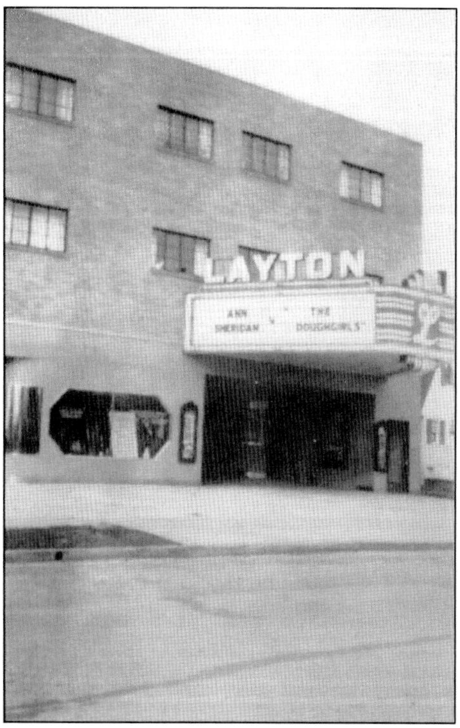

This is a picture of the Layton Theater, named in honor of the owner, Layton Ayers. The single screen, newly constructed, 1,000-square-foot theater opened in March of 1941. Movies around that time were approximately 50¢ for adults, 35¢ for students, and 15¢ for children.

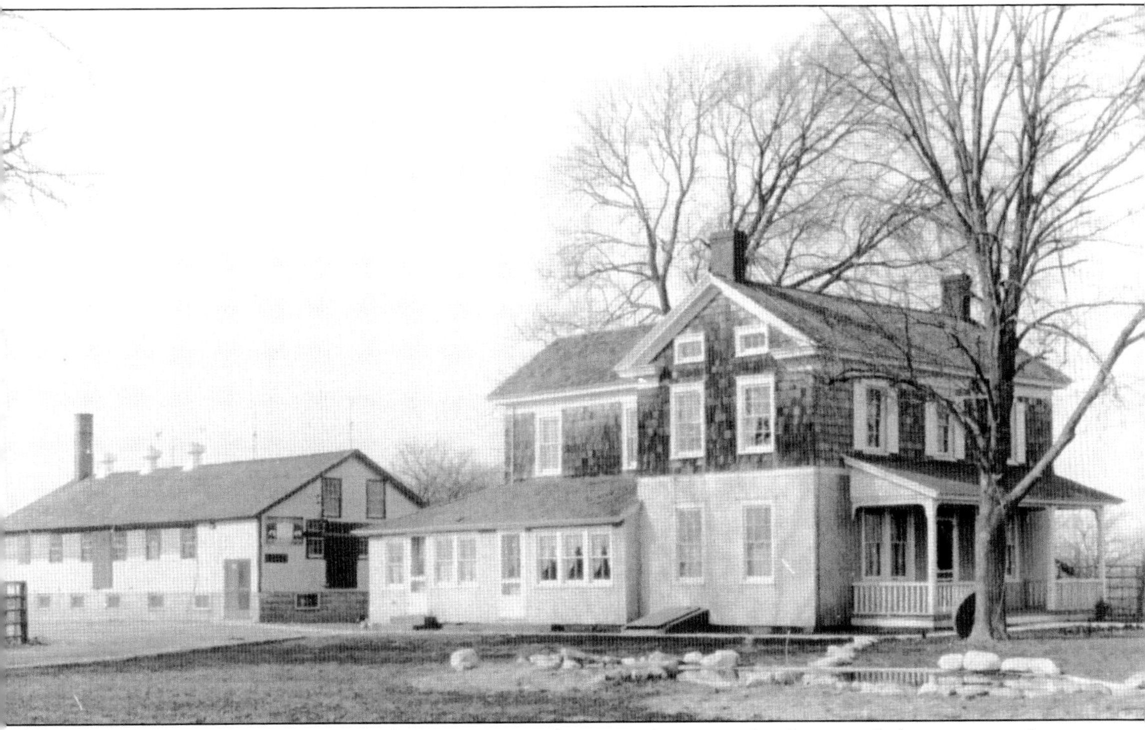

In 1919, Allen's Hatchery was begun. Shown here is what was the home of the company's founders. The original farm house was actually located off of Atlanta Road, but the Allens moved into town, to this house, around 1923 because the town had electricity. The home now serves as the Executive Offices, and the building in the back still serves as a hatchery.

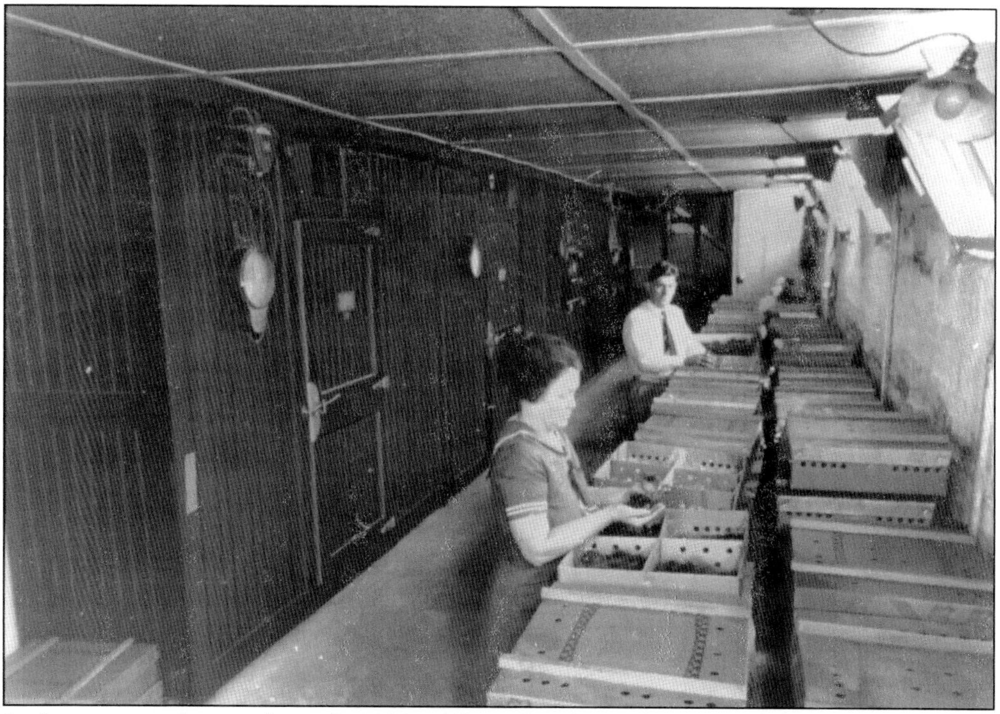

In this picture taken in the early 1930s, Allen's founders, Clarence and Nettie Allen, can be seen. They are standing outside the incubators checking chicks.

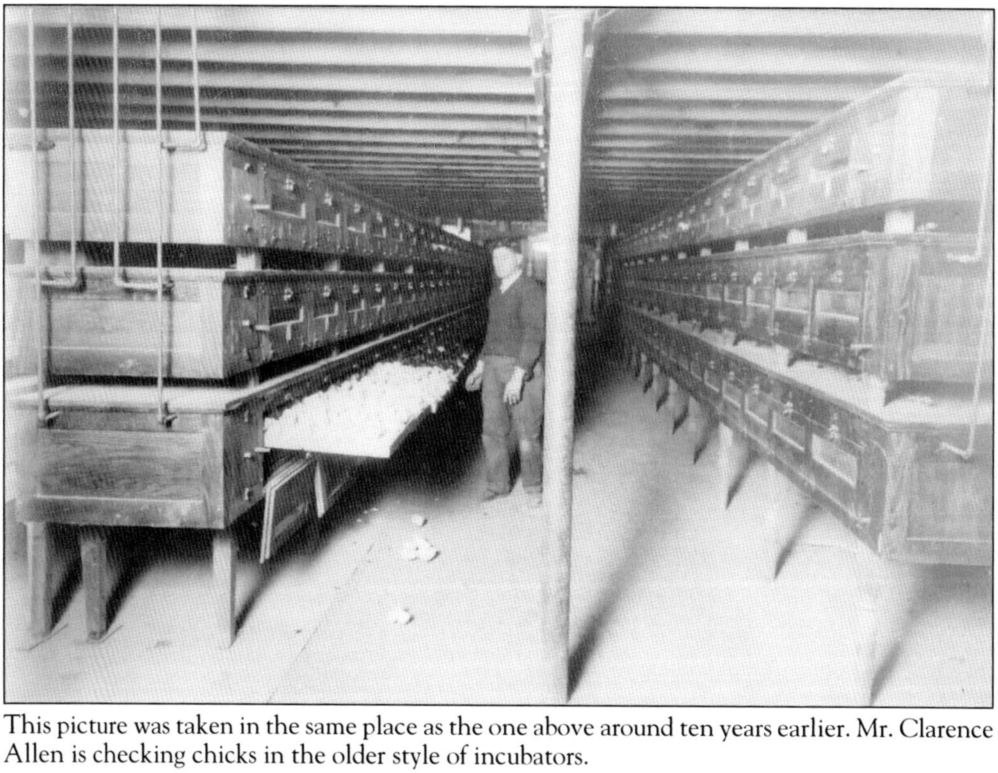

This picture was taken in the same place as the one above around ten years earlier. Mr. Clarence Allen is checking chicks in the older style of incubators.

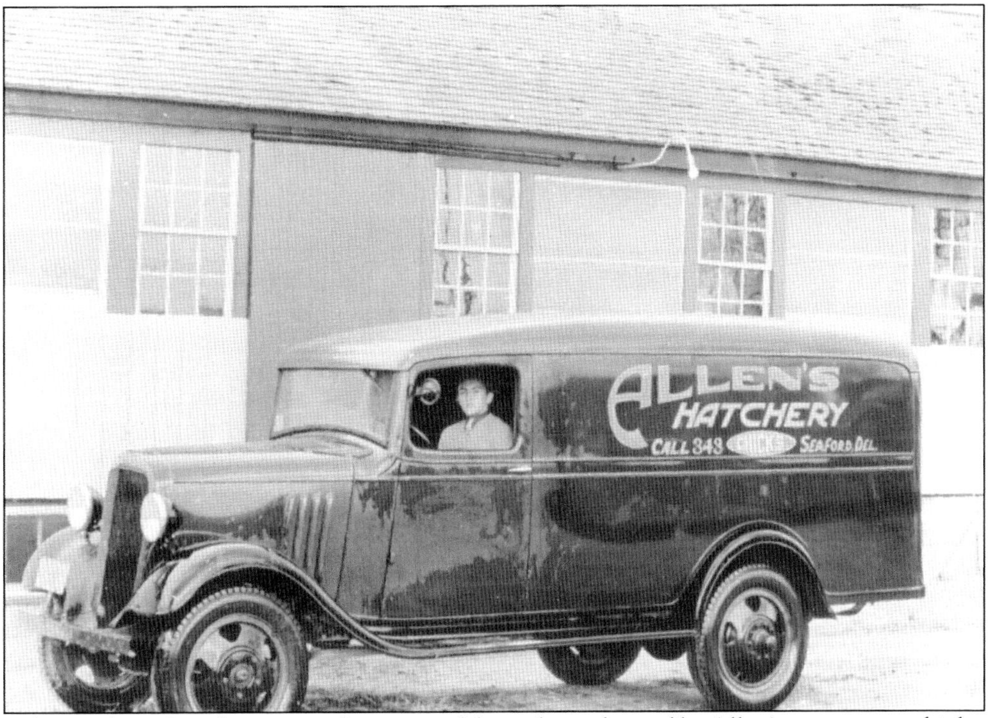

Taken in the 1930s, this picture shows one of the early trucks used by Allen's to transport chicks. What started as a small company with two employees, has grown to a corporation in its fourth generation of operation that produces 2.5 million chicks per week with 2,500 employees.

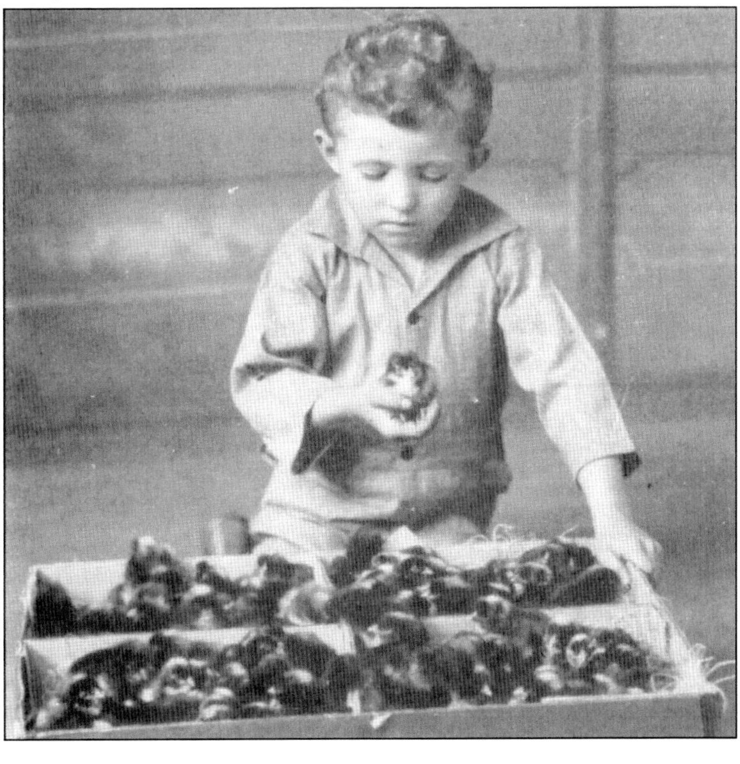

In this picture, one of Clarence & Nettie's sons, Jack, can be seen. Perhaps by studying the chicks in this way, he is attempting to learn the family business at a young age. Jack has gone on to run the company with his two brothers Warren and Charles.

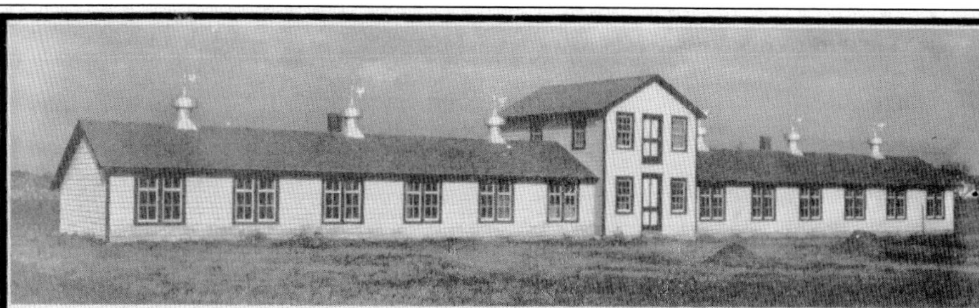

Our new long-type house fully equipped with batteries for the production of started chicks.

Allen's Range Grown Pullets

THRIFTY BIRDS FROM OUR BEST MATINGS

During the summer and fall, we have for sale several thousand Barred Rock pullets. These pullets are grown on our breeding farm of 125 acres with plenty of free range, under the supervision of an expert poultryman. Experienced poultrymen know it is very difficult to buy good pullets. On many breeding plants, it is customary to reserve the best pullets for breeders, the public getting the left overs.

Pullets are shipped express collect. We guarantee them to be healthy, thrifty birds, and to be as represented in regard to breeding. You will find them a profitable investment as letters from customers will confirm.

• • •

South Dennis, N. J.—*Let me know if you would have for sale about 500 three weeks old Pullets, if not let me know the age you have for sale. The 400 three weeks old pullets you sent me are doing nicely.*—Charles Hays.

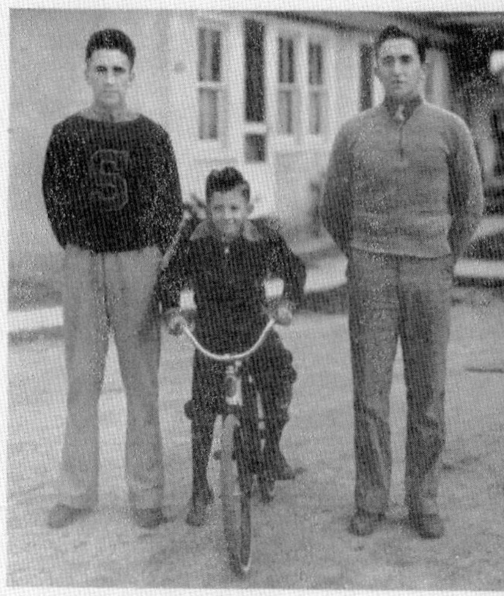

Three young members of the Allen family.

2½ POUNDS

IN TWELVE WEEKS TIME

The picture at the right shows an Allen Barred Rock Pullet tipping the scales at two and one-half pounds in twelve weeks time. Rapid growth and sturdy livability are breeding factors which have been firmly established in the strains which produce Allen's Chicks.

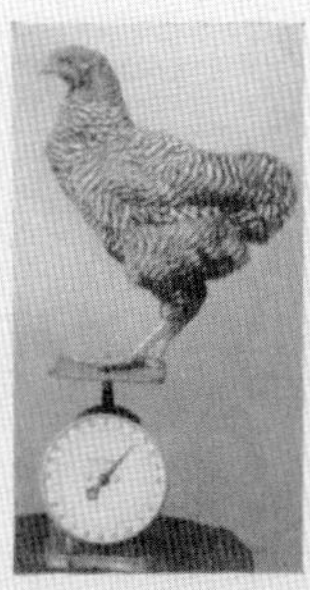

HONEST TESTIMONY

Woodbine, N. J.—We received your pullets in fine shape and I must admit we were surprised that they were so nice. It would be a pleasure to tell others about them.

When you wrote me you mentioned various ages; if you still have them how much are they. I would like to get some more soon.

Trusting to hear from you and hoping we may again do business I am.—**Paul Seache.**

Shown in this article are the original chicken house of Allen's (top), the three sons of Clarence and Nettie: Warren, Jack, and Charles (middle right), and one of Allen's chickens weighing in at 2.5 pounds in 12 weeks time (bottom center). The company gained a reputation for quality chickens that has not vanished.

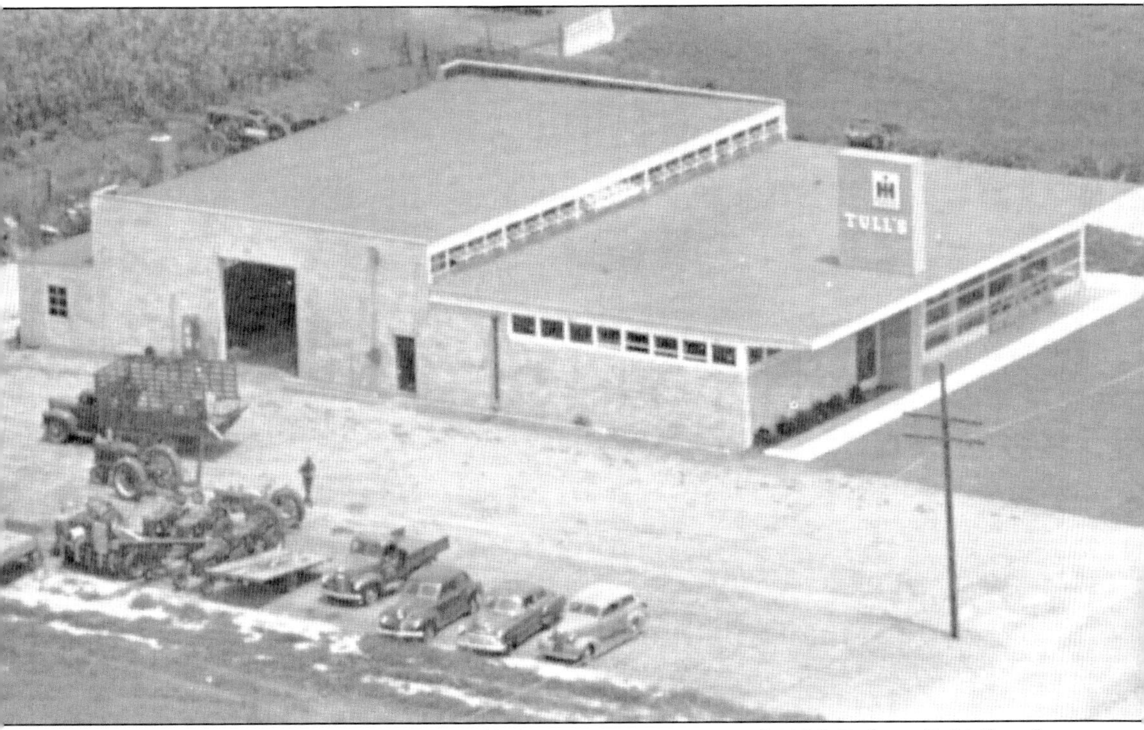

Tull Brothers, shown in this photo, actually began sometime around 1927. Robert C. Tull and Earle M. Tull started a company in the feed business that has grown into much more. The business moved to its present location in 1949 with the expanded line of products. Tull's is still a prominent business in the community in its third generation of ownership.

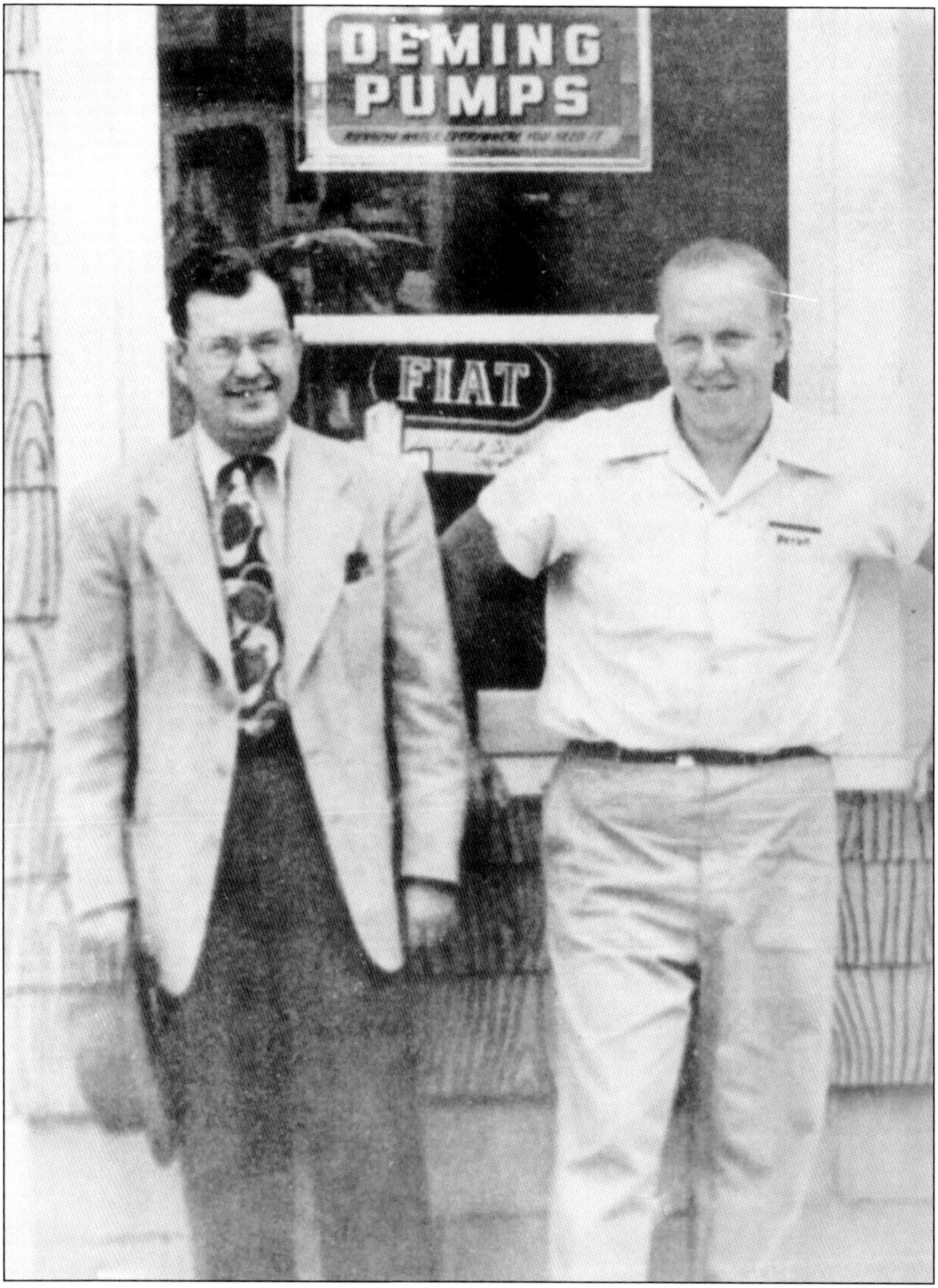

On August 3, 1949, George H. Sapna Sr. (left) and Oscar E. Peterson Jr. (right) formed a partnership using the trade name Peninsula Plumbing Supply Company. The partnership became a corporation on November 15, 1949. With its two employees, the business was conducted from a 3,000-square-foot building located on Water Street. The business has since grown immensely from one small branch into five larger ones. It continues to operate in its second generation of ownership under the trade name Penco Corporation.

Two

Downtown

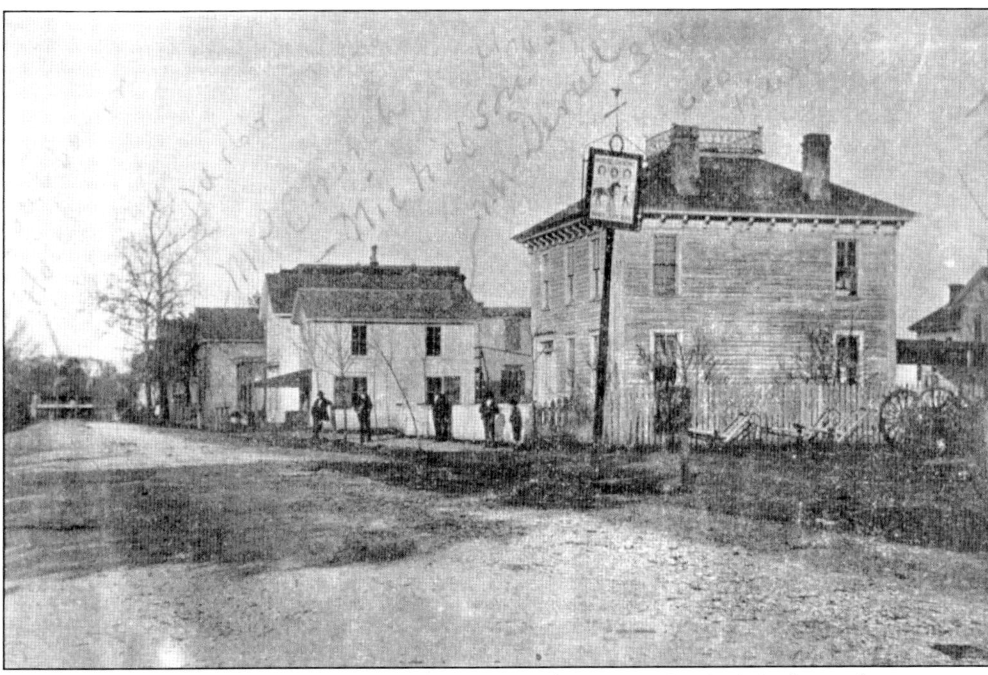

This is one of the oldest pictures of High Street in downtown Seaford. It shows the properties that stood on the corner of High and Pearl Streets around 1875. The building on the right was a blacksmith shop owned by Mr. Purse, but it was demolished in the early 1990s.

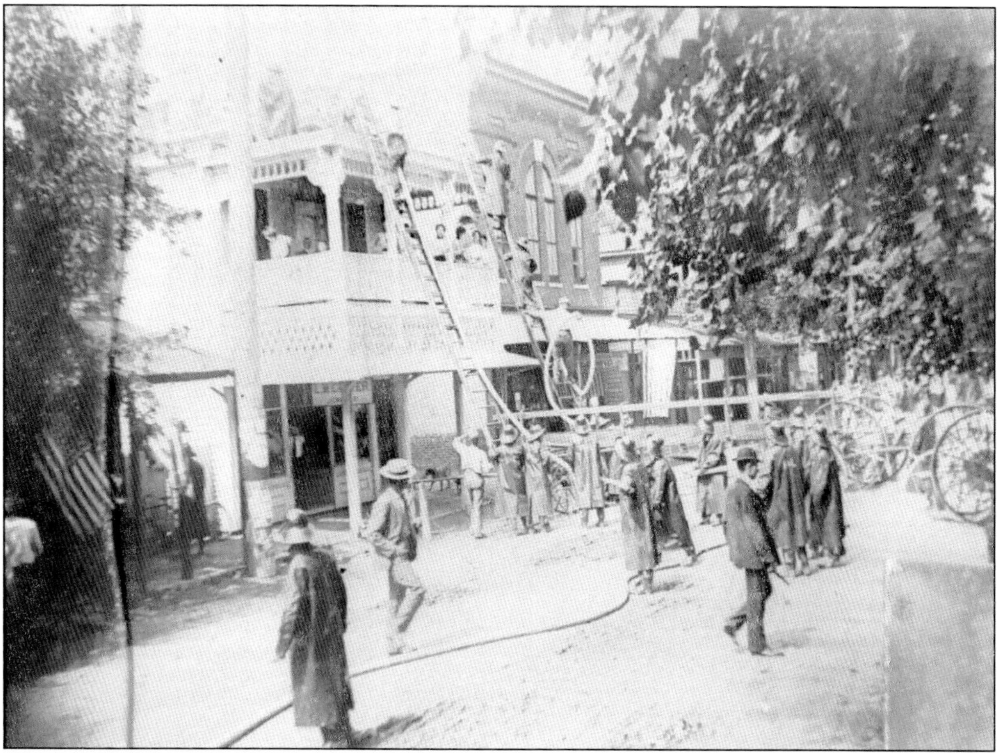

This was an example of a drill that Seaford's Fire Department staged. This particular drill took place on the Fourth of July in front of what was Mr. L.M. Culver's Jewelry Store on High Street. It was staged to show the efficiency of their hook and ladder department.

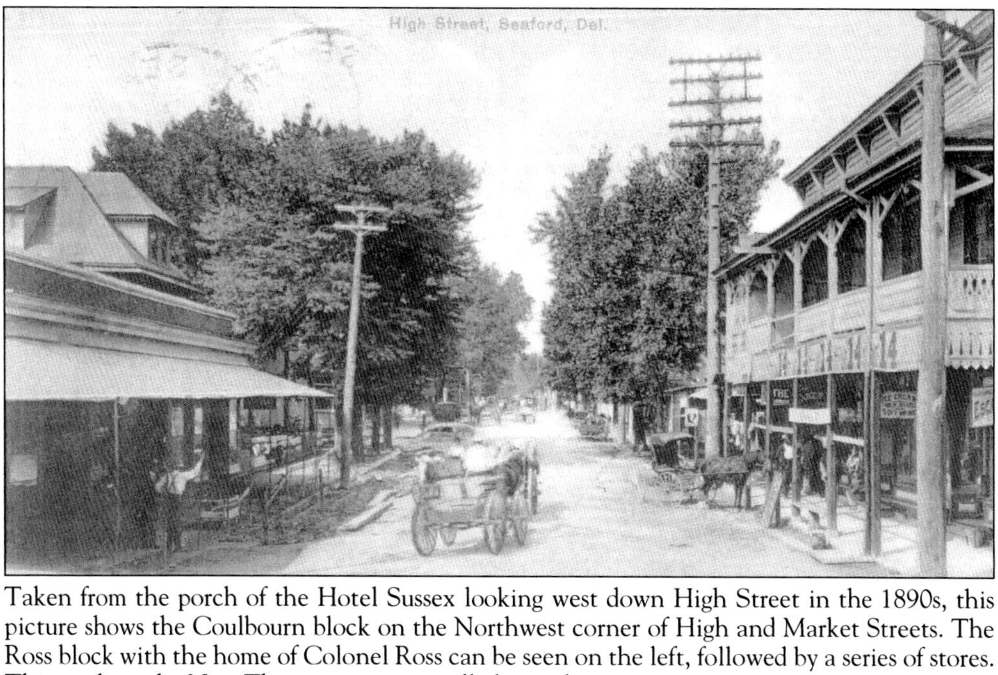

Taken from the porch of the Hotel Sussex looking west down High Street in the 1890s, this picture shows the Coulbourn block on the Northwest corner of High and Market Streets. The Ross block with the home of Colonel Ross can be seen on the left, followed by a series of stores. This is where the New Theater was eventually located.

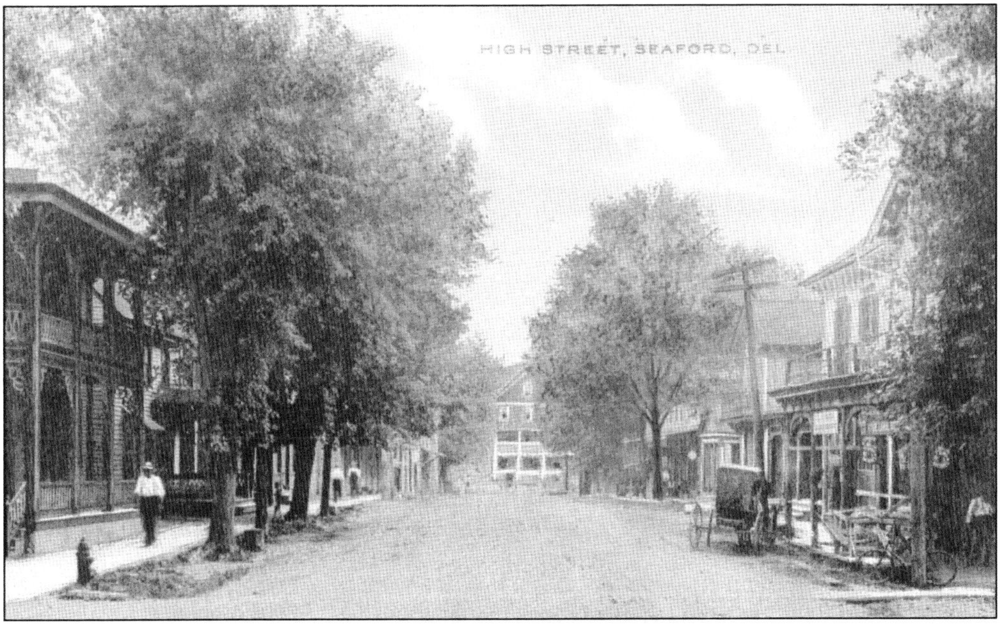

This picture of High Street was taken from Pine Street looking east, c. 1910.

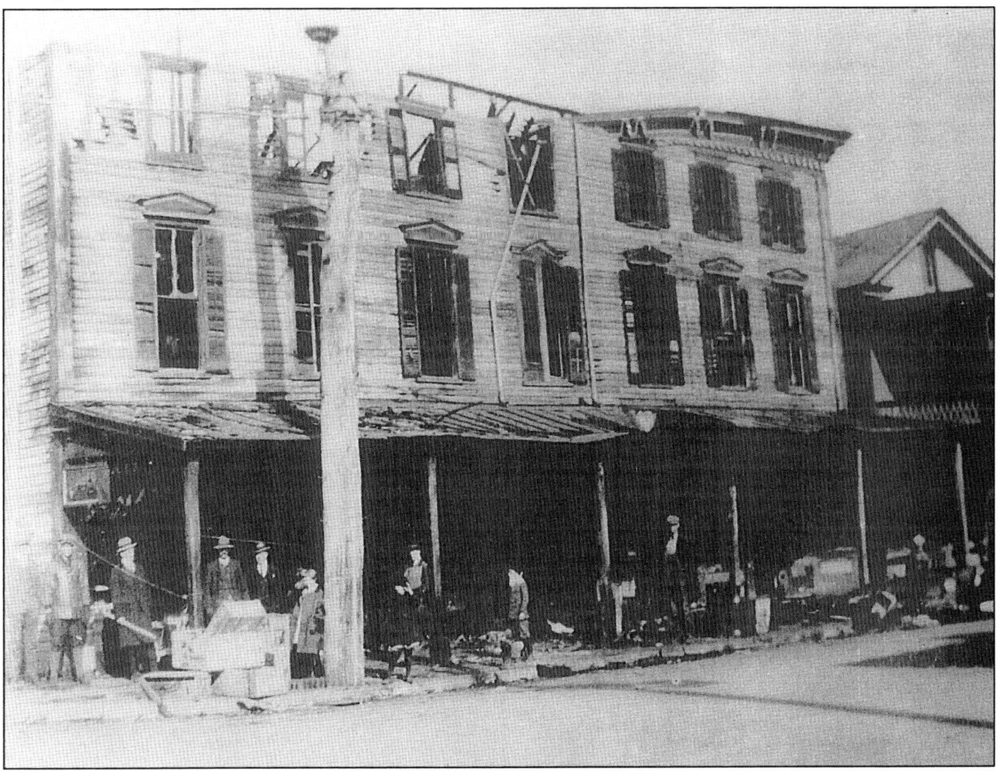

This building, which stood on the corner of High and Arch Streets, was known as the Bells Exchange Building. On the second floor, Wright Robinson's grandmother operated a private school that had around 15 to 20 students. The building burned however, approximately 80 years ago while the town's night watchman was asleep in a barbershop across the street.

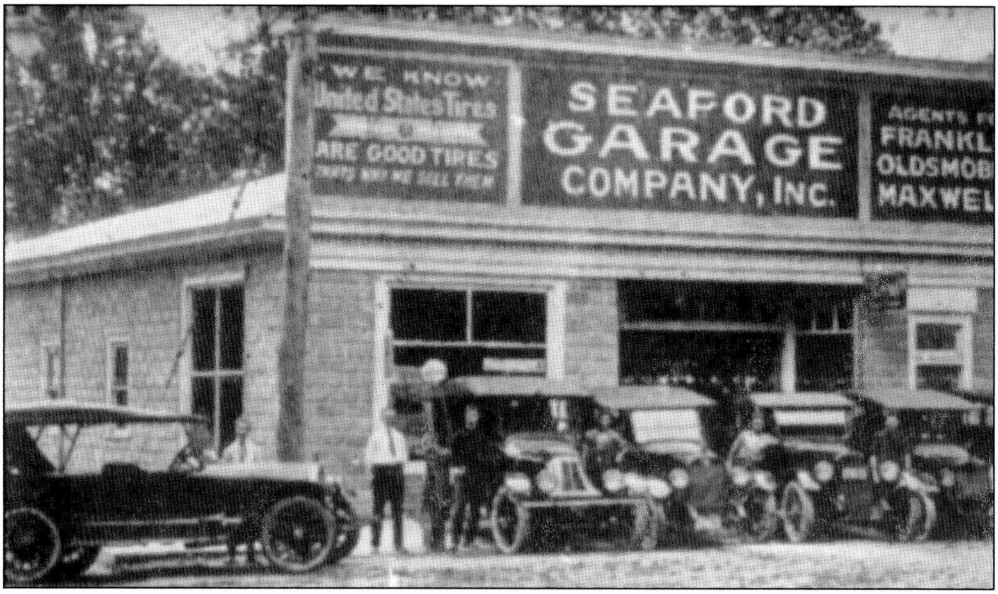

Taken sometime in the early 1920s, the building shown in this picture stood on the southwest side of High and Pine Streets. It originally housed a garage operated by Tillie Bryan, who sold Franklin Automobiles. Mr. Bryan can be seen standing beside the gas pump in the photo. He later moved his business to Blades Causeway, and this store became a 5&10 operated by Mr. Charles Hastings. At one time, the cellar of the building housed a sewing plant that was operated by N.M. Conaway.

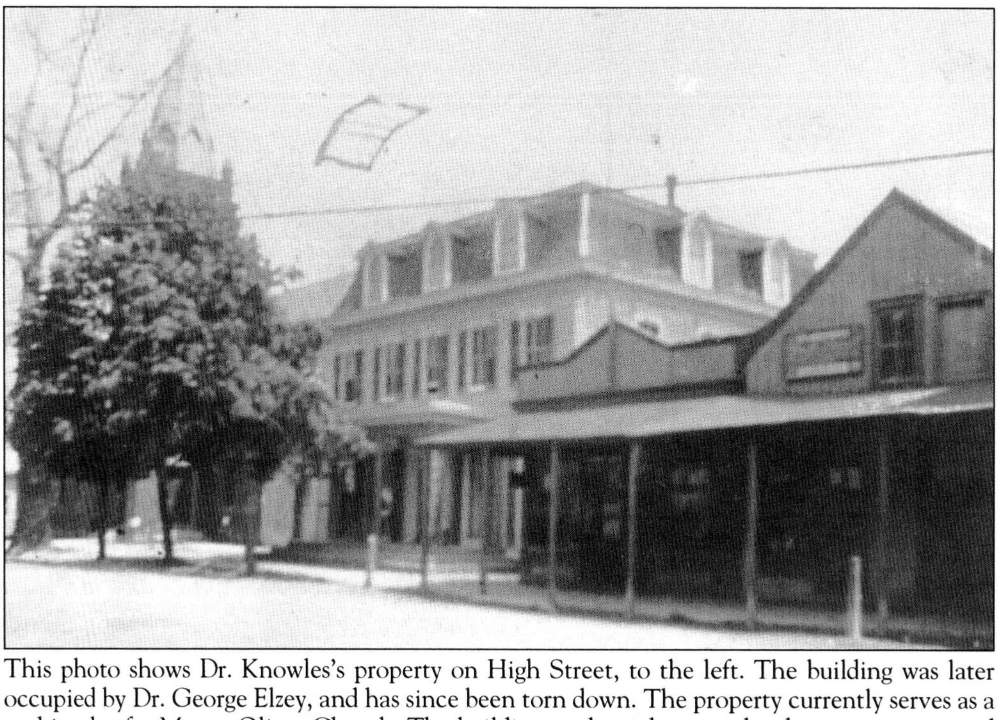

This photo shows Dr. Knowles's property on High Street, to the left. The building was later occupied by Dr. George Elzey, and has since been torn down. The property currently serves as a parking lot for Mount Olivet Church. The building to the right was a hardware store operated by Mr. L.E. Wallace, a Civil War veteran.

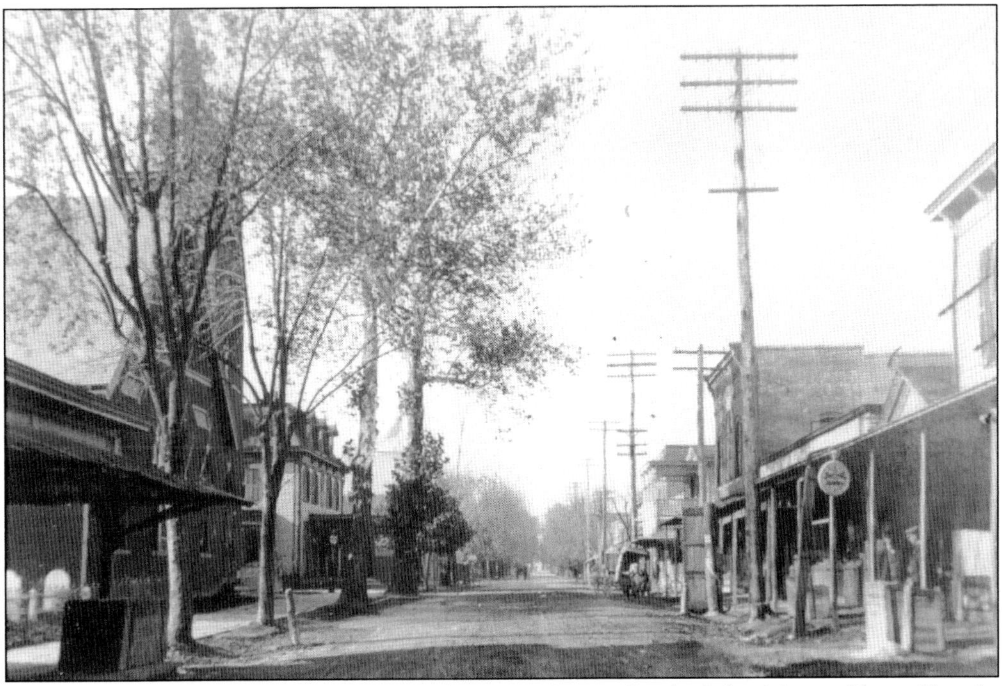

This is a view of High Street looking west from Pine Street. On the left is Mount Olivet Church, and beyond that is the house that Dr. Knowles occupied.

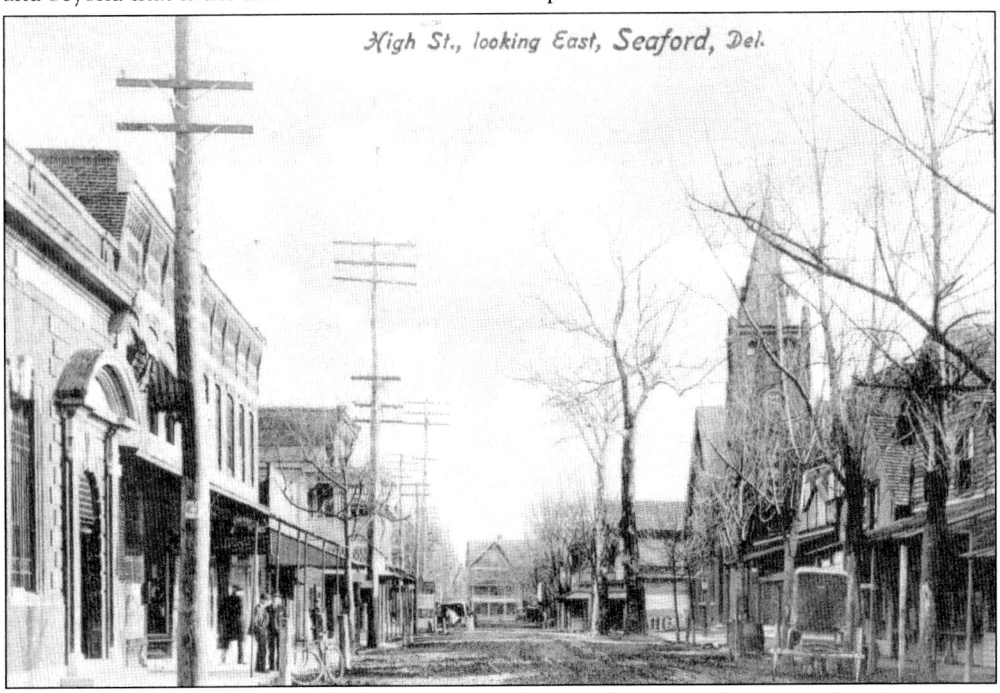

This is a picture of High Street looking east. The muddy streets shown in the picture were common during the winter months. Wooden walkways were later put across the street to make crossing the street easier. They were especially helpful to the ladies, who often wore floor-length dresses. The wooden street crossings were then replaced with paving in 1912.

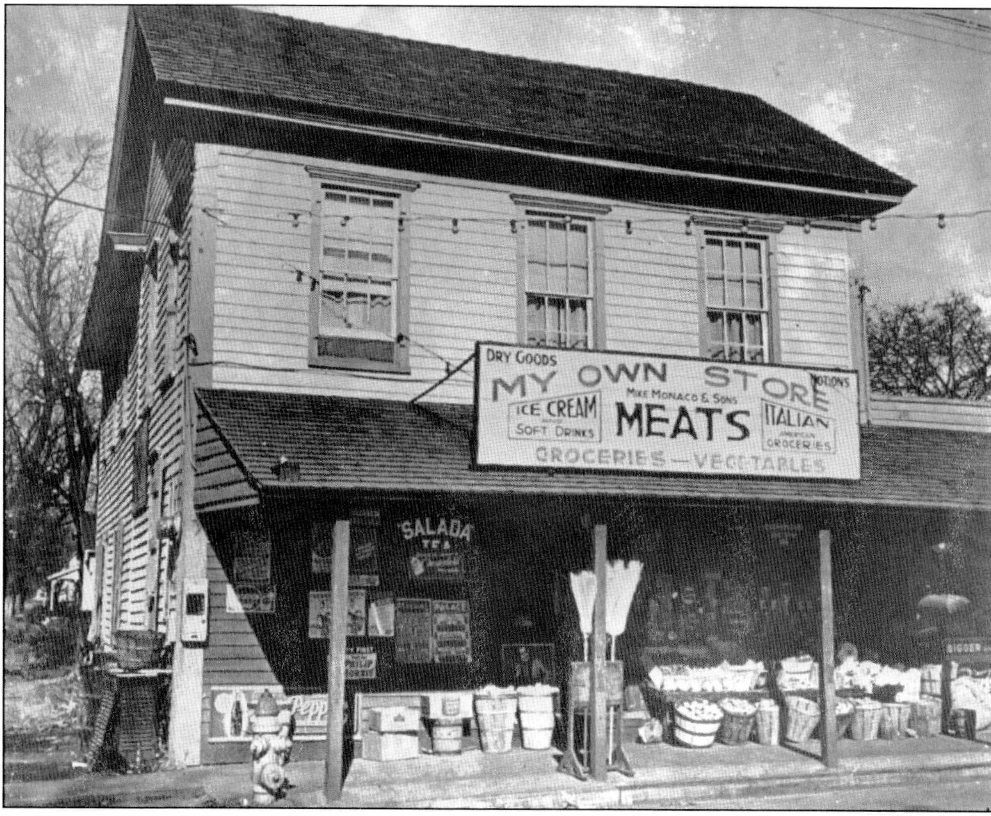

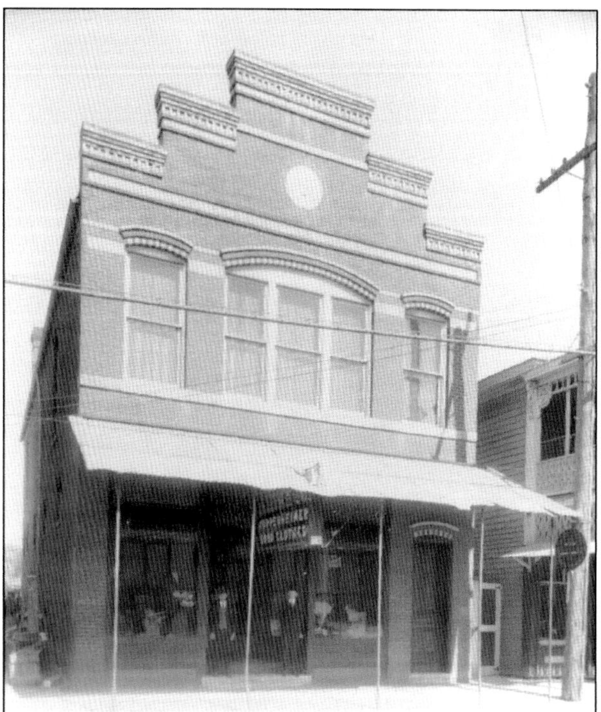

This picture was taken in the 1920s and shows the store on the corner of Railroad Avenue and High Street. It was a grocery store owned by Mr. & Mrs. Mike Monaco and was their first business venture. The Monacos later sold the property and moved across the street to operate a larger store. Prior to the Monaco's ownership of the property, a Mr. Ellingsworth and a Mr. Harry Griffith operated businesses there.

Mr. Stein, one of Seaford's great citizens, owned and operated this store, Stein & Company, at the time of this picture. Mr. Stein was a tailor and had a thriving men's store that went bankrupt in the '30s. He became most famous for his contributions to Stein Highway. Above this store is where the Masonic Lodge was housed.

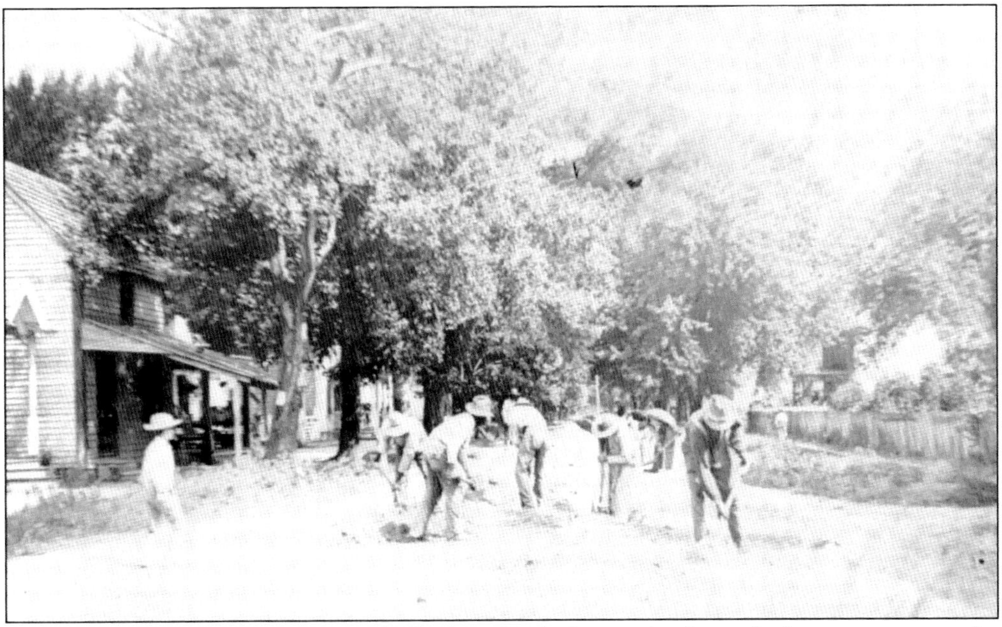

Shown here are men laying oyster shells along High Street. At the end of oyster season in the late nineteenth century, the shells were brought to High Street and laid to make the street solid. Horses would walk down the street and pound the shells into a pulpy hardness that made travel much more pleasant in the summer months.

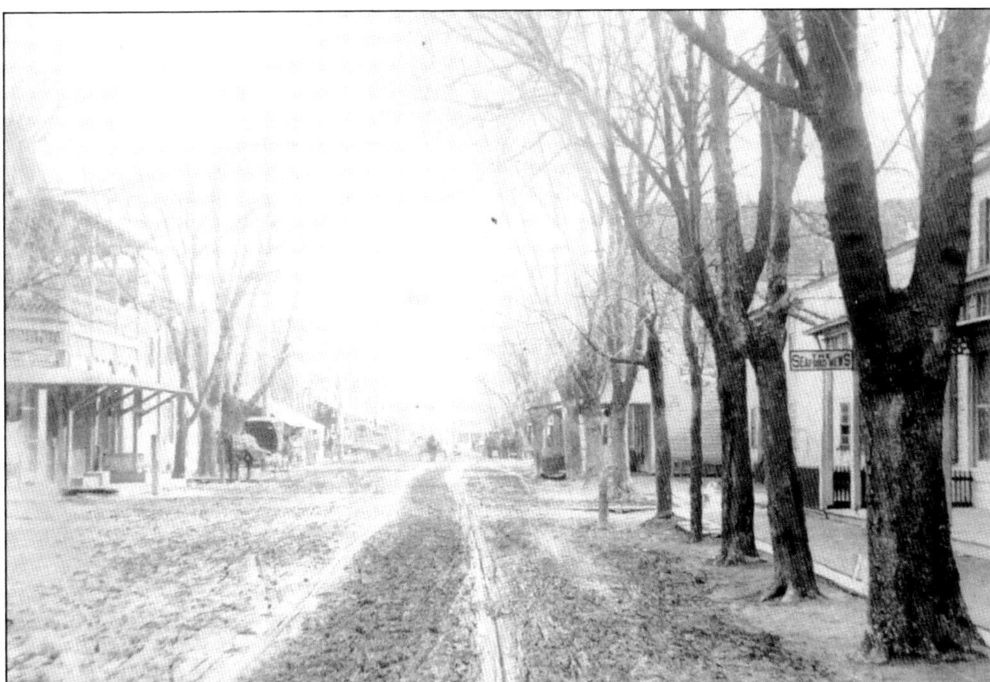

This is a view of High Street when trees lined the roads. The trees were later removed when concrete was laid from curb to curb.

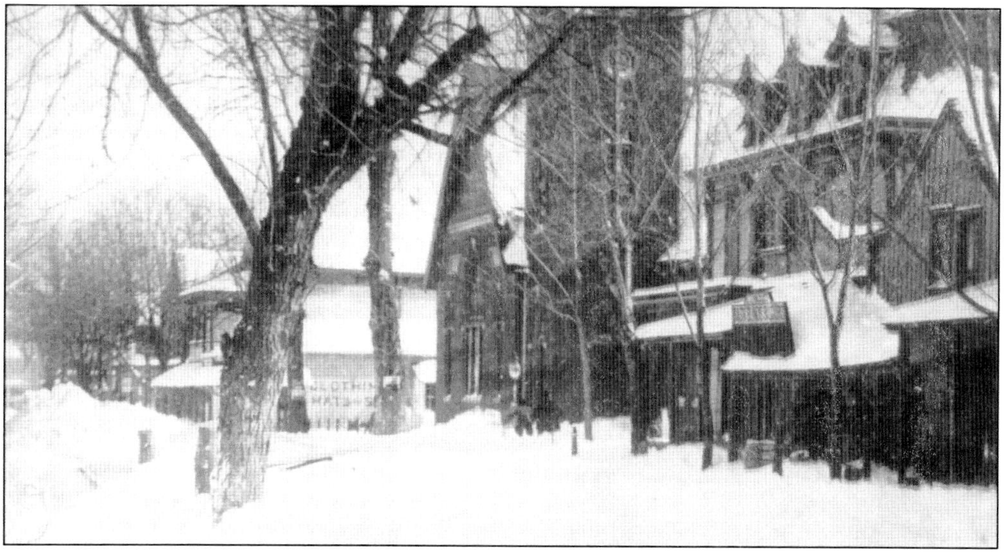

This is a picture of a snow scene along High Street. When it snowed, High Street was a popular place for sledding, skating, and playing.

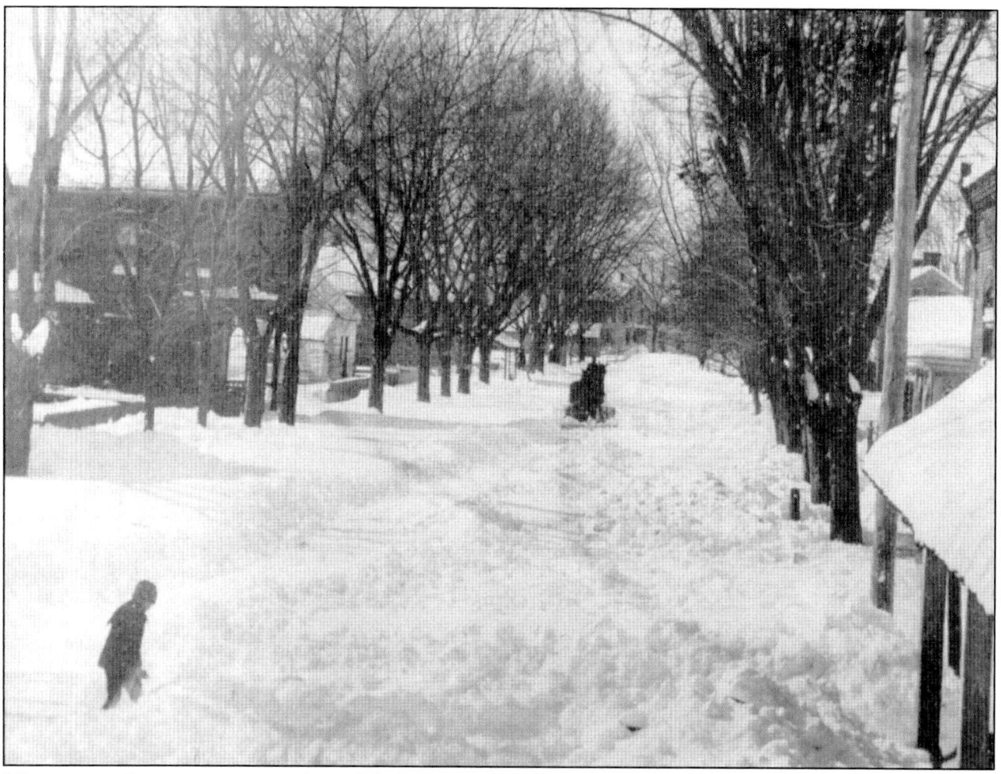

This is another snow scene along High Street. In the 1890s, there was a snow storm so severe that the community was paralyzed.

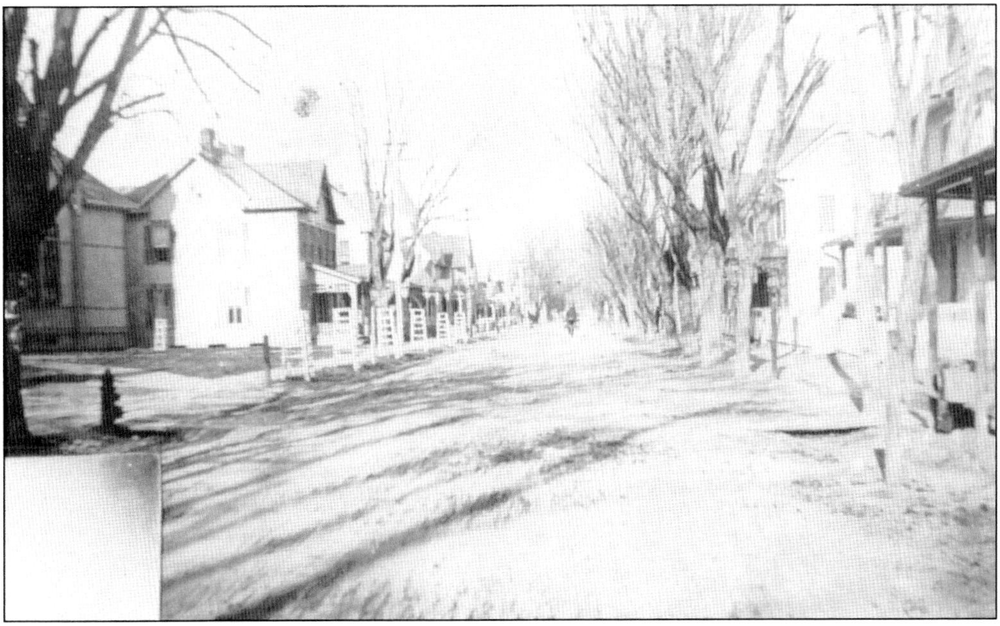

This is a view of Pine Street in downtown Seaford. The view is looking north from High Street during the winter months.

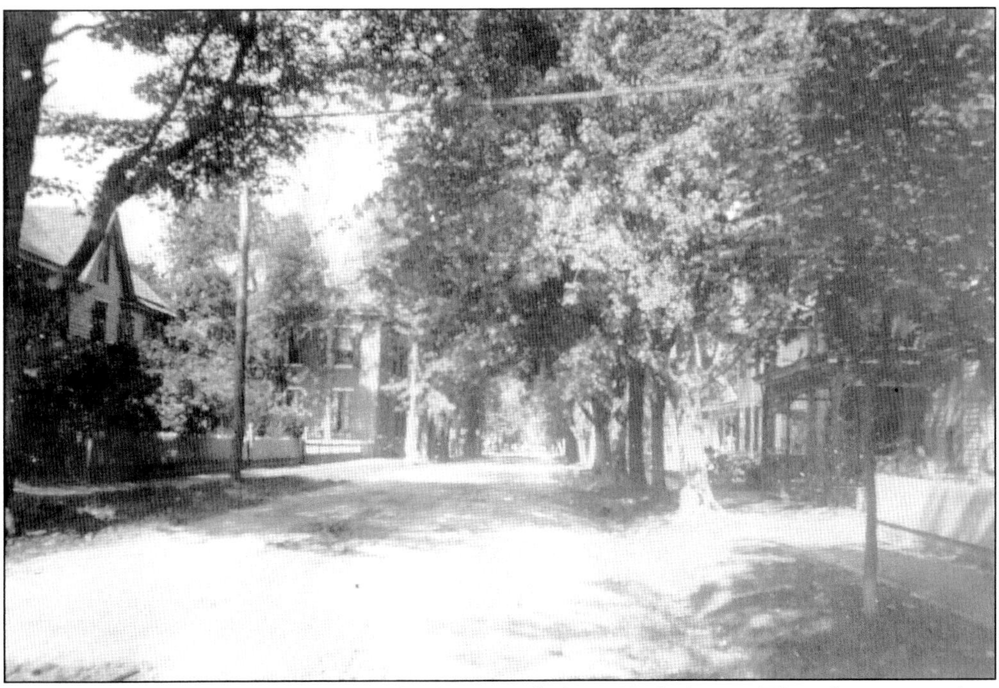

This is another view of Pine Street looking north from High Street. This photo was taken during the summer months.

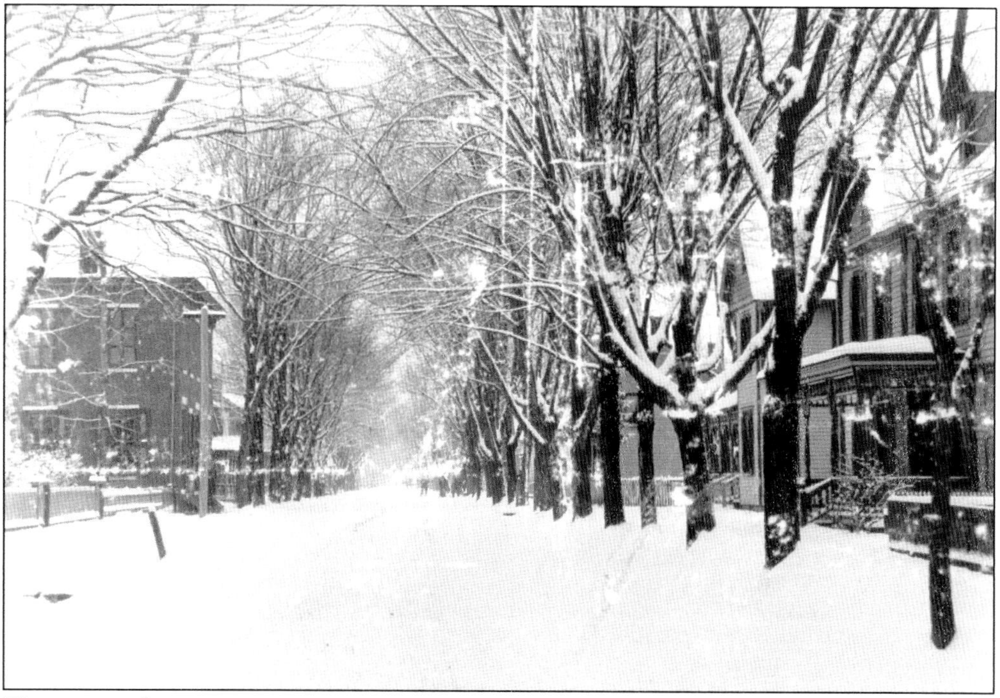

This picture shows a snow scene on Pine Street.

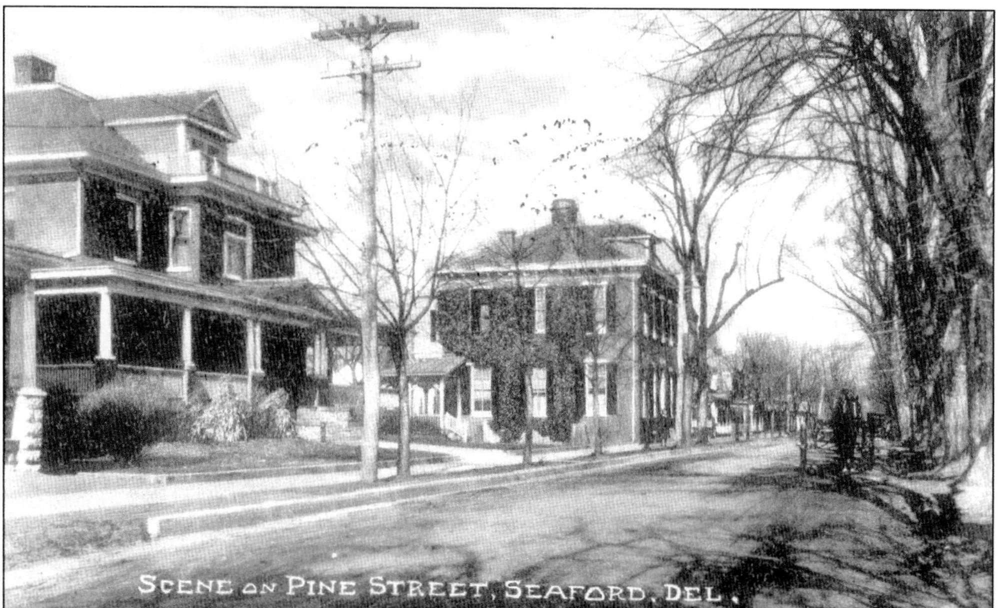

This is a scene on Pine Street in the early part of the twentieth century. To the left was the home of Mr. J.A. Morgan, one of Seaford's produce brokers. The building next to it was Seaford's first bank, First National. It was owned by Mr. Henry White Baker, who was the town banker. Both buildings are still standing today.

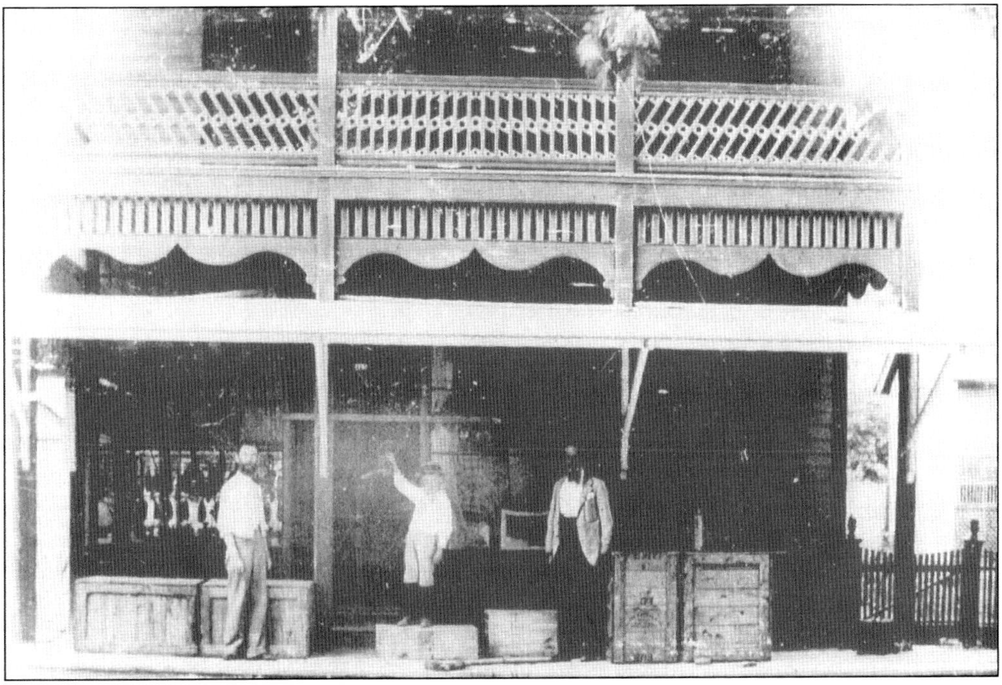

This was MJ Cox & Company Store that stood on the corner of Pearl and High Streets. The business was operated by Mr. Harper Cox. His son Joe (shown standing on the box in the picture) later took over the business. The building has since been demolished.

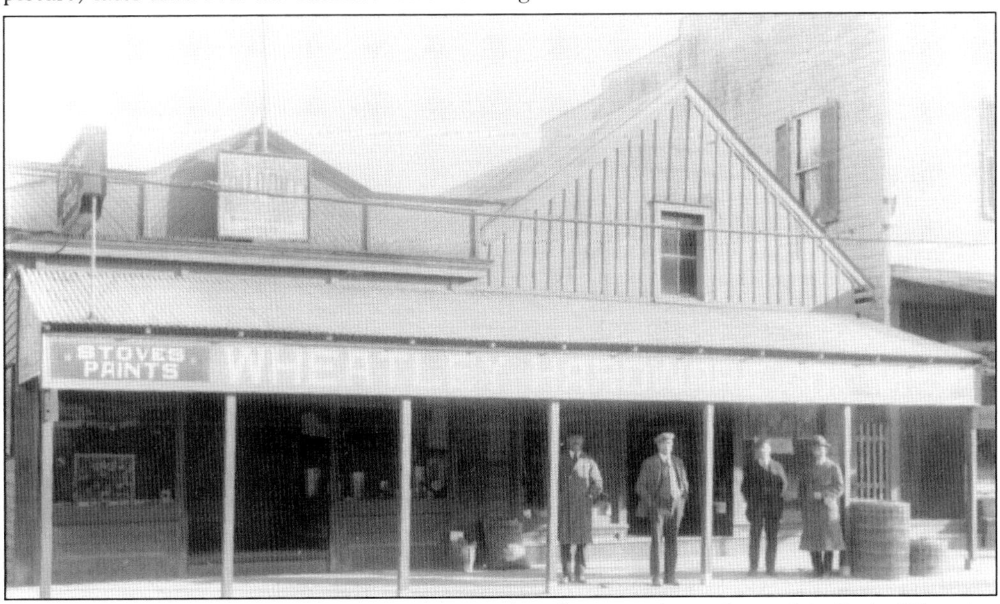

At the time of this picture, this business was Wheatley's Hardware Store. Mr. R.A. Wheatley purchased the property from Mr. L.W. Wallace, who had operated his own hardware store from the building. Wheatley's Hardware sold the DuPont paint line, and when the DuPont Plant was constructed in Seaford, Mr. Wheatley did very well selling the paint for the new plant. In addition to serving as a store, this business functioned as a community gathering place. There was a little stove in the store, and many would gather around it to socialize.

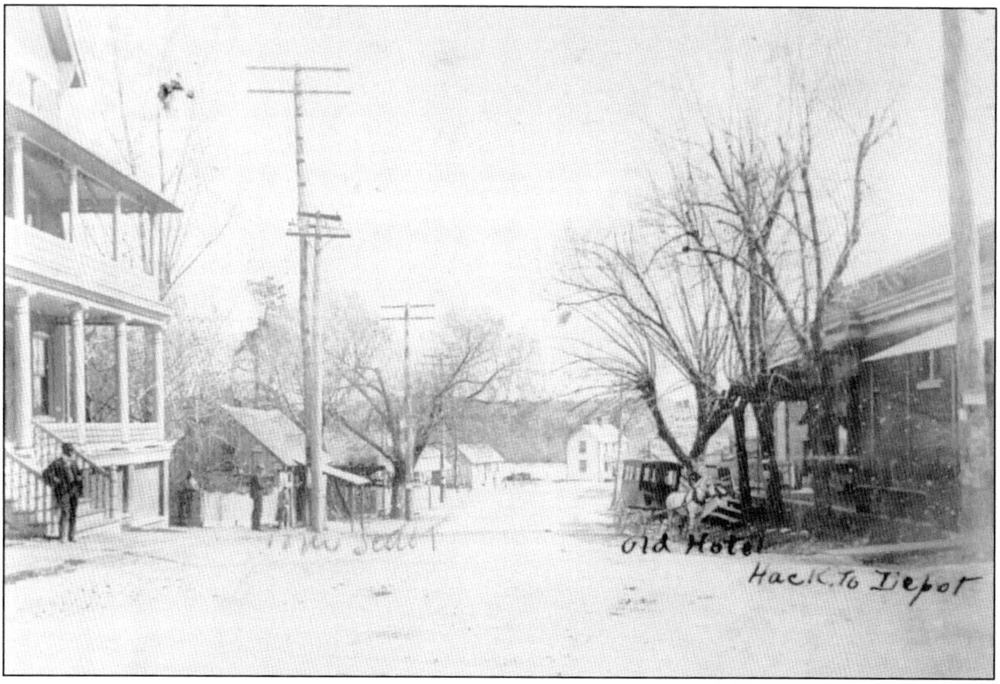

This is a picture of South Market Street leading down to the bridge. To the left is the Sussex Hotel, and to the right is a building that was owned by the Ross family. There is also a depot hack to the right of the photo. It was operated by the Hurley family and would carry passengers from the RR station to the Hotel.

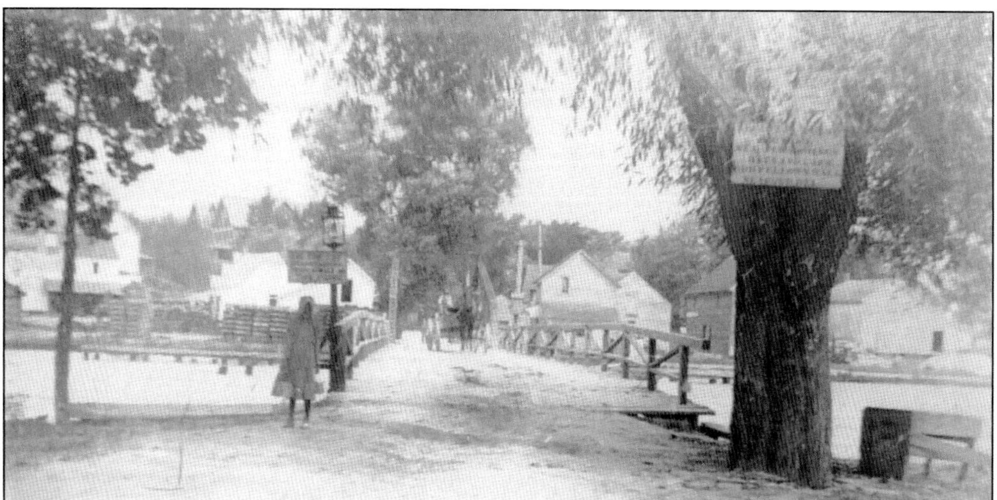

This is a picture of the Market Street Bridge from the Blades side looking toward Seaford. Before the State purchased it, the bridge had a toll. The toll keeper in 1880 was Alfred Webb, and the toll was 2¢ to walk across and 5¢ to drive a team.

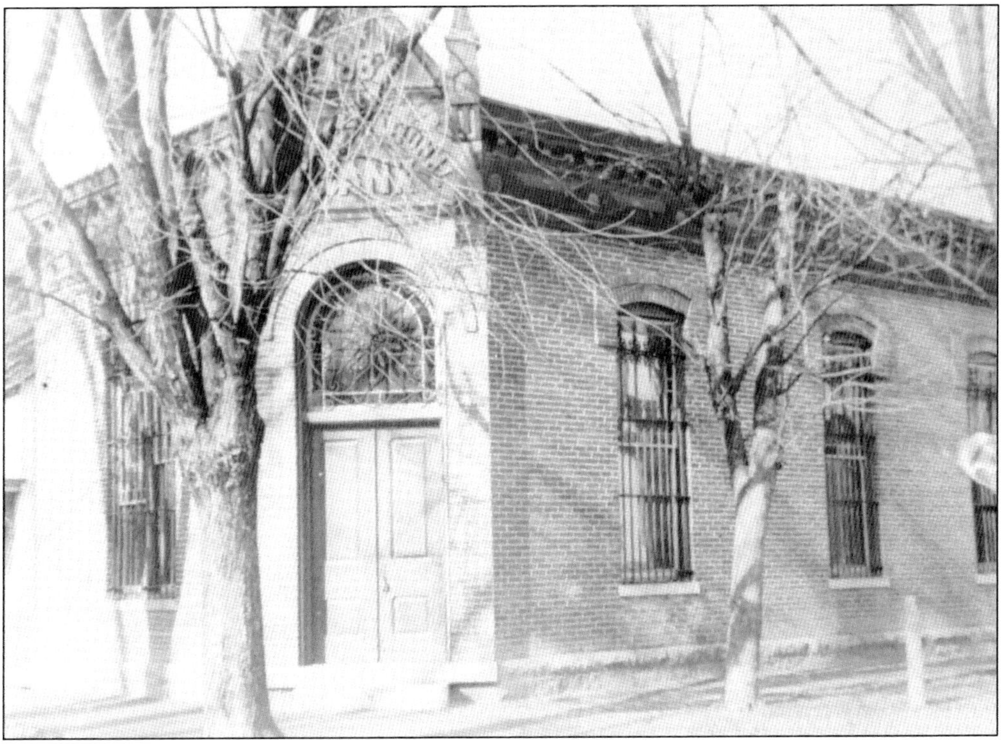

This building, still standing at the corner of High and Conwell Streets, was the Sussex National Bank. It was started in 1898.

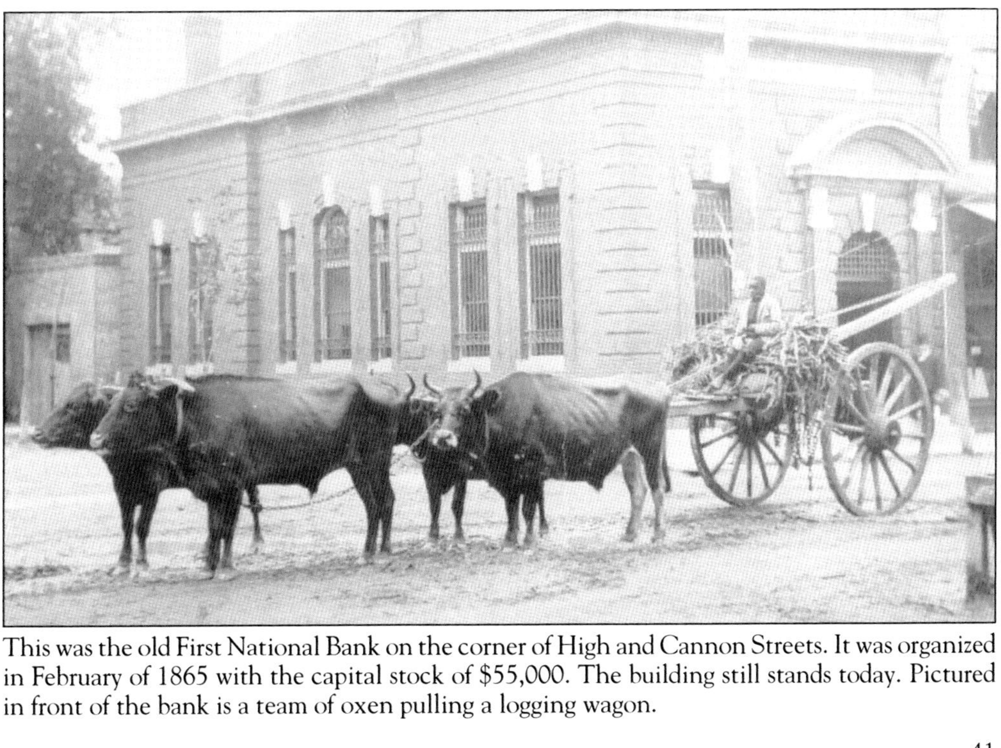

This was the old First National Bank on the corner of High and Cannon Streets. It was organized in February of 1865 with the capital stock of $55,000. The building still stands today. Pictured in front of the bank is a team of oxen pulling a logging wagon.

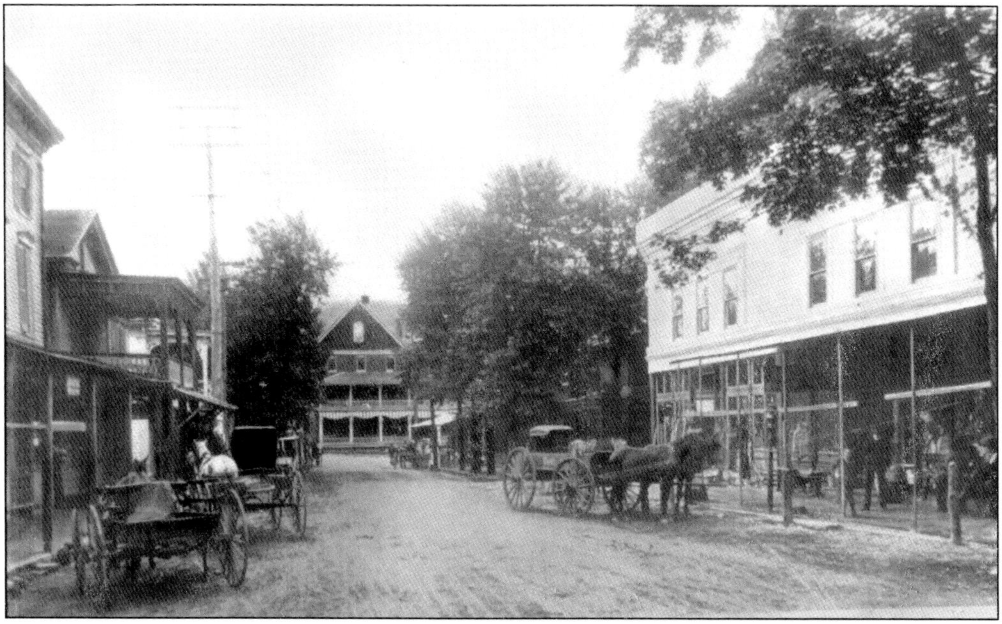

Shown in the right of this picture is Burton Brothers Hardware Store. Constructed in 1893, this building still stands on High Street. The builders made use of everything during construction. Even the crates that carried the galvanized tin for the building became the wooden structure beneath the tin. The Burton brothers opened a hardware store in the section of the building to the far left, which is still open today. The section to the right housed a theater with apartments above. The hardware store has since expanded, taking over the entire building.

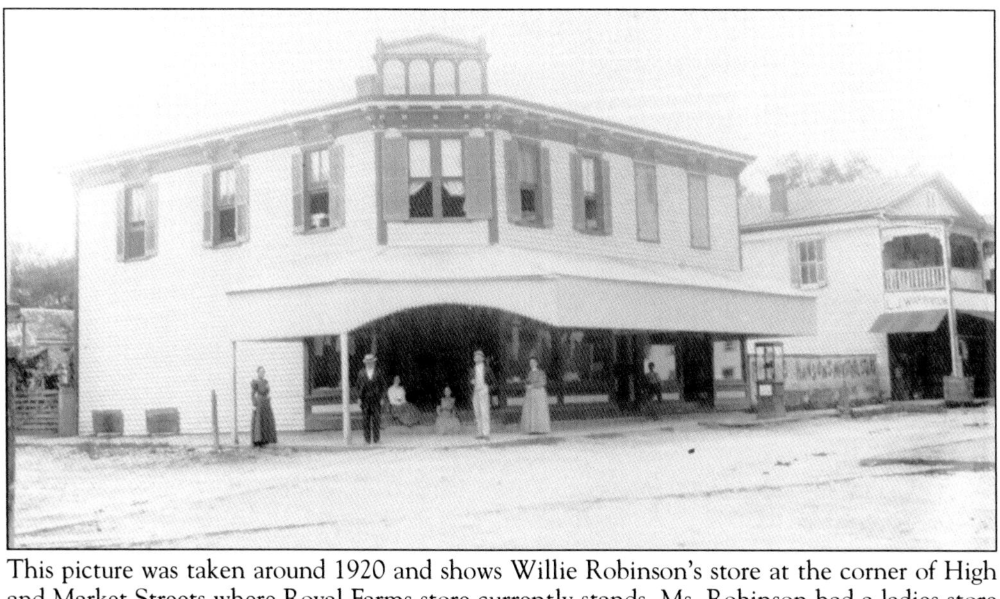

This picture was taken around 1920 and shows Willie Robinson's store at the corner of High and Market Streets where Royal Farms store currently stands. Ms. Robinson had a ladies store where she sold dry goods, buttons, pins, etc. that ladies used for sewing and around the home.

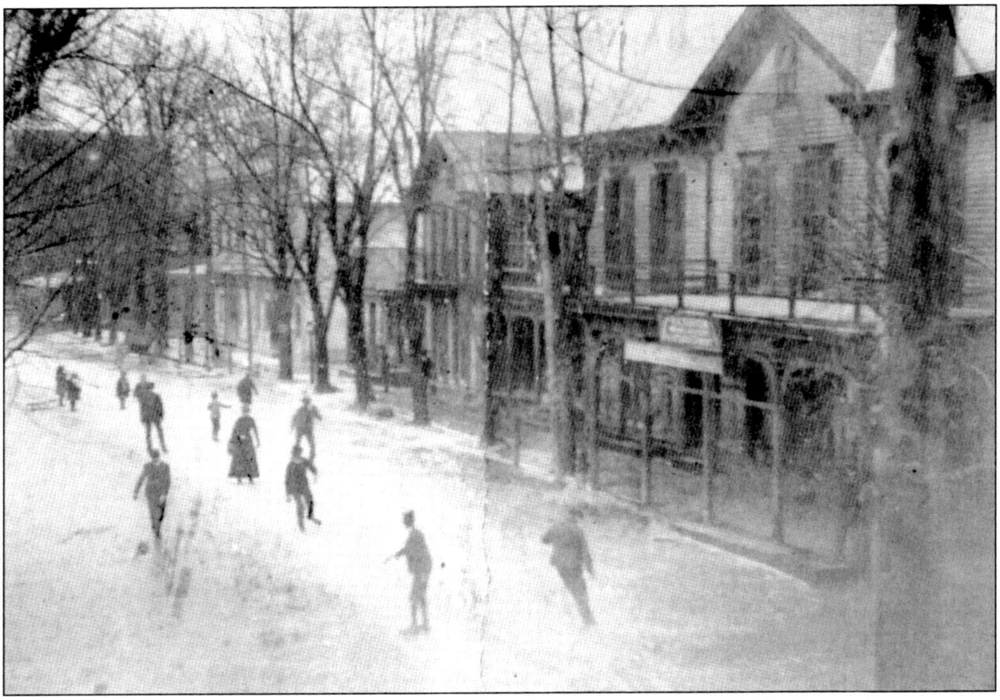

In both of these photographs, people can be seen ice skating along High Street during an ice storm. This happened on several occasions downtown. On one occasion in the 1920s, some of the skaters made it all the way to Bridgeville.

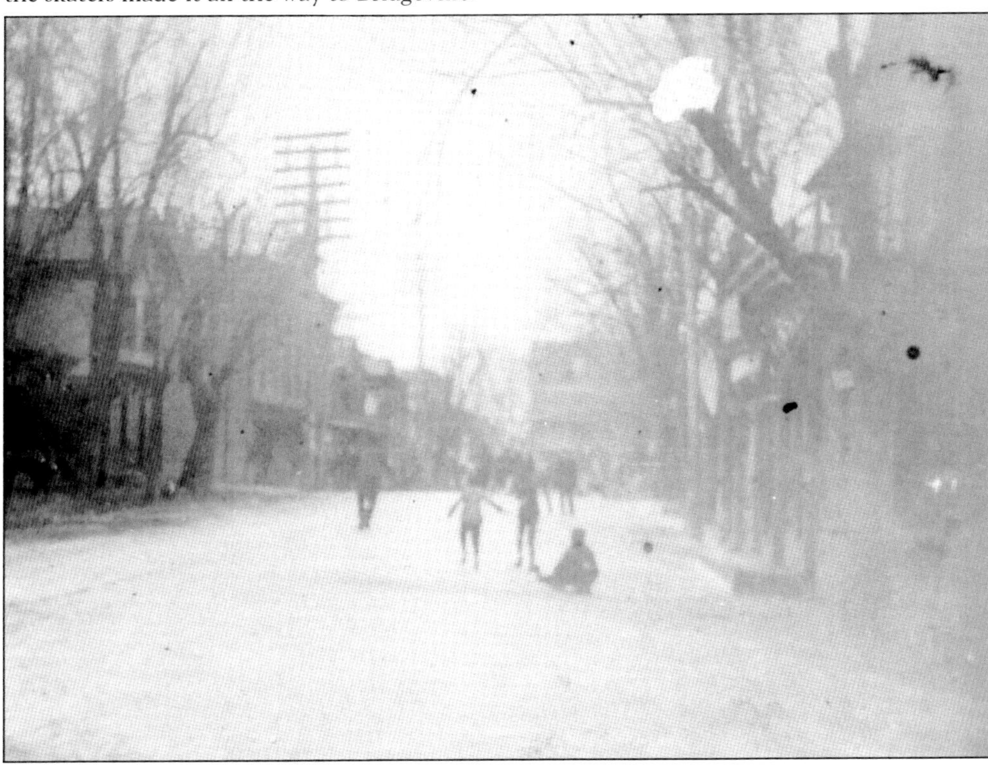

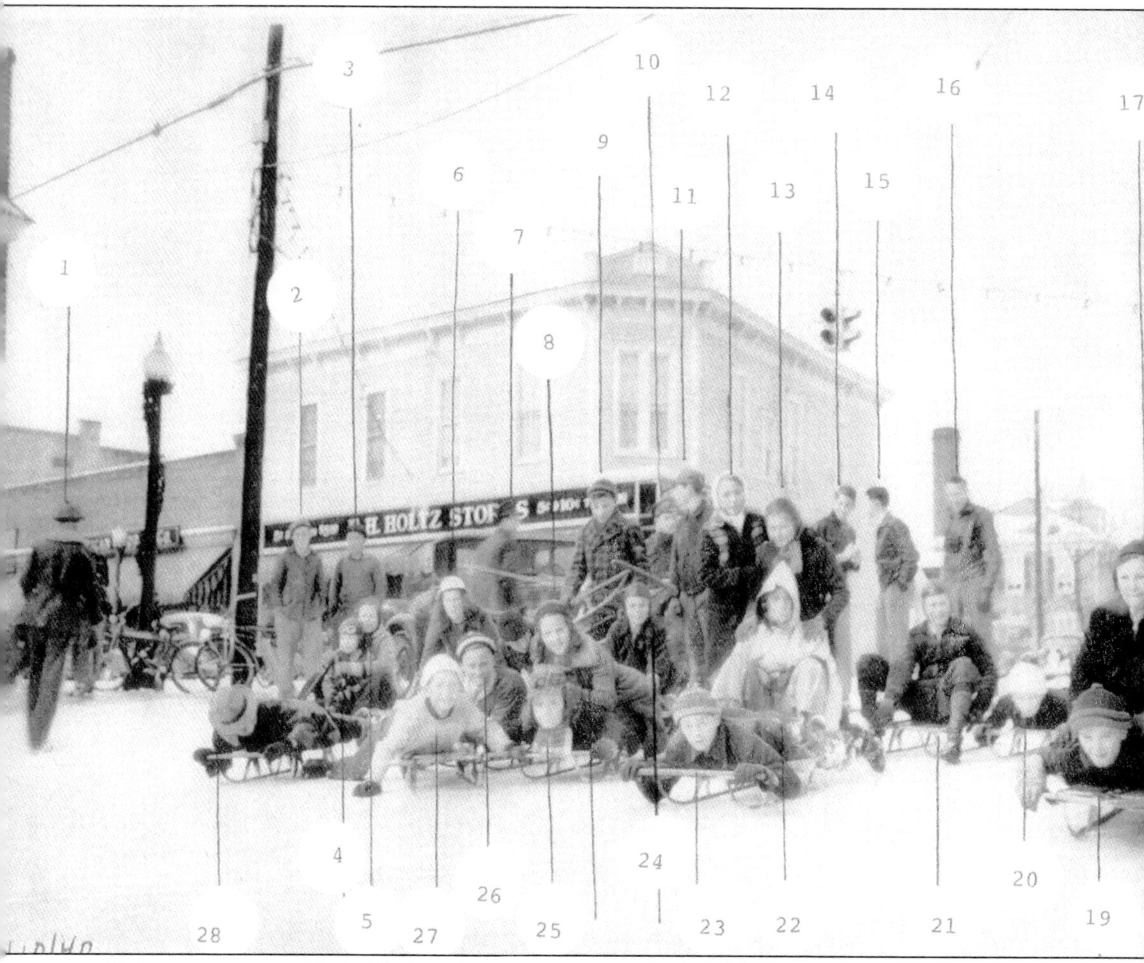

Taken on January 10, 1940, this photo shows a group of children assembled on what was known as Darbie's Hill on Pine Street for a day of sledding. Pictured here are 1) ?, 2) ?, 3) Marvin Harrold, 4) John Purse, 5) Barbara Purse, 6) Joanne Snyder, 7) ?, 8) Patsy Thompson, 9) Lou Parris, 10) Allen Morgan, 11) ?, 12) Margaret Carmean, 13) Helen Myers, 14) Wesley Salisbury, 15) Charles Simon, 16) Charles West, 17) Jack Allen, 18) Harry Records, 19) Bill Easom, 20) Jack Fulling, 21) Jennings Spicer, 22) Inez Spicer, 23) Donald Swetland, 24) Shelley Spicer, 25) Janet Culver, 26) Dean Betts, 27) Edward Morgan, and 28) Jack Embrey.

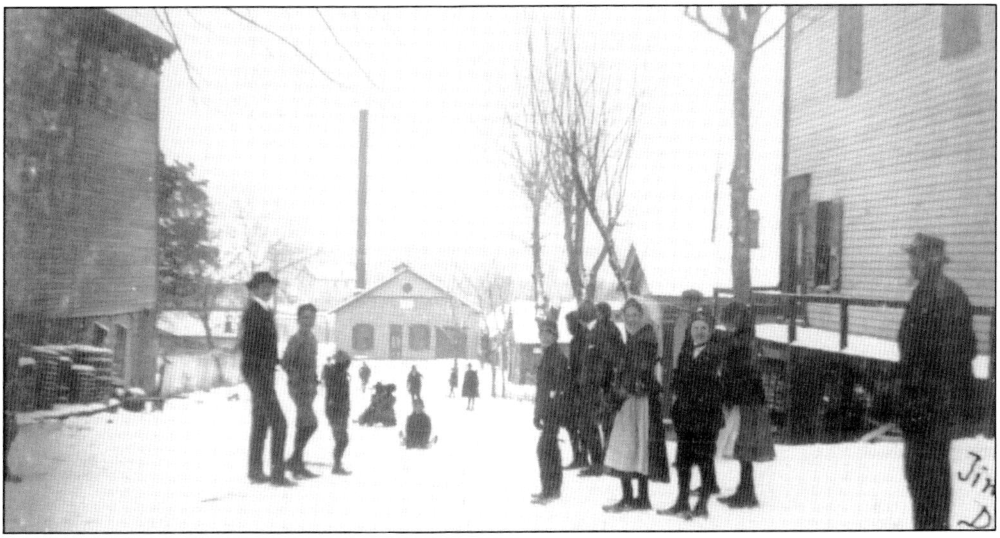

This is another shot of Darbie's Hill looking from High Street down toward the River. During snowstorms, the hill was a mecca for children. The town would always stop traffic on the hill so that there would be plenty of snow for sledding.

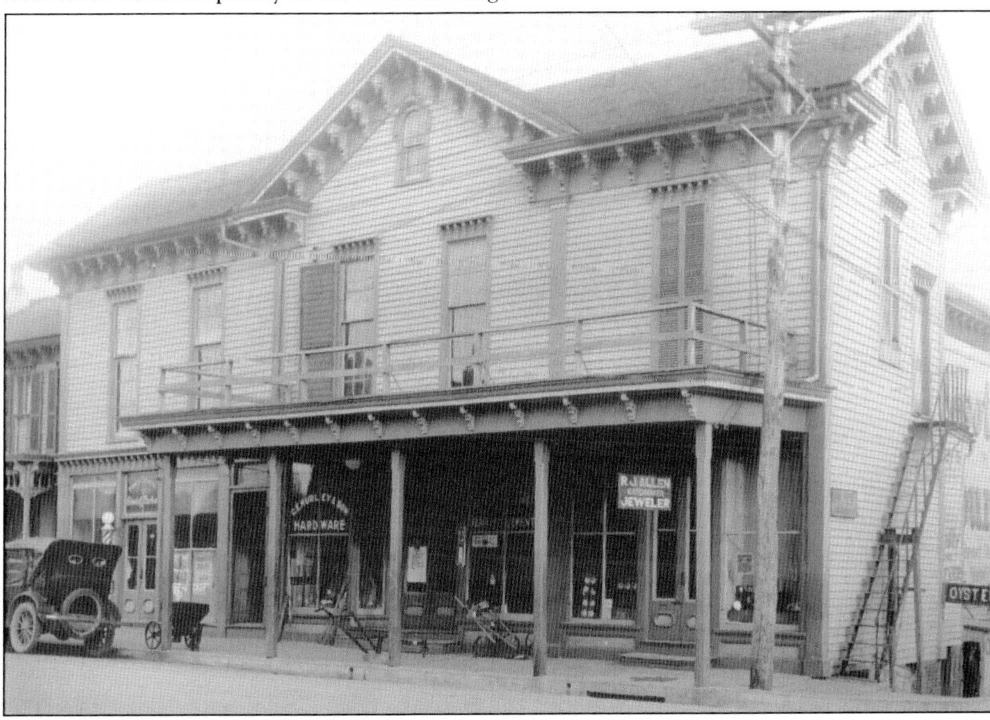

This picture was taken during the 1920s. Pictured is Mr. C.E. Hurley's hardware store (in the main part of the building). The second story housed a young men's social club called the Crescent Club. Young Seaford men would assemble there and sit on the upstairs porch and watch the traffic go by, shoot pool, and socialize. The steps to the right led to Seaford's only dry cleaning establishment, operated by David Boyce, a well-respected African American in the community. The store to the right was a jewelry store operated by Mr. Allen, and to the left was a barbershop operated by Mr. Ernest Fields.

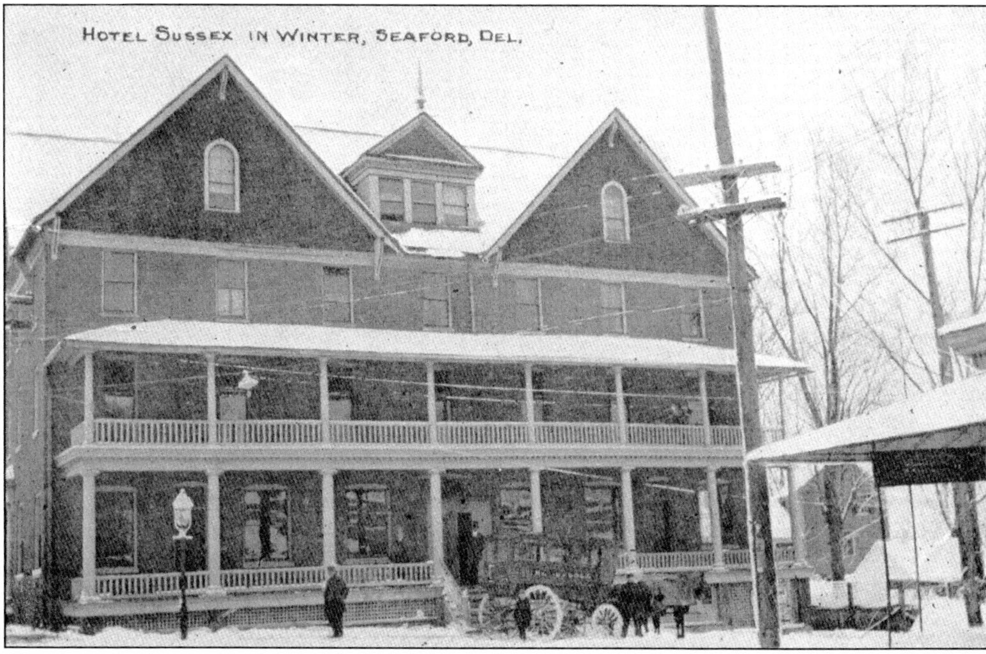

This is an early picture (most likely taken in the early 1900s) of the famed Hotel Sussex that stood in downtown Seaford. It was built around 1896, and is shown in this picture with two porches; but years after, the top porch was taken down. The Hotel burned, however, on October 4, 1954, which was a huge devastation to the community. The fire was fought by Seaford, Blades, Bridgeville, Delmar, Sharptown, Georgetown, Federalsburg, and Salisbury fire companies. The picture shown below was taken during the fire by an amateur photographer.

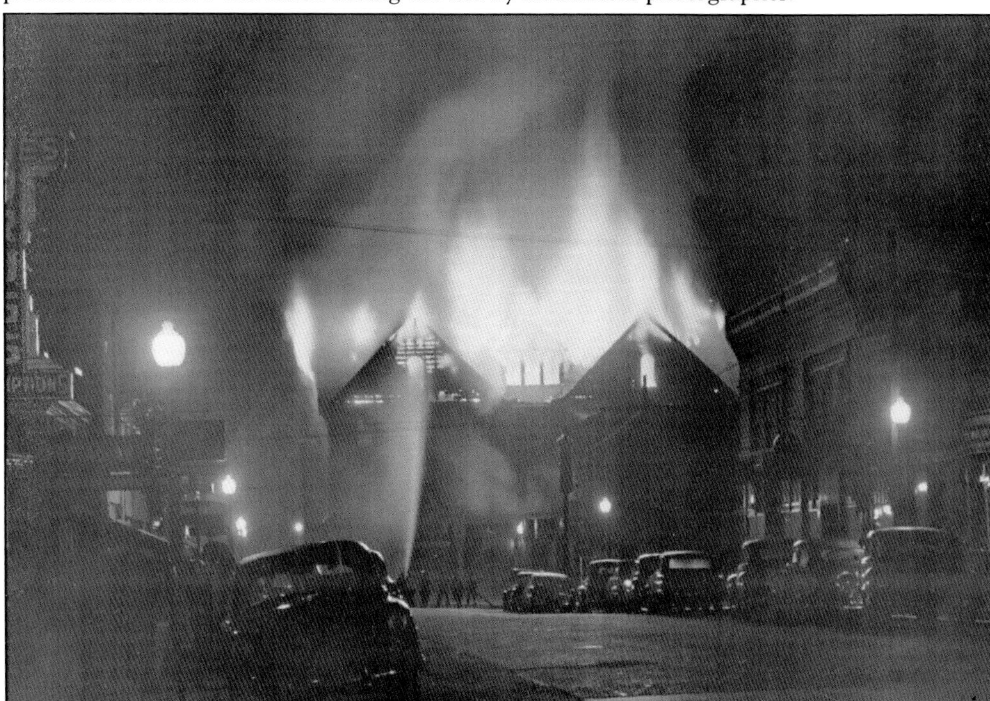

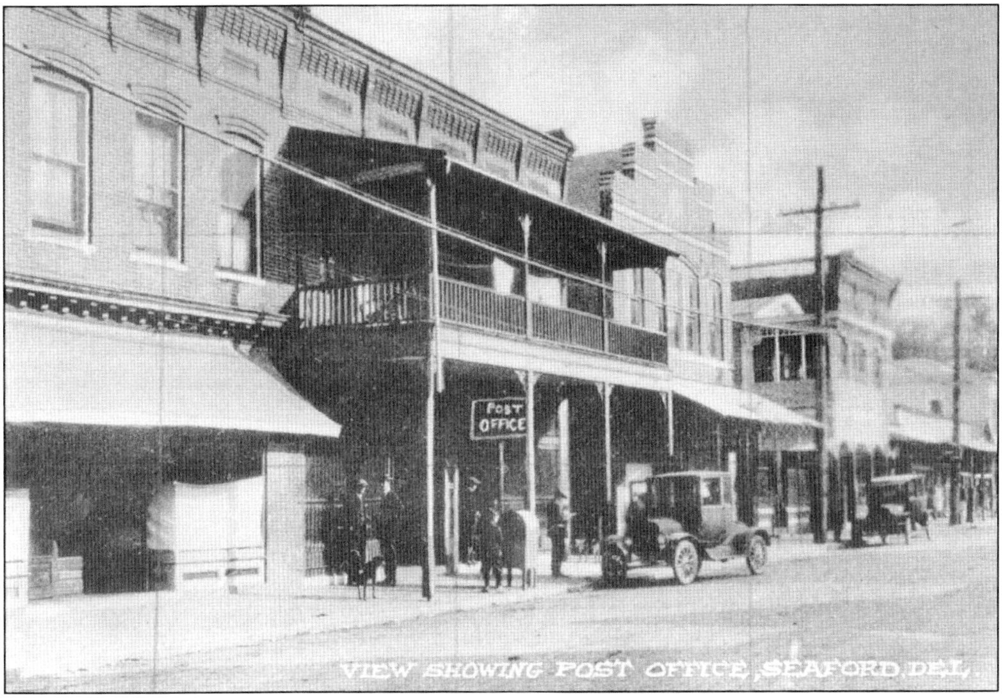

This view of High Street, taken around 1918, shows where the post office was housed during WW I. The building later became Manning's Drug Store. The property to the left housed a store operated by a merchant by the name of Mr. Goodman, and later, became First National Bank.

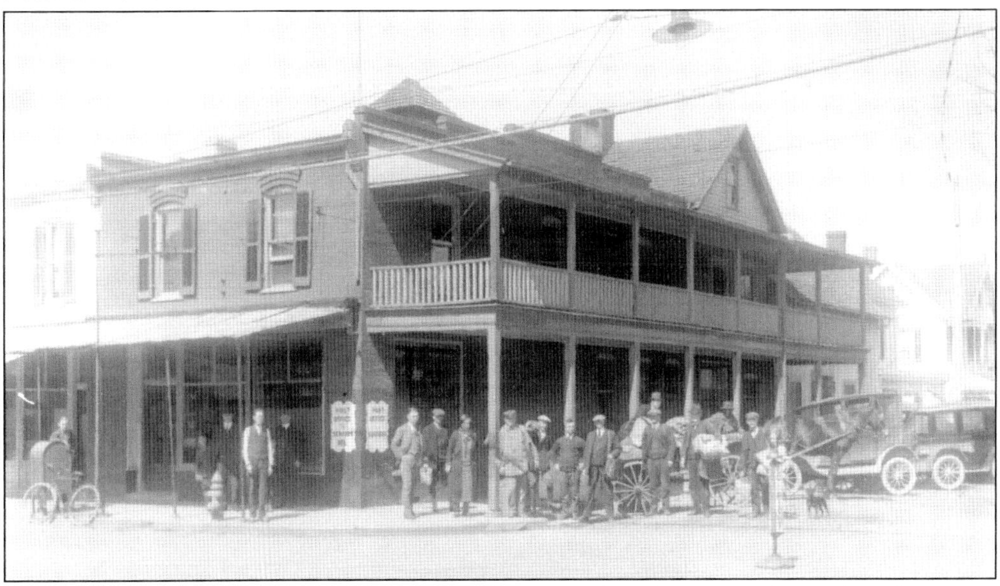
This picture, taken in the early 1930s, shows the post office when it was located on the corner of High and Cannon Streets. The group standing in front of the building represented the postal force at that time. Prior to the post office, the building housed a drugstore that was operated by Mrs. Kitty Rogers. Years after the post office, it was bought by Milton H. James, a real estate operator.

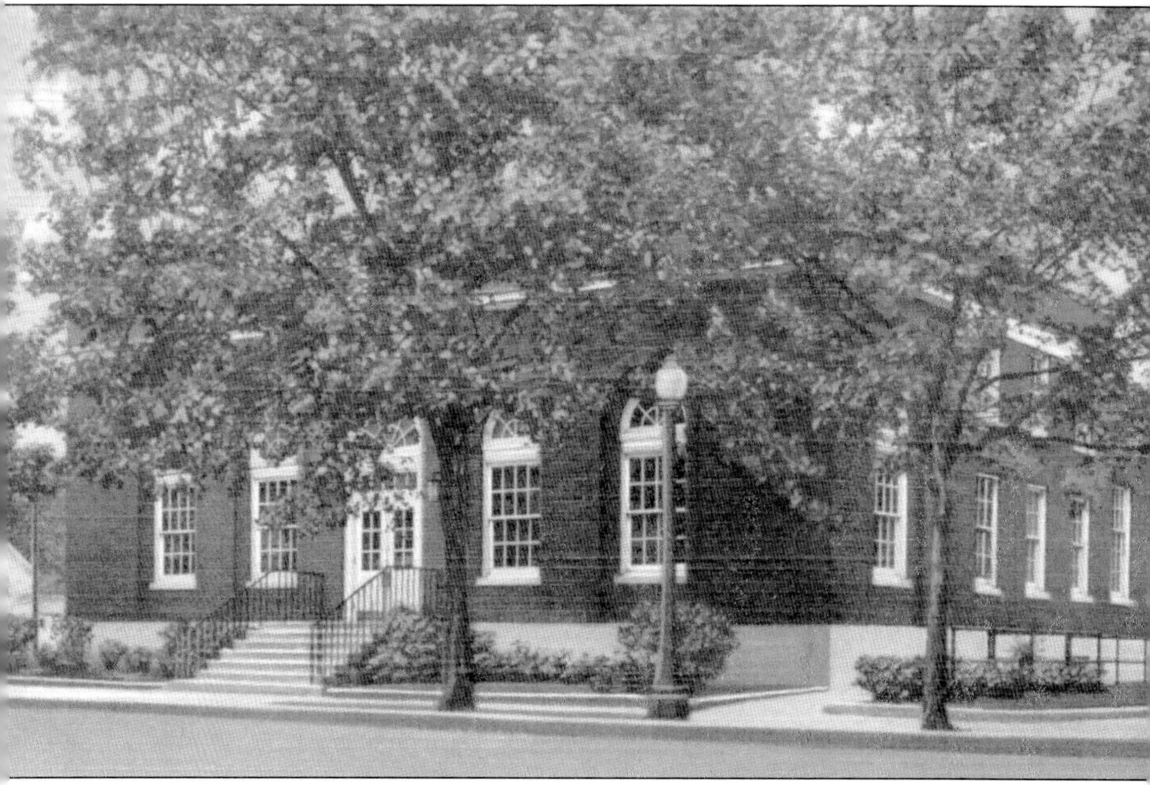

This picture, taken in the mid-to-late 1930s, shows the post office in its current location, at the corner of High and Conwell Streets. The building was constructed in the 1930s solely for the purpose of housing the post office.

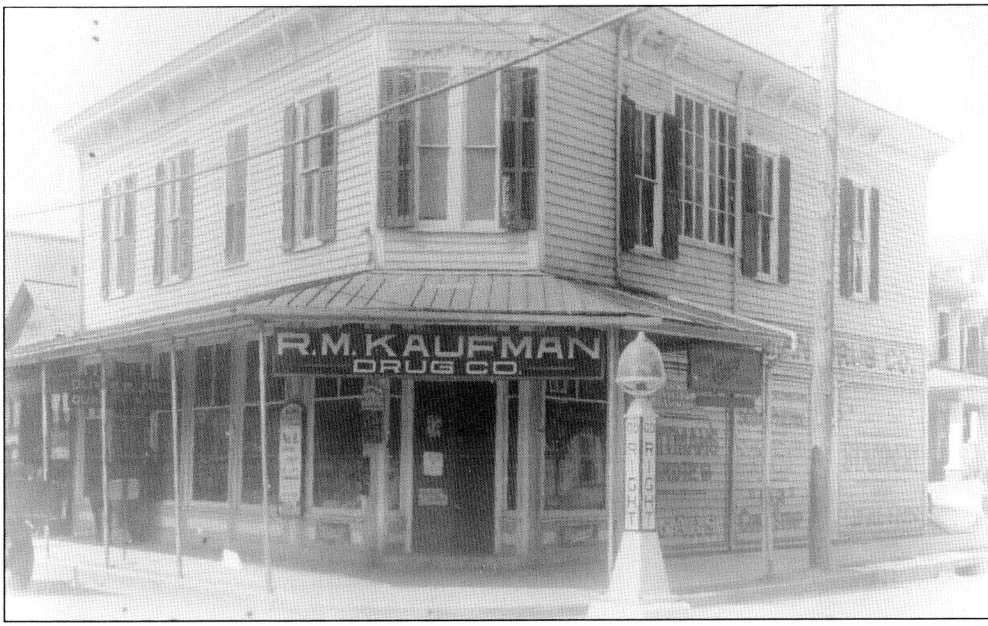

This picture, taken around 1925, shows the Collison Block (as noted on the cornerstone on top of the building) on the corner of High and Pine Streets. It was named for Mr. Joe Collison, a Civil War veteran who owned the property. Dr. R.M. Kauffman had his drugstore here. The traffic signal shown in front of the building was Seaford's first. It was hand operated and turned by crank.

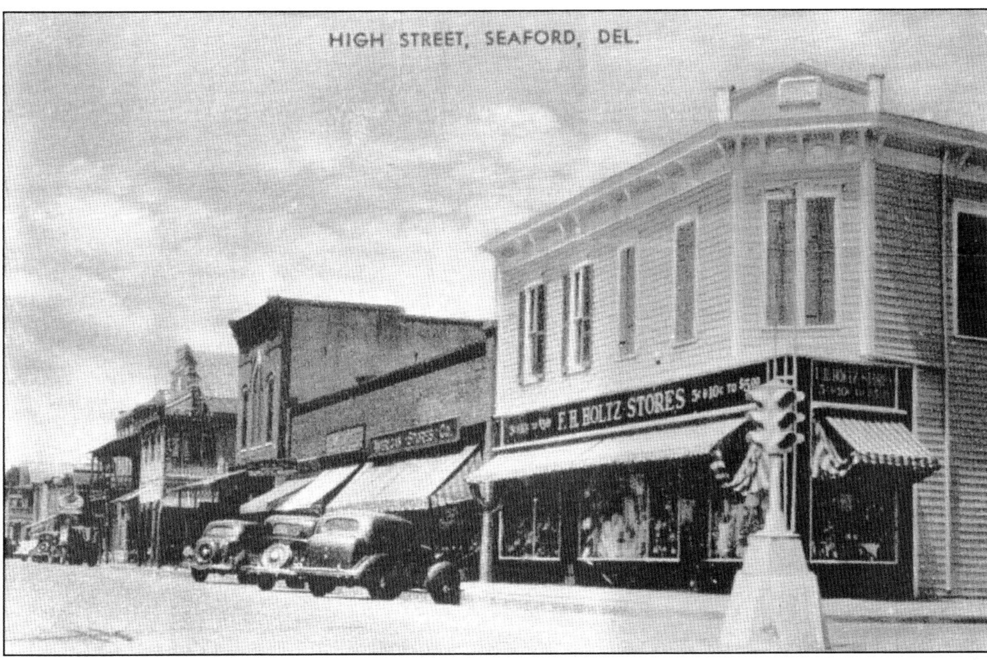

This picture also shows the Collison Block at the corner of High and Pine Streets in the early 1930s. The traffic signal in front of the building was no longer hand operated, but was automated, another first for Seaford.

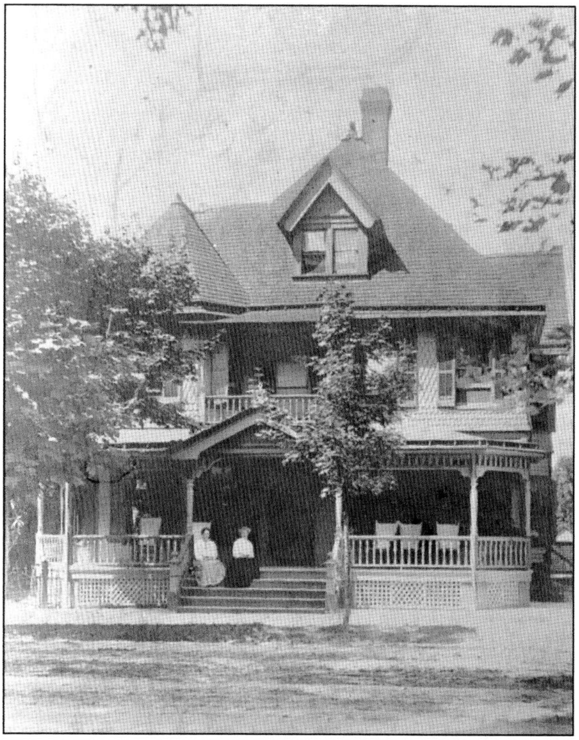

This was the Greenabaum home on High Street. It was owned by Emmanuel Greenabaum, who owned Greenabaum's cannery. Pictured on the porch are Mr. Greenabaum's wife and sister, Lizzy Greenabaum.

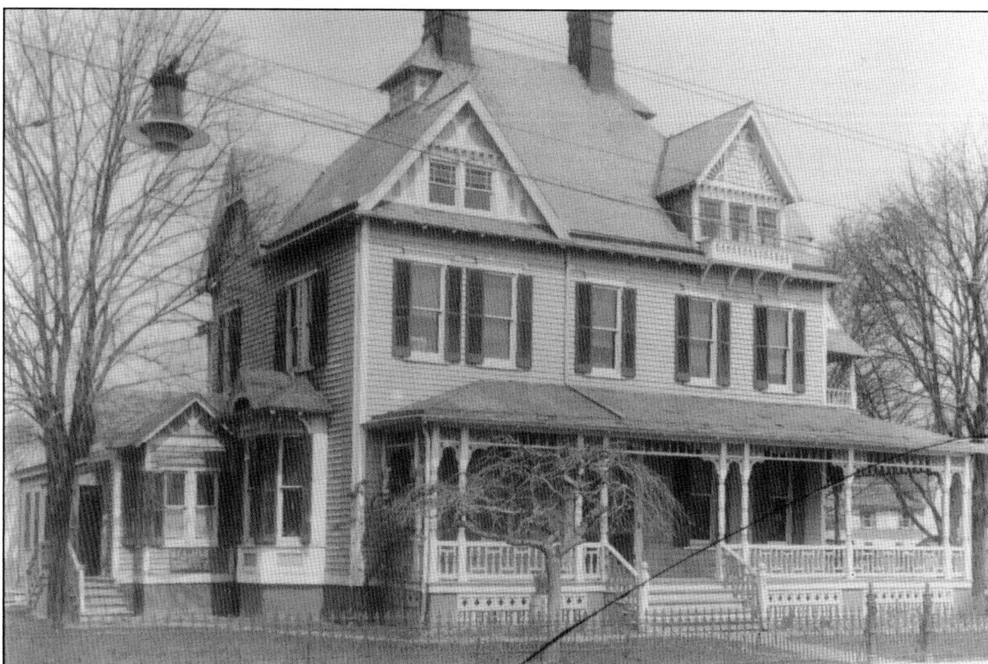

This is a picture of the Ross home that stood adjacent to the Greenabaum home on High Street between Railroad Avenue and Conwell Street. The home, still standing, was later remodeled by Mr. William F. Allen.

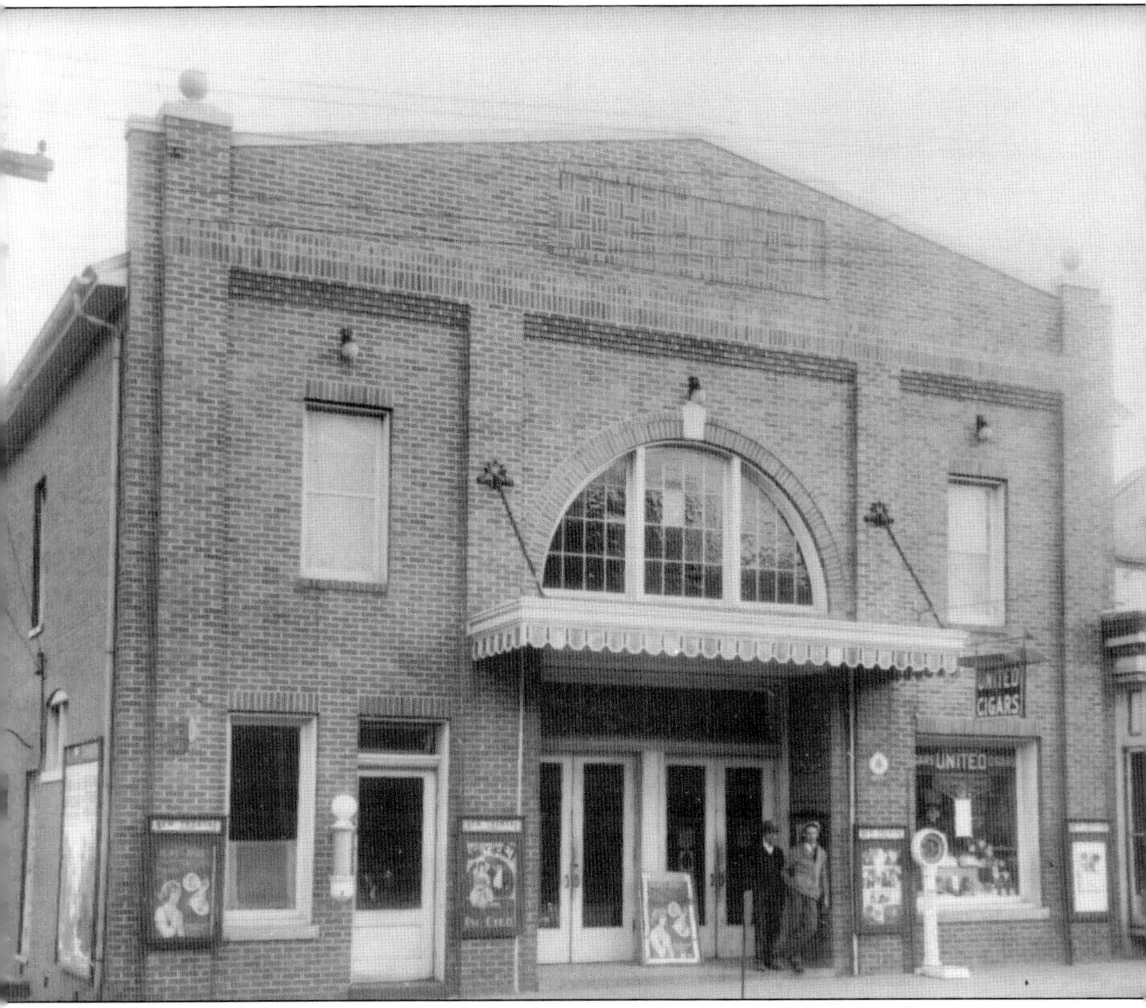

This is a picture of the New Theater that stood at the corner of High and Market Streets. It was owned by Ford Breeding. To the left was a barbershop, and to the right was a cigar shop. The Theater burned twice, and after the second fire, was replaced by the Palace Theater.

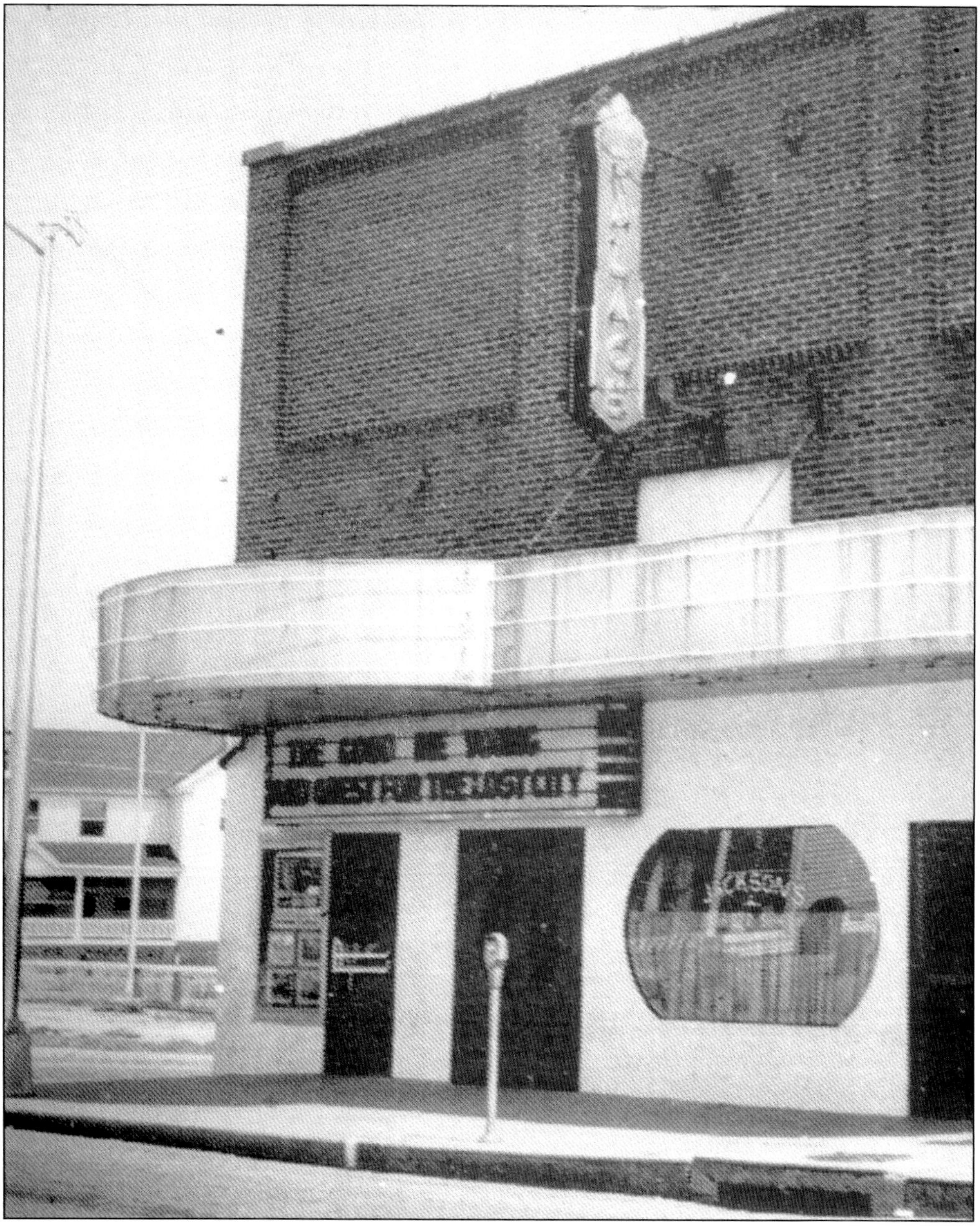

This photo shows the Palace Theater that replaced the New Theater after it burned. It was owned by the Ayers family in the picture. A barbershop remained on the left, but the cigar shop that was on the right was replaced by a beauty shop owned by Albert Jackson. At the time of this picture, Mr. Ted Hatten owned the barbershop. He also sang baritone in the famed Hobbs & Longendyke Minstrel show.

Three

The River & the Railroad

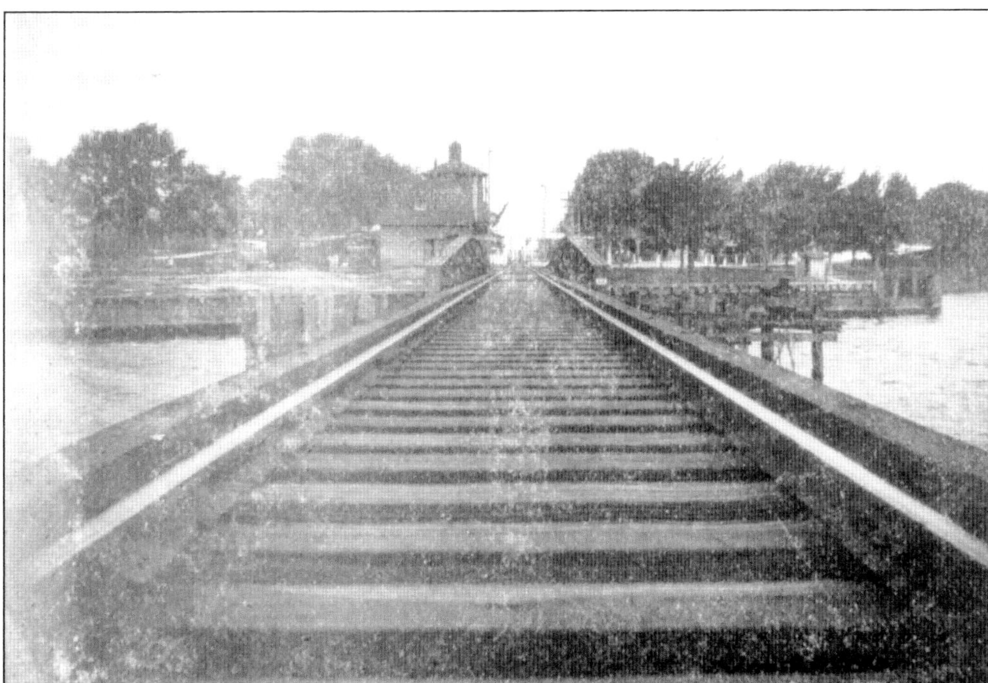

Seaford was blessed with two valuable resources: the Nanticoke River and the railroad. The existence of these were a large part of the reason Seaford experienced the growth that it did. This picture shows the railroad bridge that crossed the Nanticoke looking north.

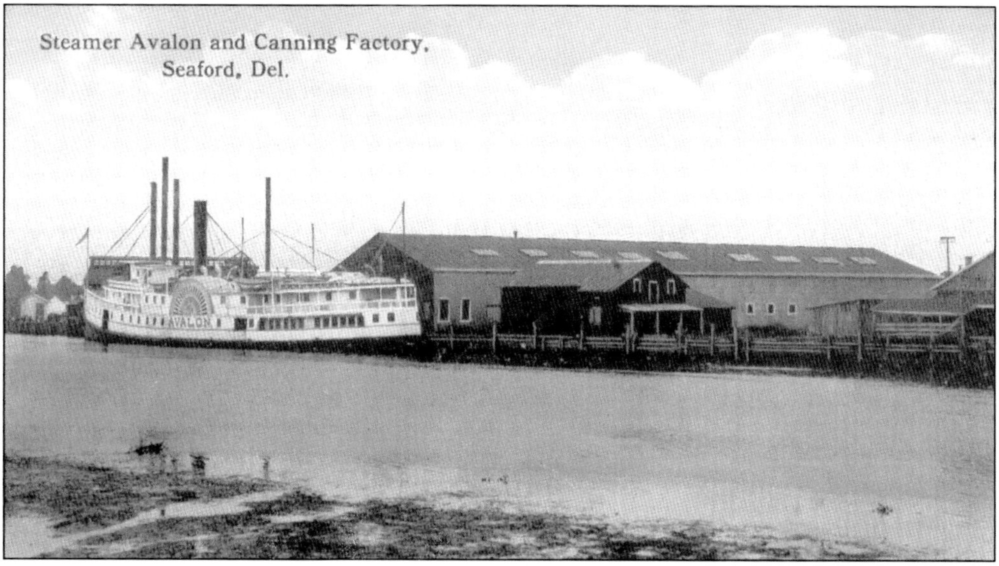

Here, the steamboat *Avalon* can be seen. During the later part of the nineteenth century and early part of the twentieth, steamboats came to Seaford on a daily basis. They came so much, in fact, that they had their own docking space near the railroad depot at New Street. The boats brought merchandise from Baltimore wholesalers to Seaford retailers and businessmen. They were an important part of the community until around 1915. The *Avalon* was not regularly in the Seaford area. The *Joppa* and the *Tangier* most often made voyages here. The *Avalon* was a much larger ship and was generally used when churches had Sunday school picnics. Everyone would board the ship and sail to Sandy Hill for a days outing and swimming.

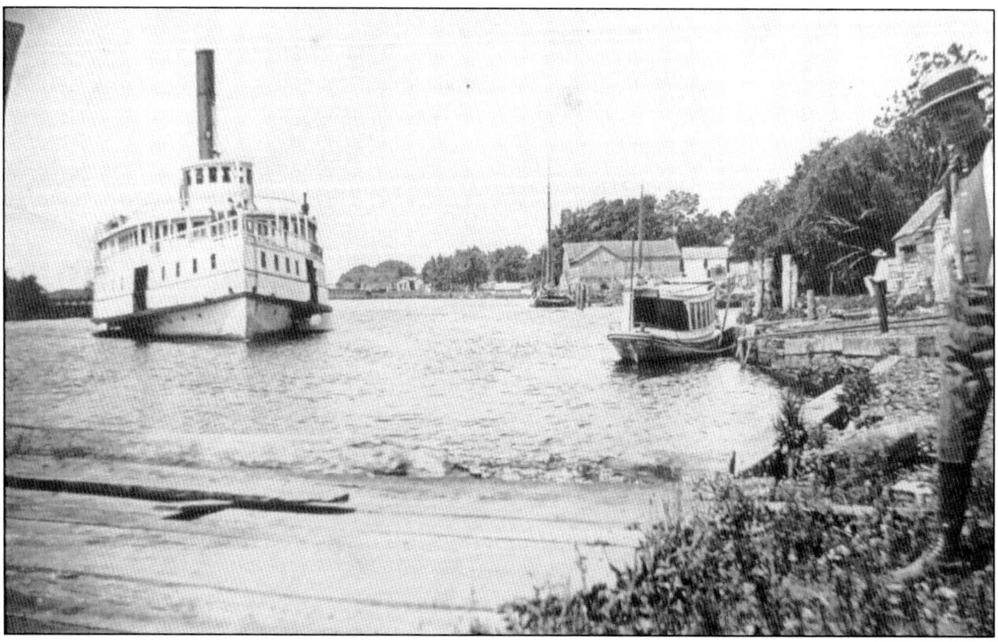

This picture shows another steamboat coming into Seaford. To the right, the old steamboat wharf where the steamboats docked can be seen.

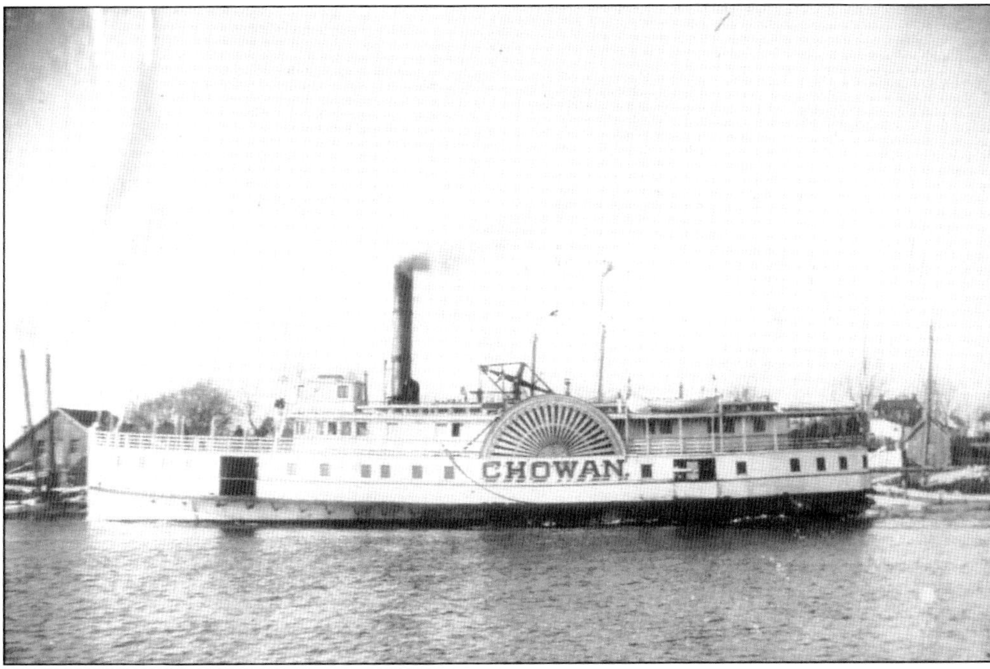

The *Chowan*, shown here, was another steamboat that frequented Seaford. It was named for the Chowan River in North Carolina, and actually frequented that area more so than Seaford.

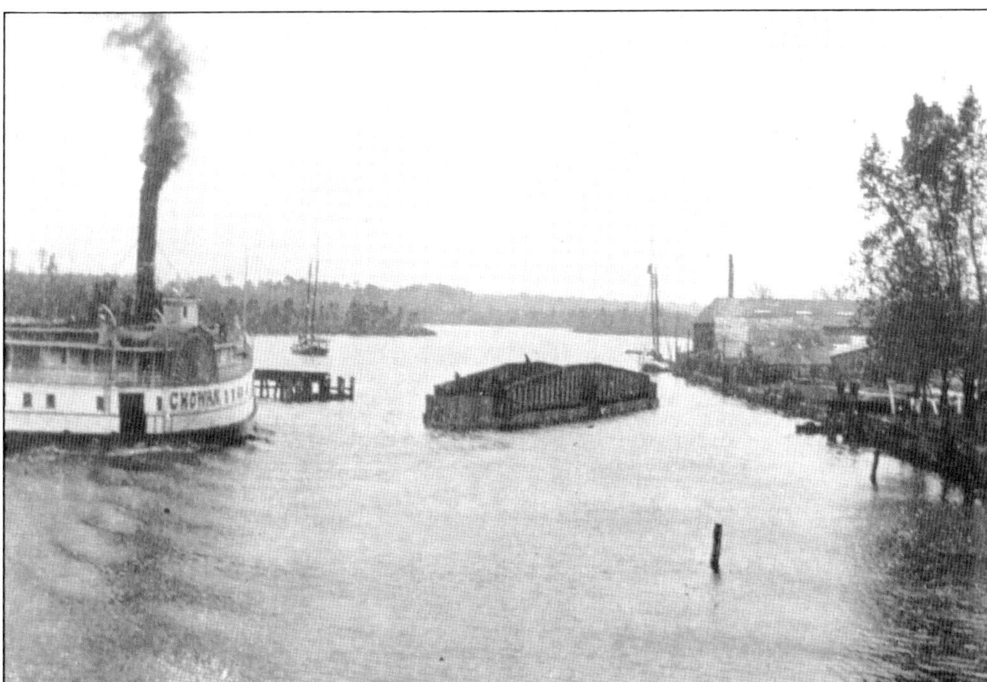

The *Chowan* is shown in this picture backing away from the wharf and preparing to go out through the railroad draw bridge, which is shown open.

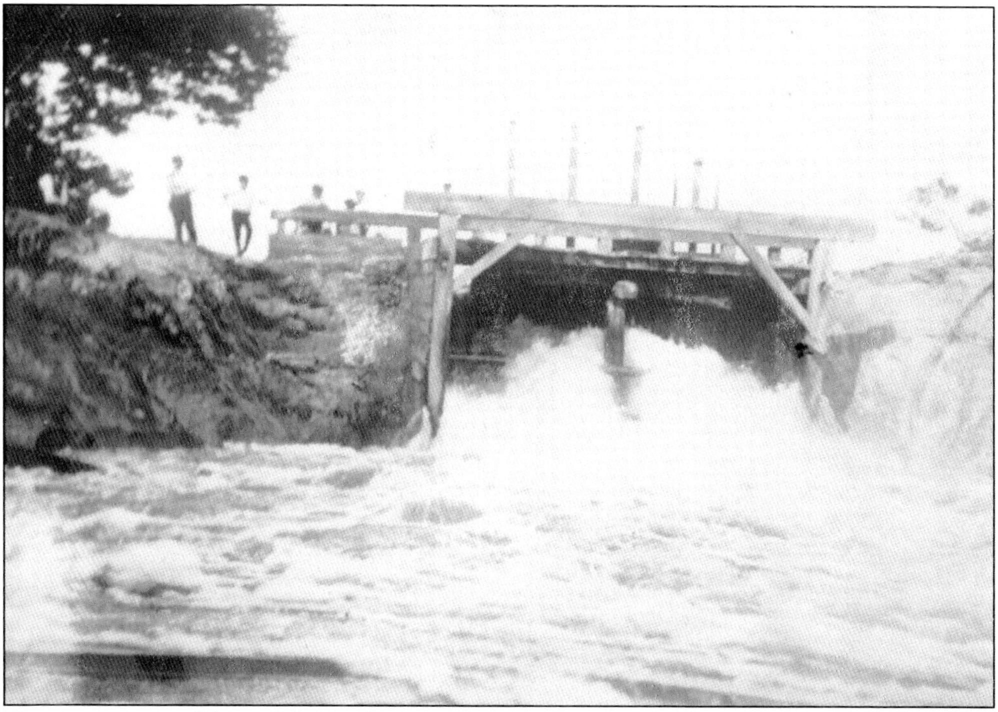

This is a picture of the milldam spilling water. It stood just west of where Nanticoke Memorial Hospital is currently located. It was built over a big dirt dike that went over and dammed water rather effectively. The milldam remained until the 1930s when a flood destroyed it.

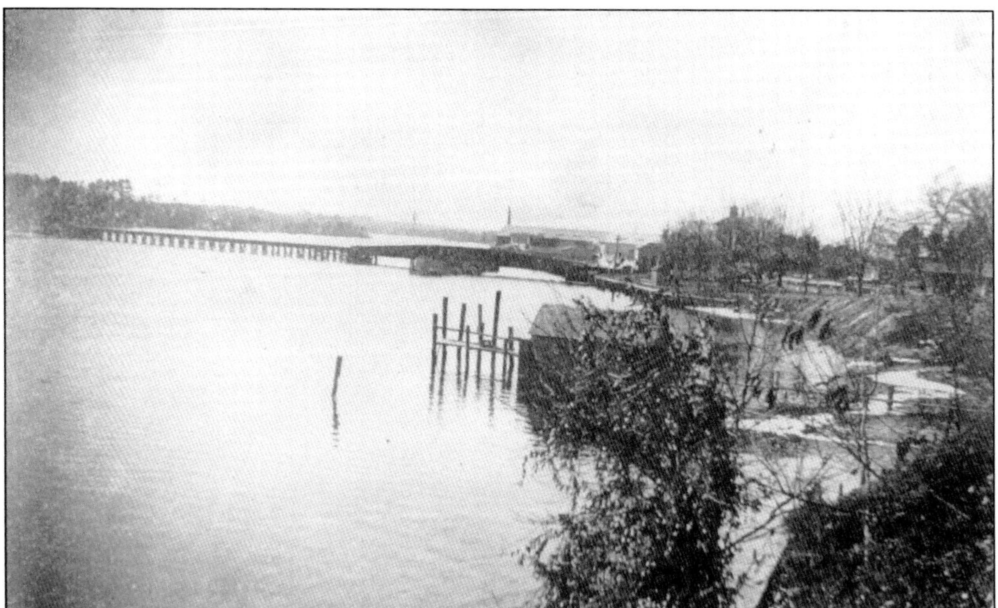

This picture, looking from south Cannon Street, shows the railroad bridge that crossed the Nanticoke River. A new bridge has since been installed.

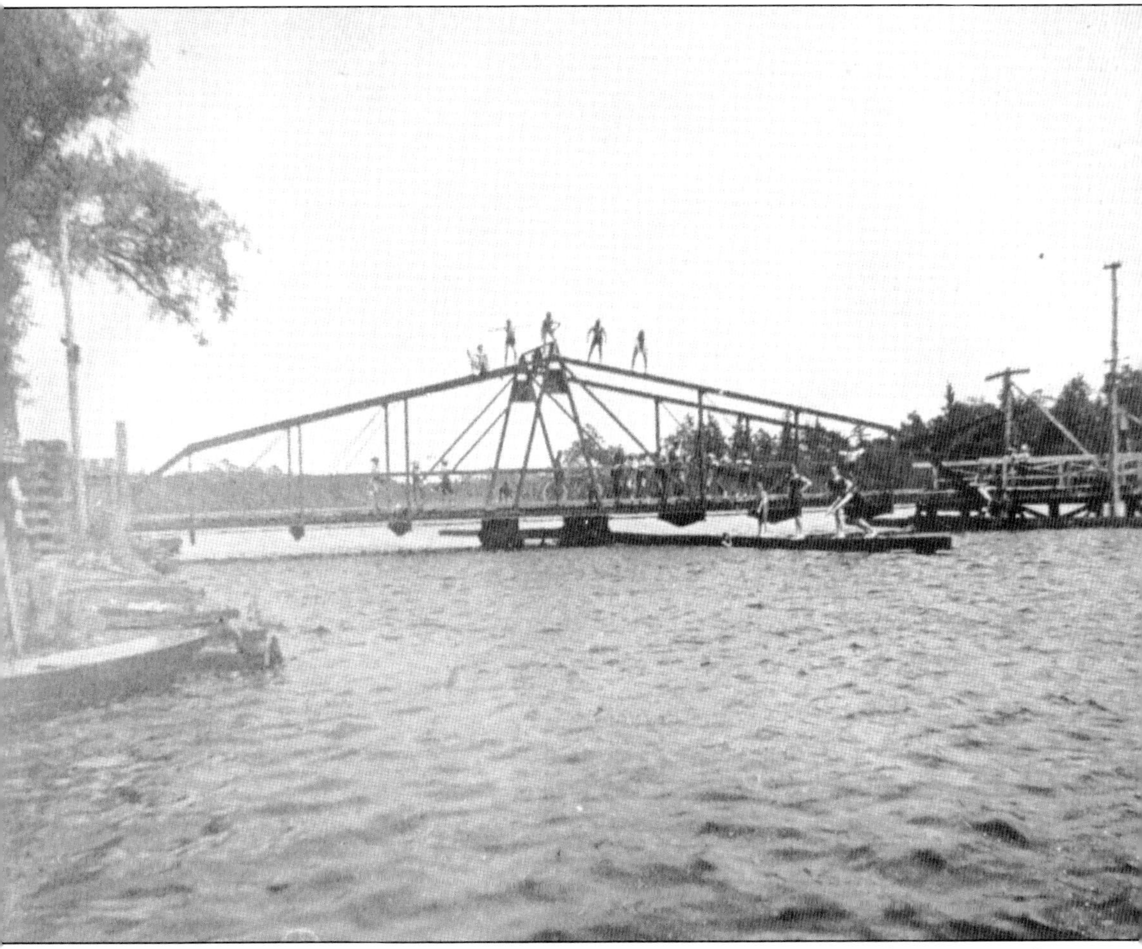

This is a picture of the toll bridge that spanned the Nanticoke between Market Street and Blades Causeway. On top of the bridge are local youth about to jump into the river. This was not an uncommon sight, as many boys learned to swim this way (including Mr. Wright Robinson).

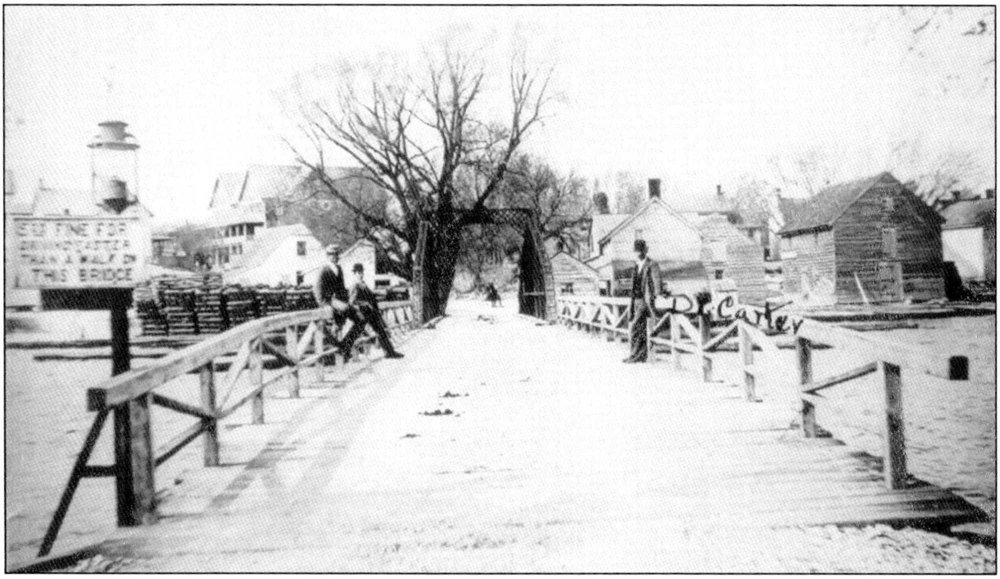

This shows the wooden toll bridge that was built over the Nanticoke in 1832 by the Seaford Bridge Company. It was a toll bridge until 1865 when it became public property. Prior to that, a franchise was granted from the State to Hugh Martin and his family to collect the tolls.

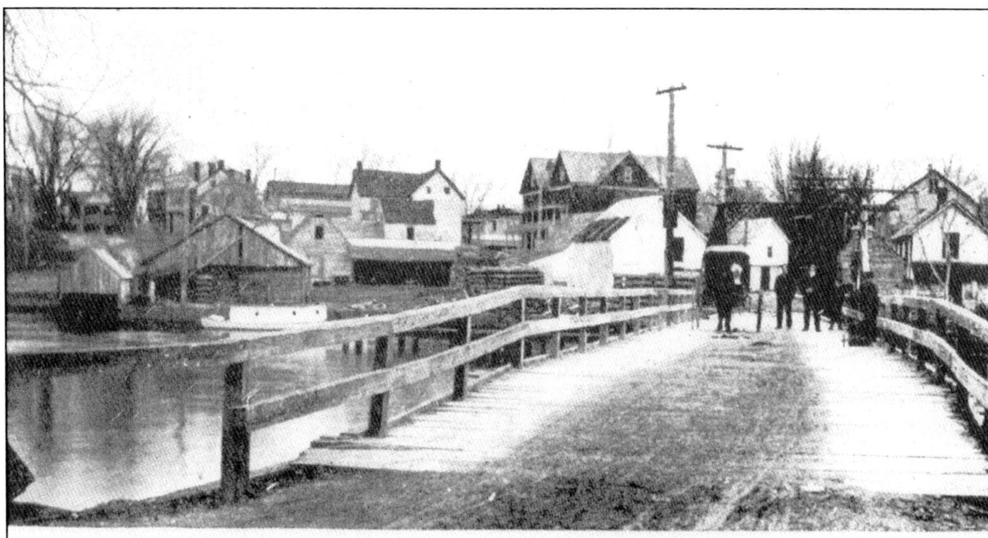

This is another view of the old bridge that crossed the Nanticoke at the foot of Front Street. It was actually a draw bridge; the middle part would swing out to allow boats to go to Concord.

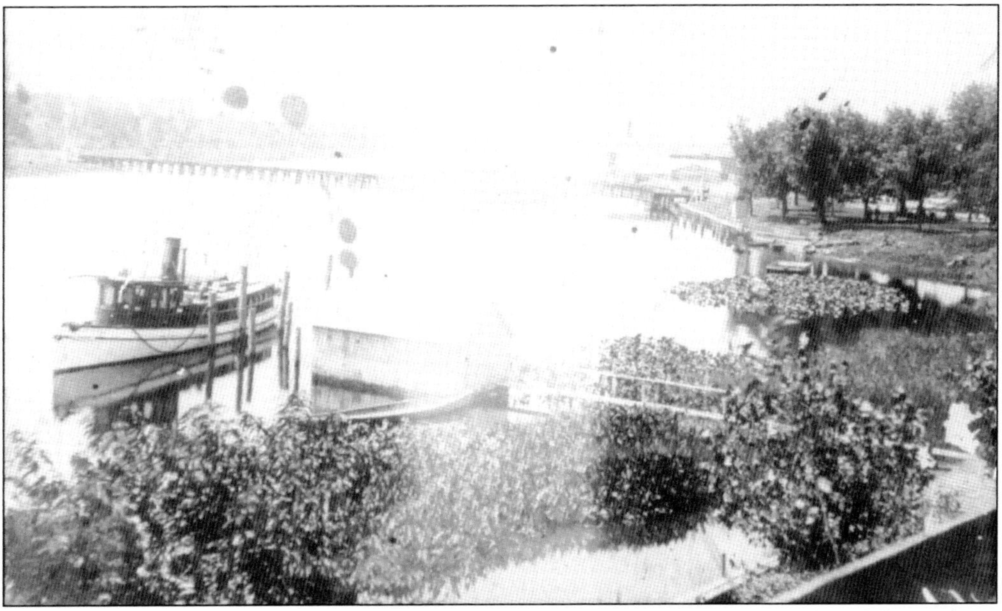

On the left of this picture, Mr. Will Ross's yacht can be seen. Just to the right of the yacht, a small boat house at the foot of New Street that was built by Martin Willey can be seen. Mr. Ross lived right up the alley from New Street and kept his yacht berthed at this location.

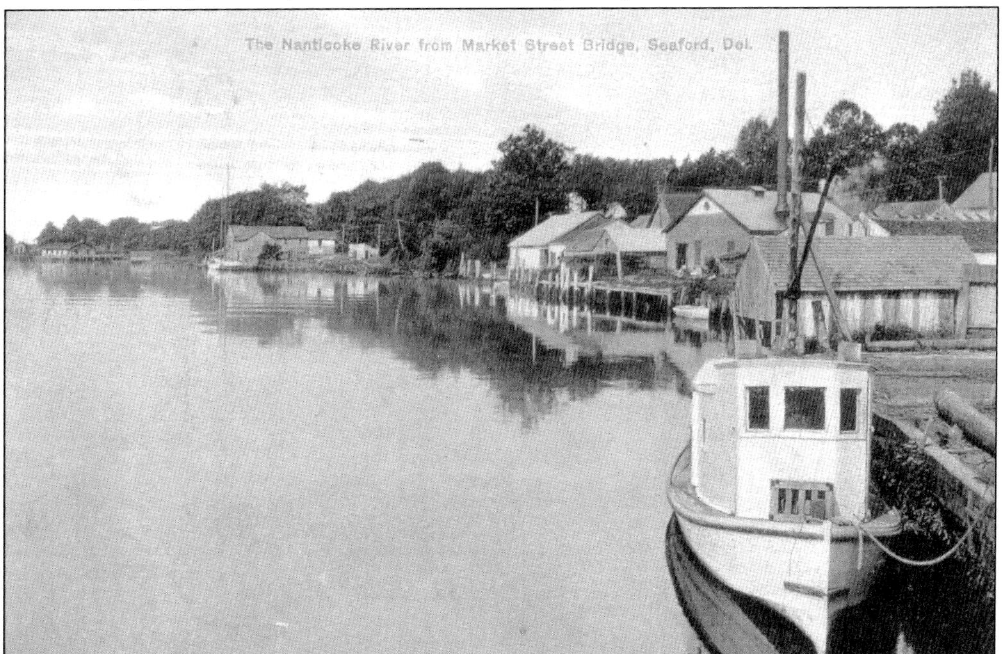

This picture shows the Nanticoke River from the Market Street Bridge around 1910. The dock area was utilized by many different types of water vessels in the early twentieth century. In the left center of the photo, one of the Oyster houses that flourished in the late nineteenth and early twentieth centuries in Seaford can be seen. This one was JB Robinson and Company, which stood at the foot of Cannon Street. The smokestacks at the right-hand side of the picture are from the City Power Plant.

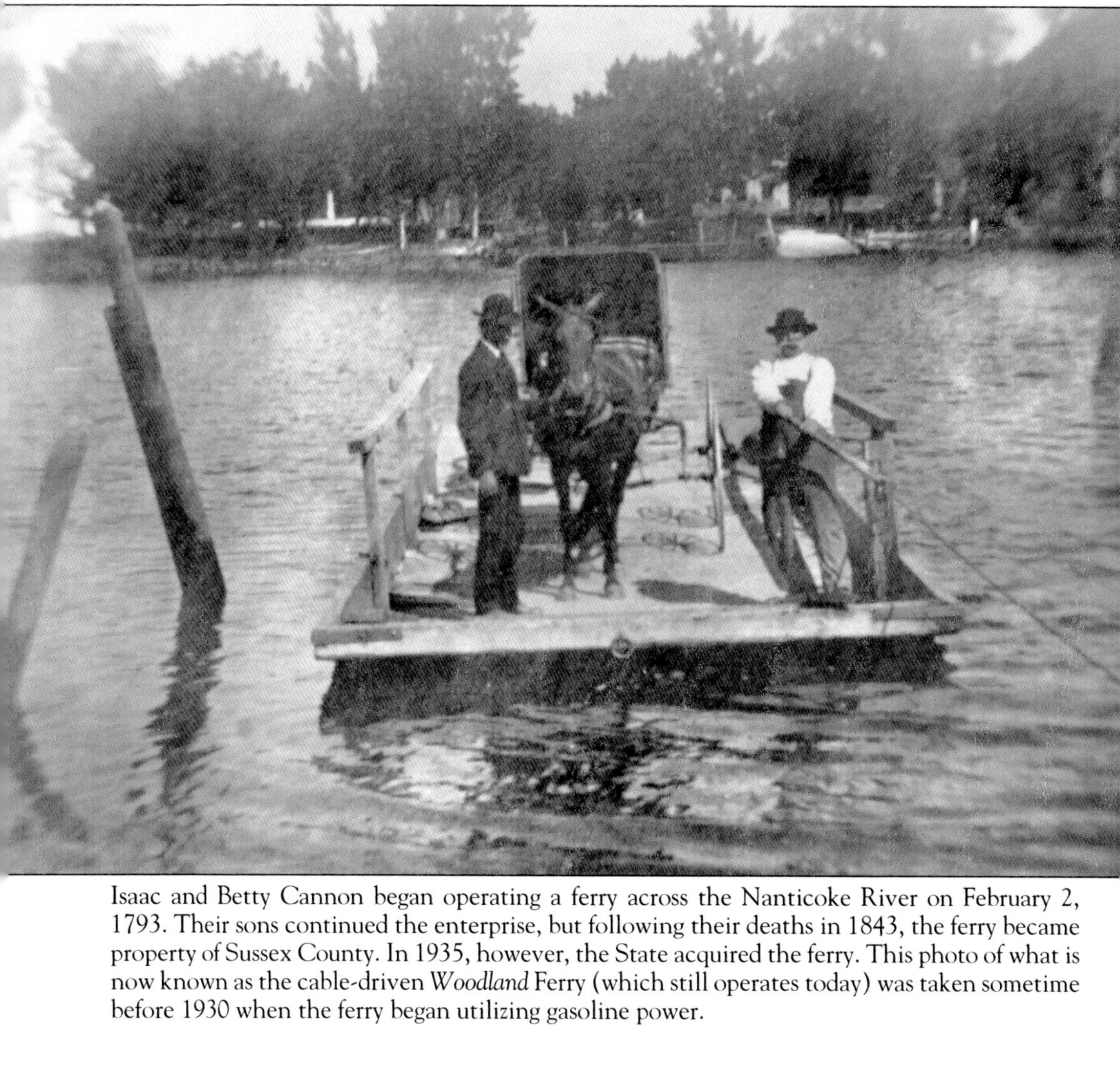

Isaac and Betty Cannon began operating a ferry across the Nanticoke River on February 2, 1793. Their sons continued the enterprise, but following their deaths in 1843, the ferry became property of Sussex County. In 1935, however, the State acquired the ferry. This photo of what is now known as the cable-driven *Woodland* Ferry (which still operates today) was taken sometime before 1930 when the ferry began utilizing gasoline power.

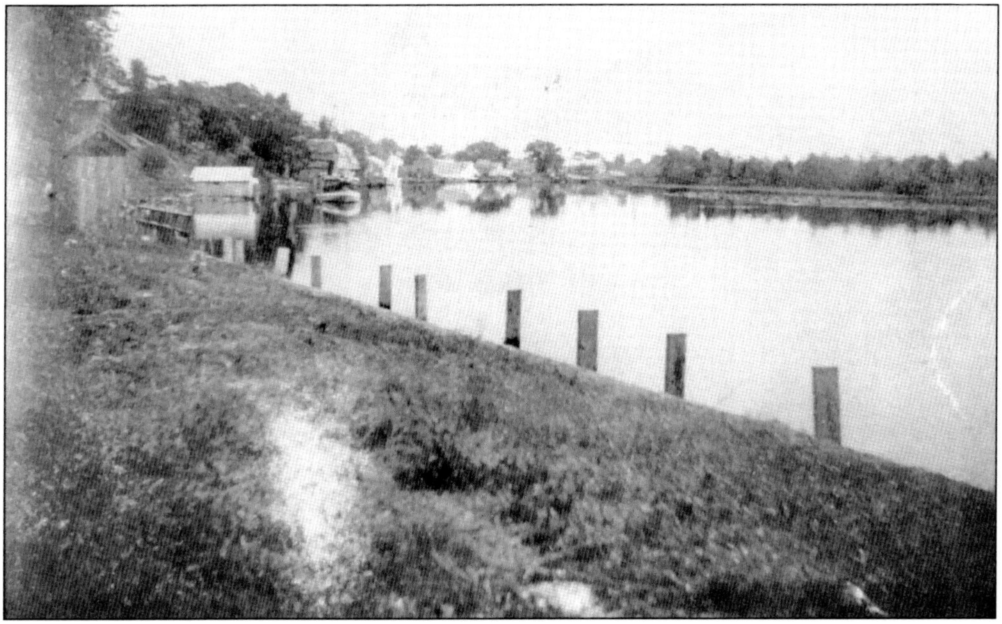

This picture of the Nanticoke River was taken from the Railroad property looking east. In the background, some of the many oyster houses that lined the river can be seen.

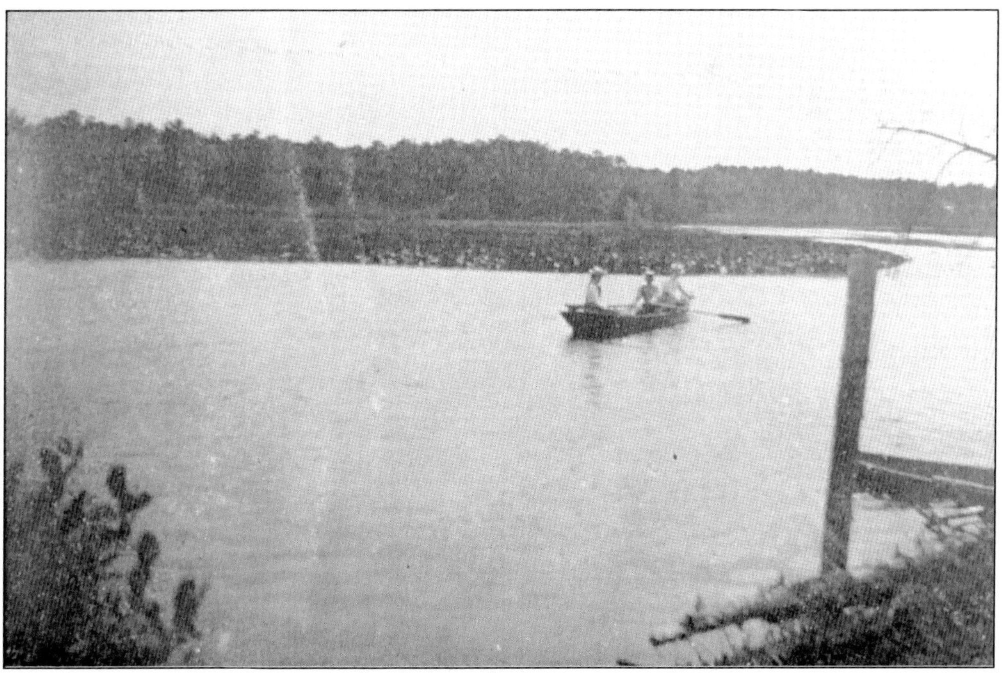

This photograph shows boaters enjoying the pristine Nanticoke River as they often do in Seaford.

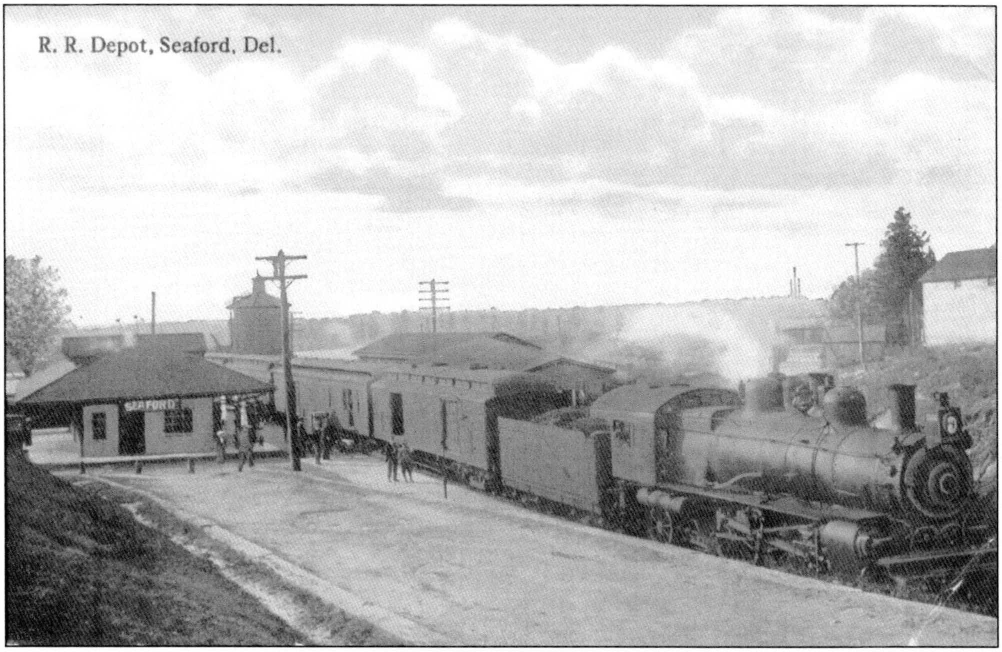

Taken around 1900, this picture shows a passenger train arriving in Seaford. The train would carry people back and forth from Seaford to Cambridge until it closed in 1949. In the background, a water tower can be seen. The trains would have to stop at the tower to get water for their boilers to make steam, which propelled the trains at that time.

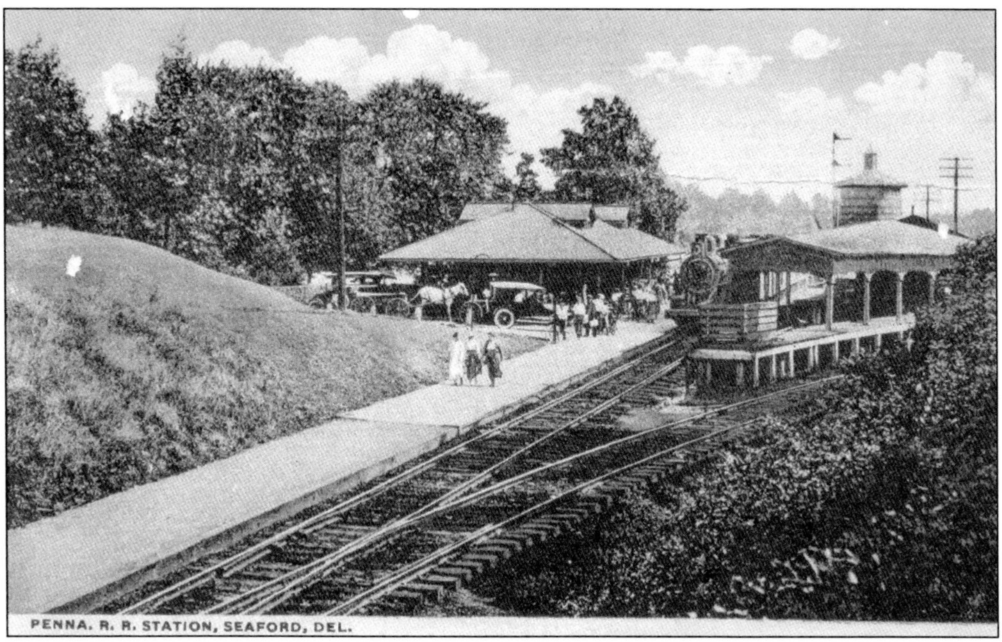

A later view of the Seaford Railroad Station can be seen here. The walkway lead from the depot to High Street, enabling people to walk into town easily. People could also hire a horse-drawn hack, like the ones shown next to the depot, to get into town. The branch of the track to the right was the one that went to Cambridge, Maryland.

This picture shows some locals posing on the front end of a train coming into Seaford.

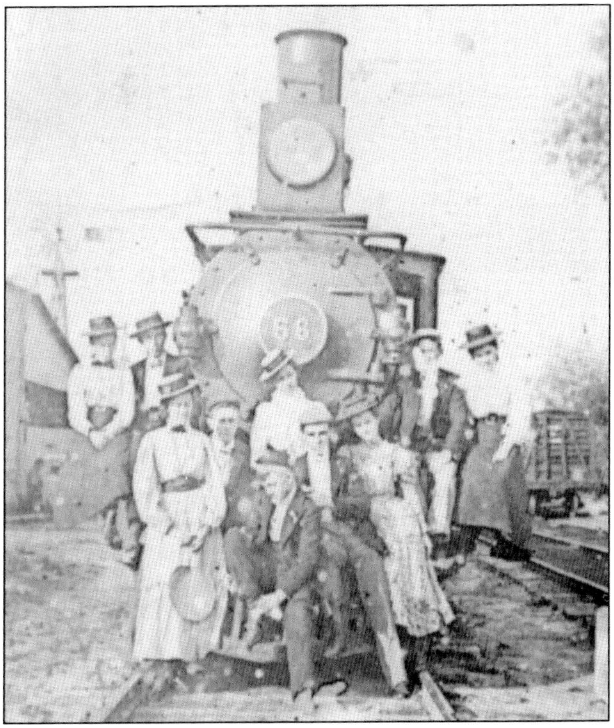

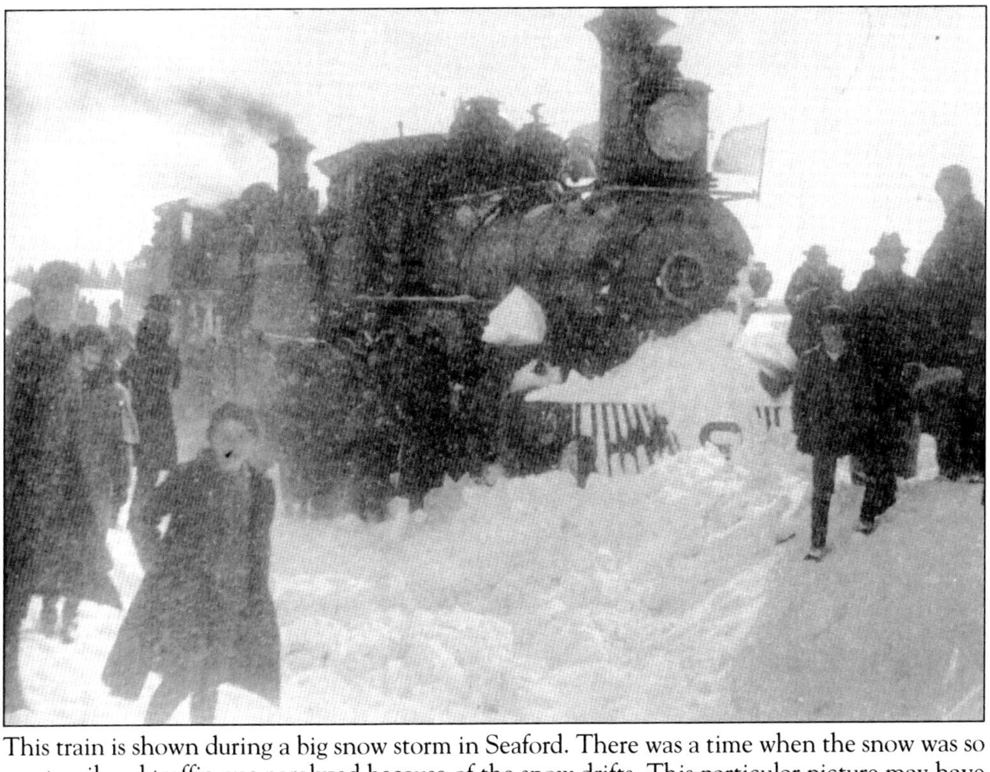

This train is shown during a big snow storm in Seaford. There was a time when the snow was so great, railroad traffic was paralyzed because of the snow drifts. This particular picture may have been taken around the turn of the century.

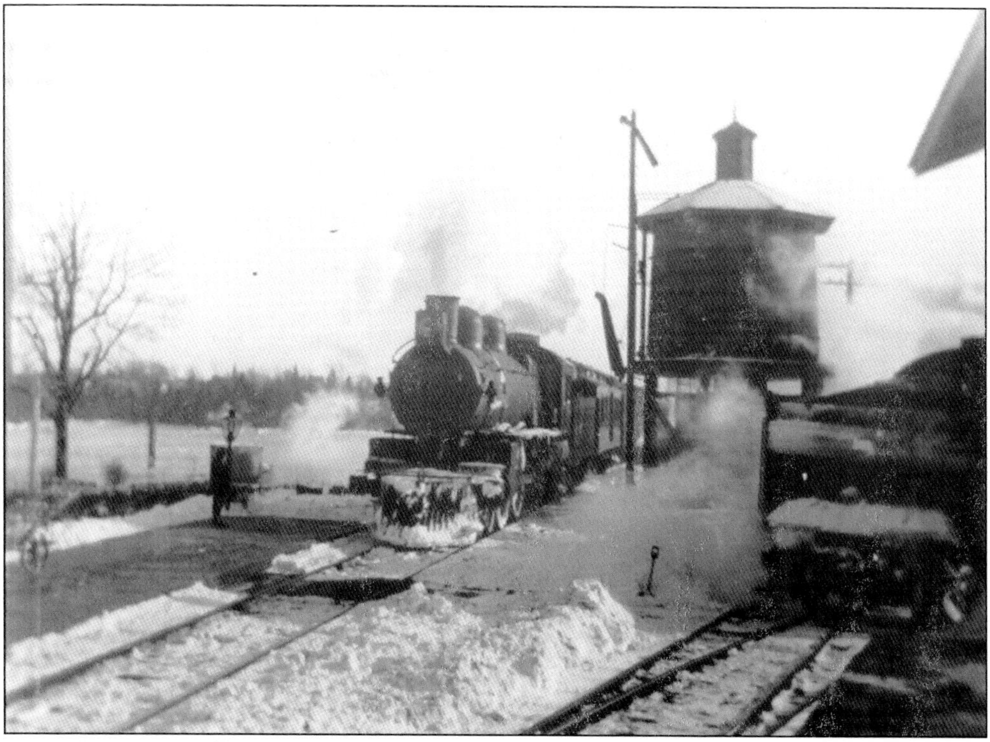

It was Governor Will Ross that fought for a railroad station and line in Seaford. It was in 1856 that the Delaware Railroad extended its service to Seaford from Wilmington, Delaware, giving Seaford two outlets to metropolitan markets—the river and the railroad. This picture shows a train in front of the water tower passing through Seaford.

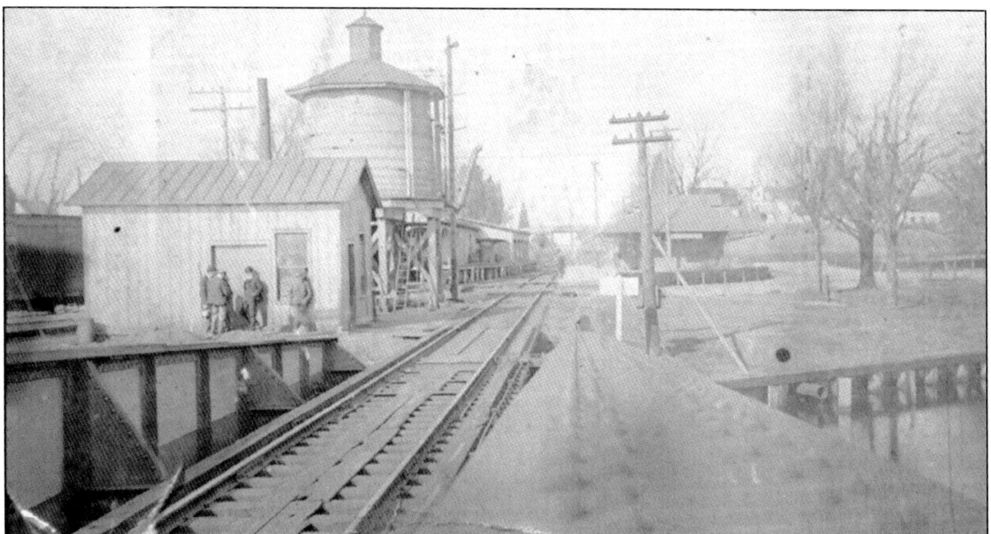

This is another view of the railroad station and the water tower from the early 1900s.

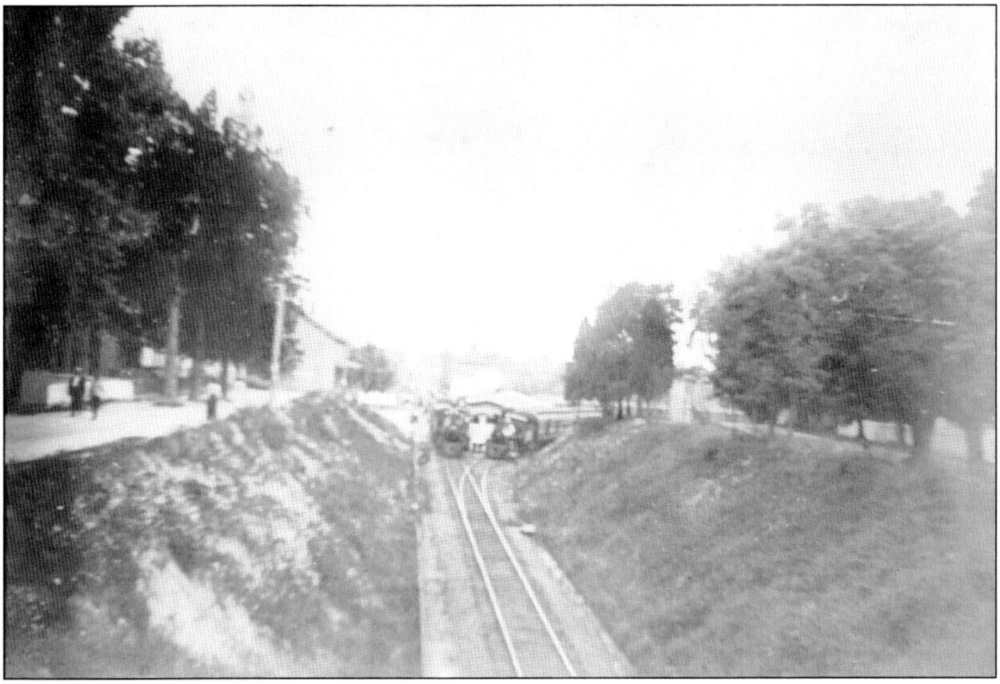

This is a picture of the Deep-cut. This entire area was dug by mules and immigrants utilizing scoop shovels. The men followed behind the scoop shovels, which were being pulled by mules.

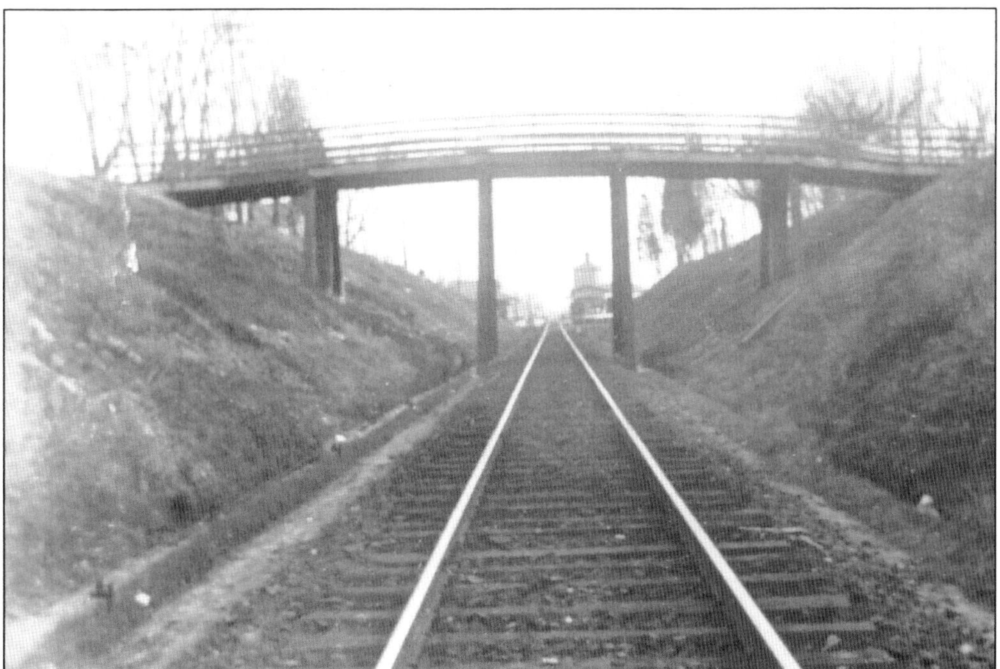

This photo shows the railroad and bridge. The bridge shown was a drawbridge that was maintained by the railroad. During the Civil War and WW II, the bridge was guarded by troops because it was very important for transportation between the north and south.

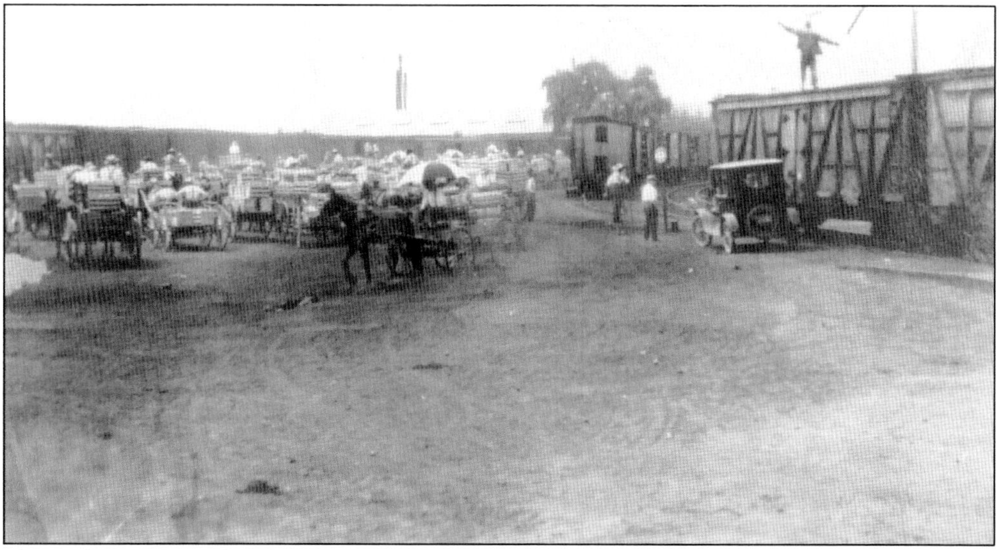

Shown here is the railroad yard with wagons full of produce. This is where produce buyers would assemble and buy fruits and vegetables from the farmers. Produce would then be placed in ice freight cars, like the one shown in the right of the picture, and transported to city markets.

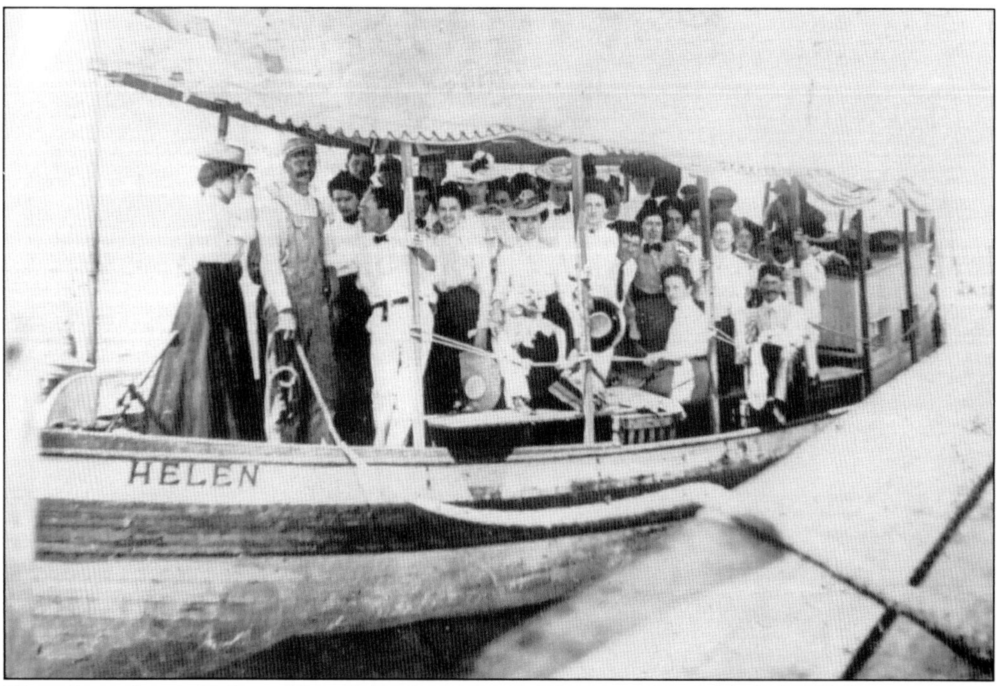

This photo shows the boat *Helen* full of passengers. They were most likely headed to Bivalve or Sandy Hill for a day's outing.

Four

People

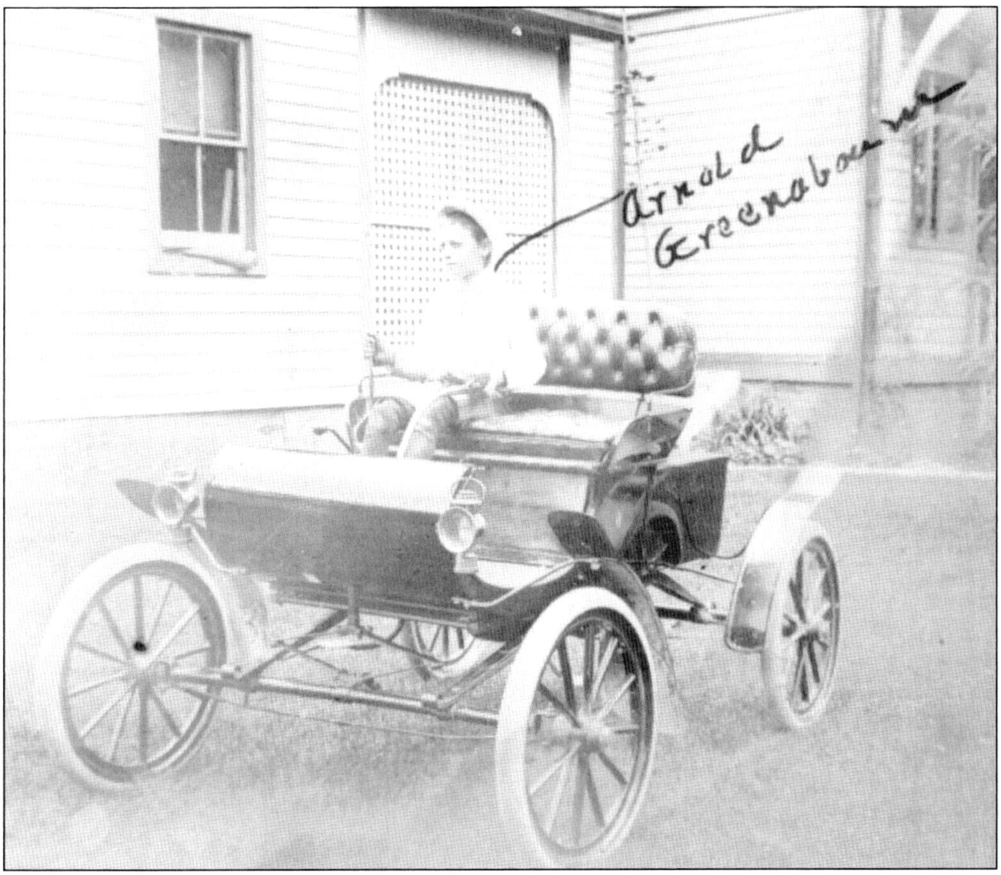

Pictured in this car is Arnold Greenabaum. The Greenabaum family was into automotive equipment early; they actually had a couple of automobiles at that time. Adventurous Young Arnold at one time built an airplane, but he never flew it because his mother gave him $100 to tear the plane down after he had built it.

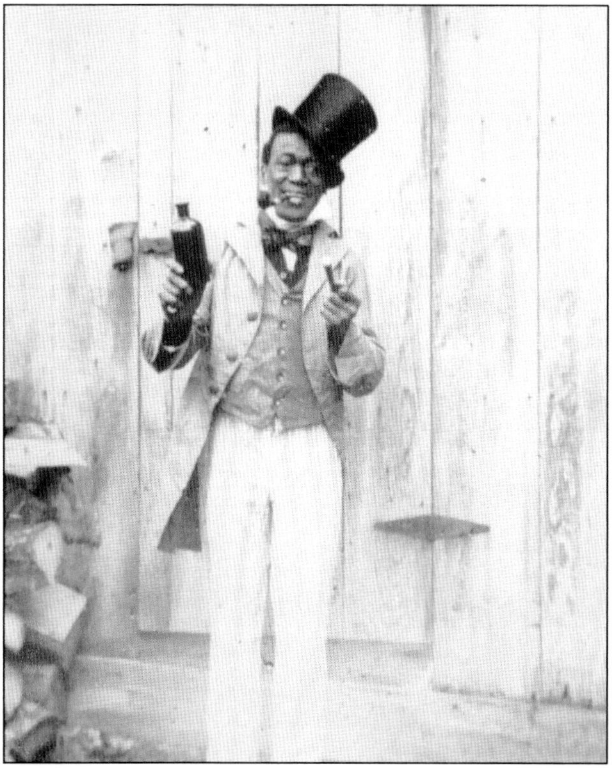

In both of these, Arthur Adams, better known in the community as "Sloppy" Adams, is pictured. He was well liked by everyone and ended his days washing windows for Seaford merchants.

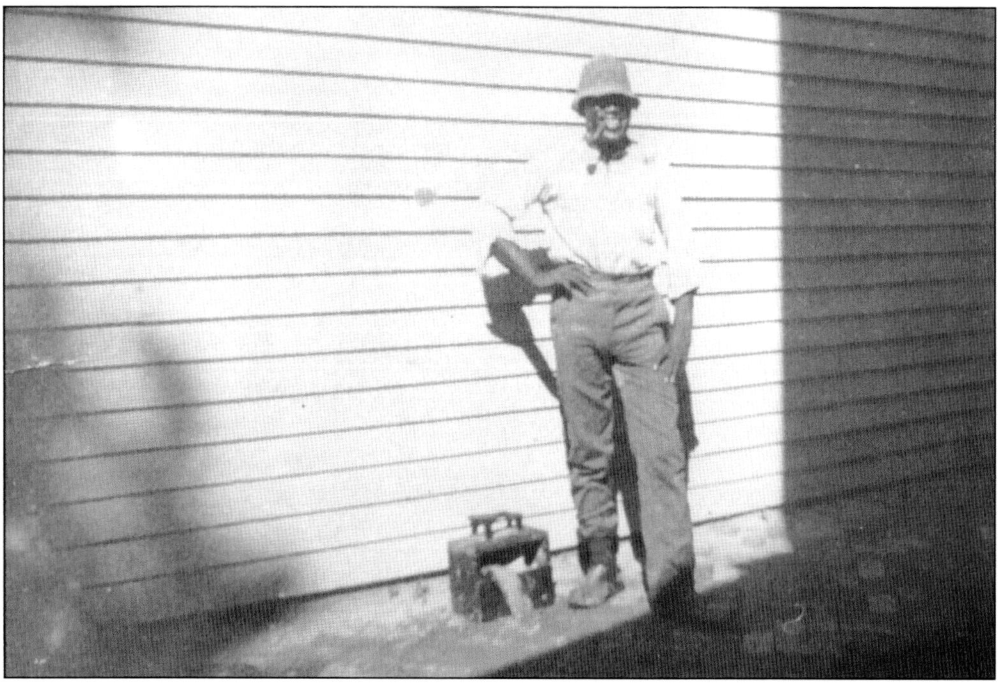

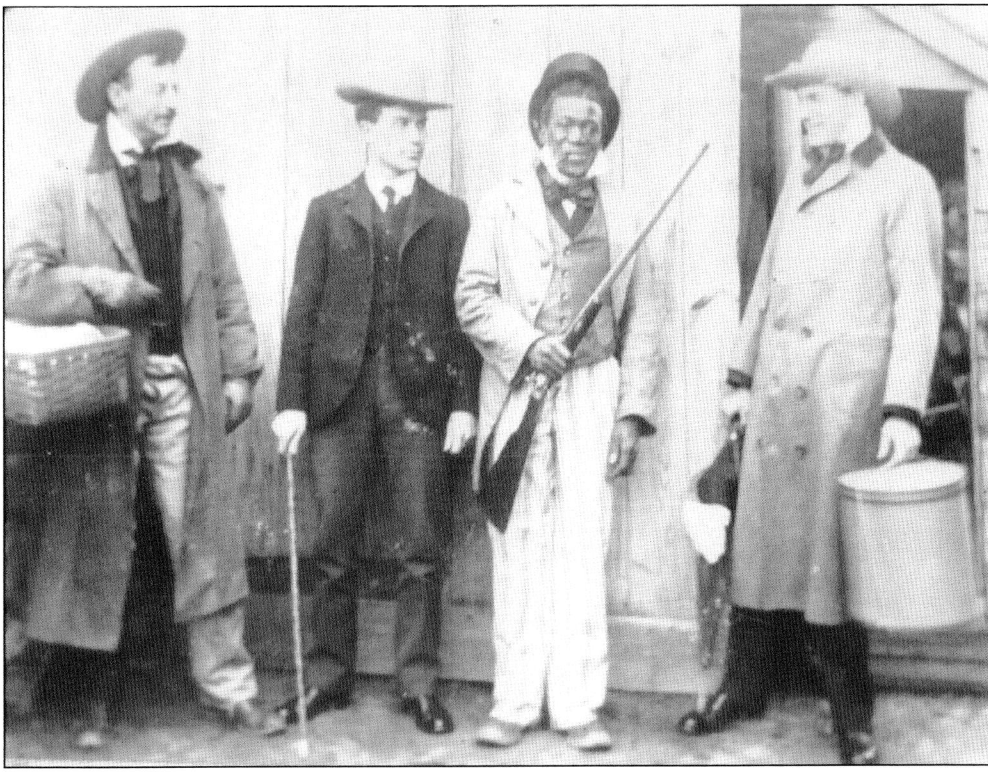

In this picture, "Sloppy" Adams is seen standing with, from left to right, Sam Fields, Walter Wallace, and Theron Stewart.

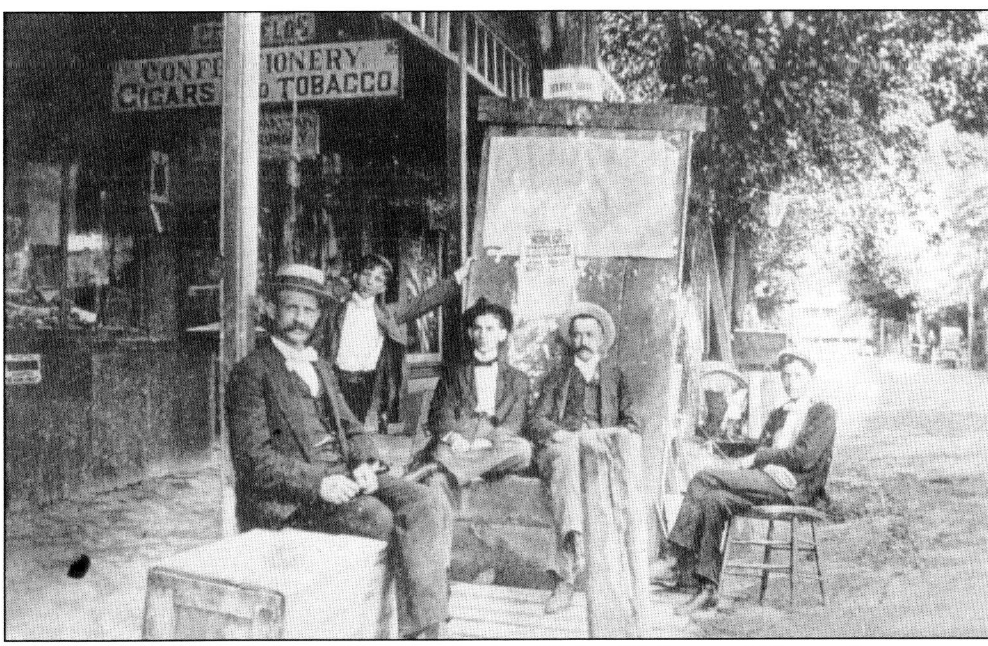

This picture, taken in downtown Seaford, displays Walter Wallace and Theron Stewart sitting with some other Seaford gentlemen.

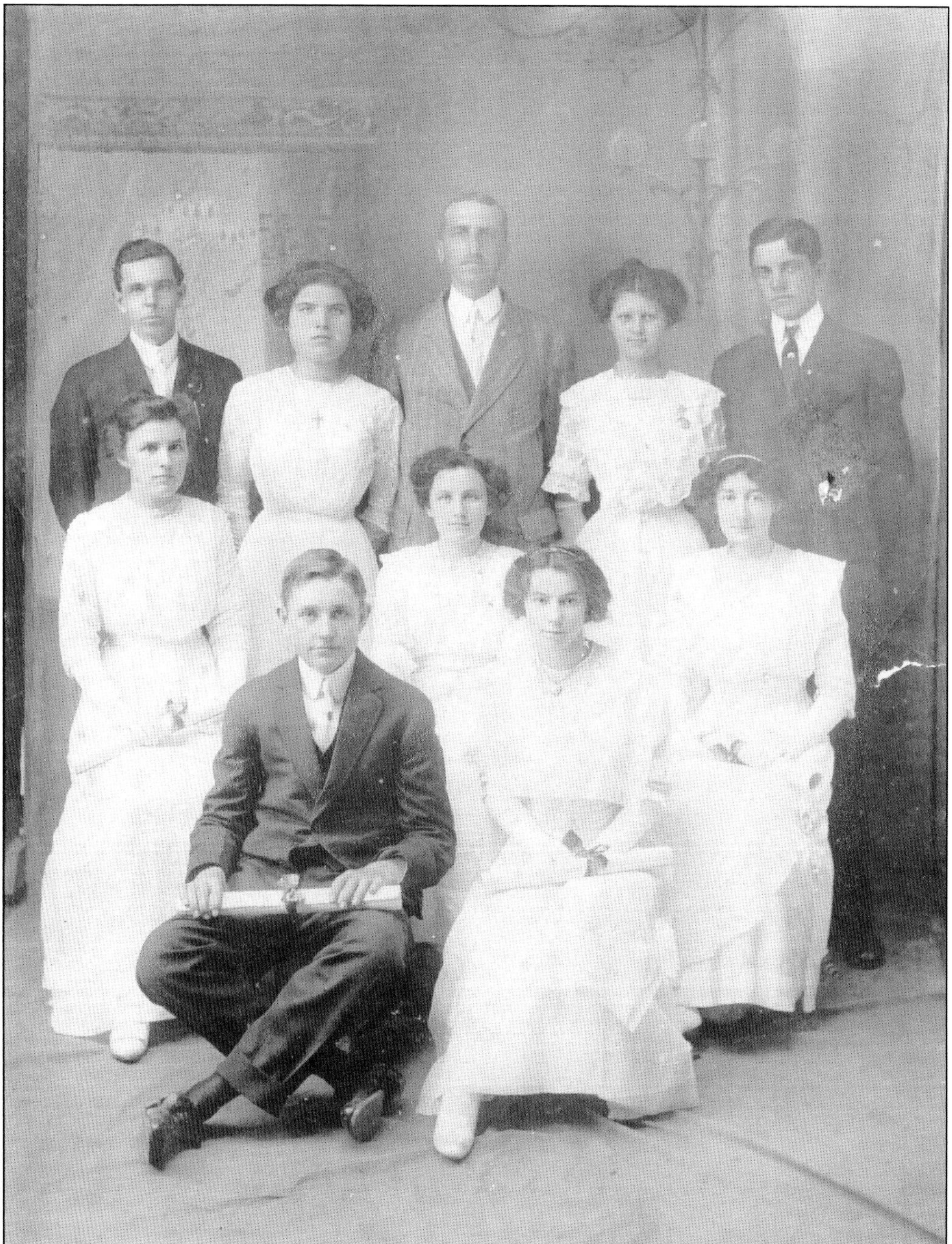

Pictured here is one of Seaford High School's graduating classes. From left to right, front to back, the people can be identified as William Allen, Holda Donahoe, Ethel Robinson, Mollie Dawson, Rachel Elliott, Albert Elzey, Kitty Allen Rogers, Professor Alexander Harrington, Nettie Tull, and Delbert Dolby.

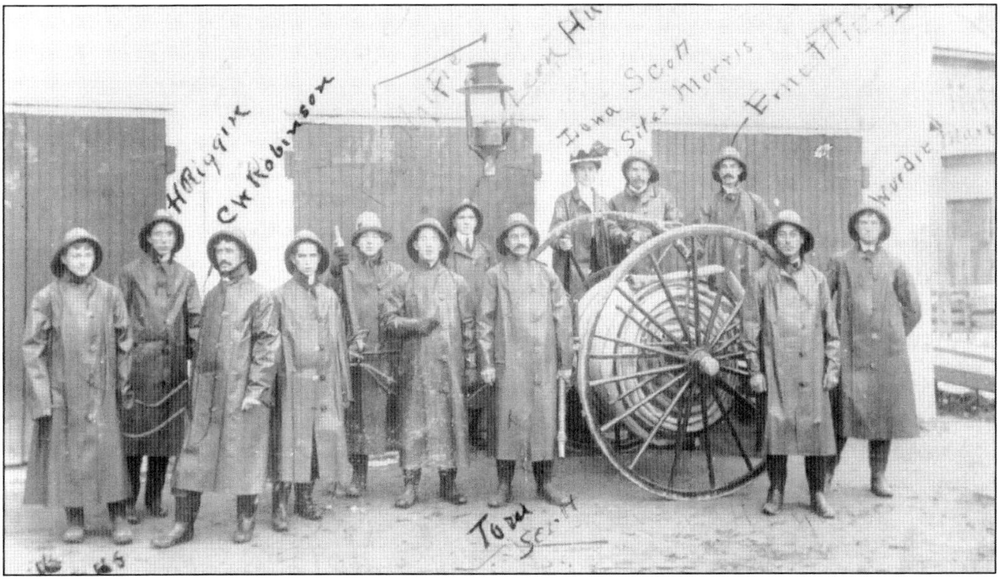

This is a picture of Seaford's early fire department, organized in 1901. Some of these firemen are identified by writing on the picture.

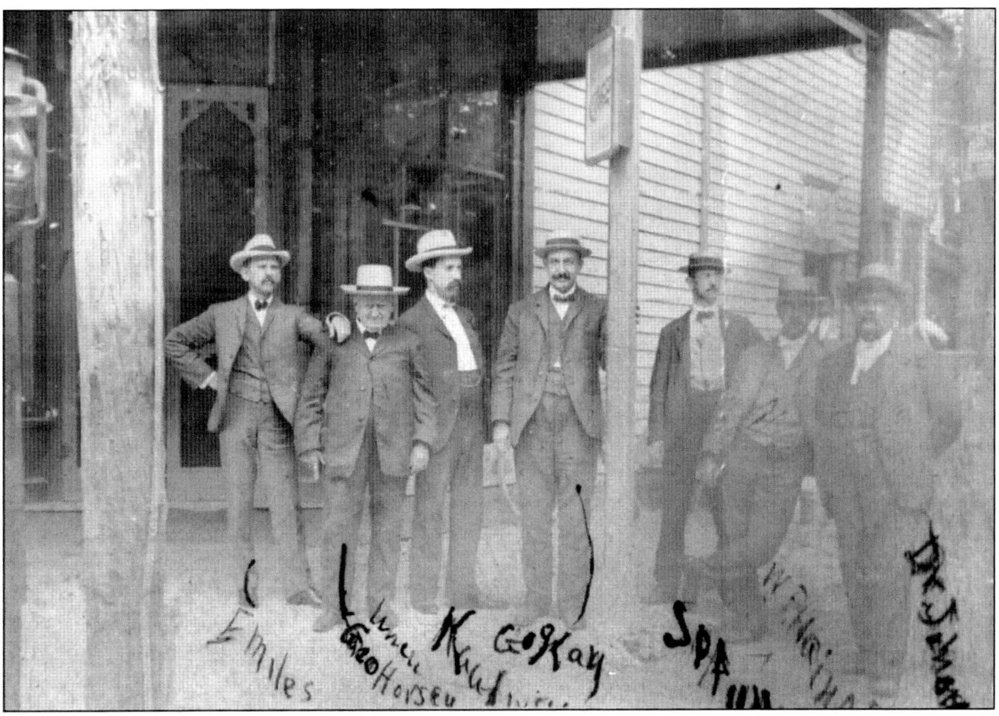

Pictured here in front of Dr. Haines Drug store on High Street are some of Seaford's better-known citizens, including, from left to right, Emory Miles; George Horsey; Dr. Kauffman; George Kay, a journalist who was killed by Poncho Villa in the Mexican uprising in New Mexico; Sam Fields; Dr. W.F. Haines; and Dr. Johns.

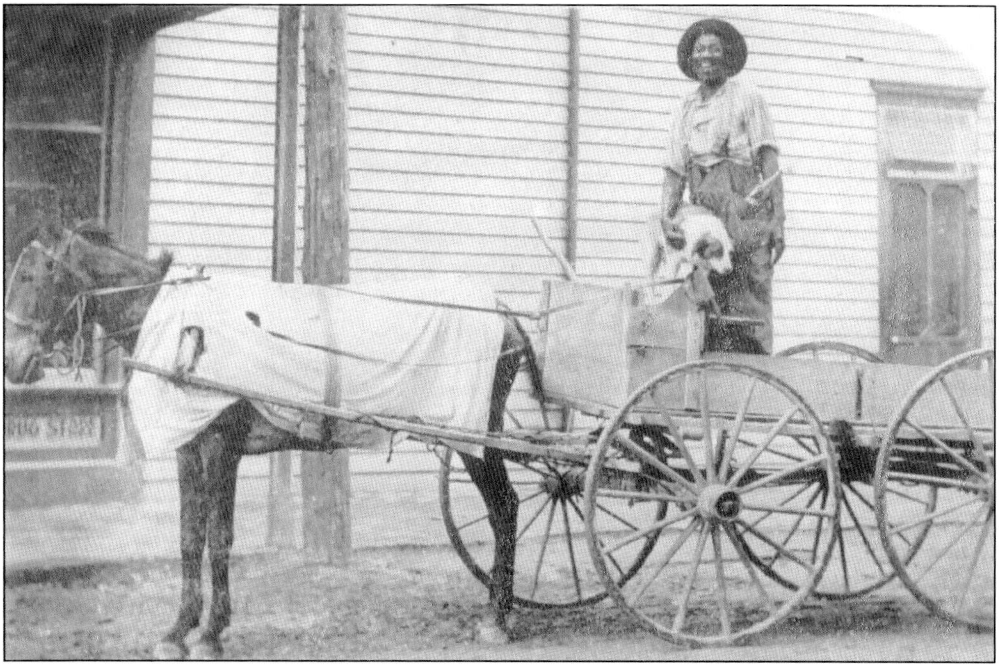

Leonard Ross and his mule are pictured here. Leonard was a highly regarded man in the community. He collected garbage and did odd jobs for people.

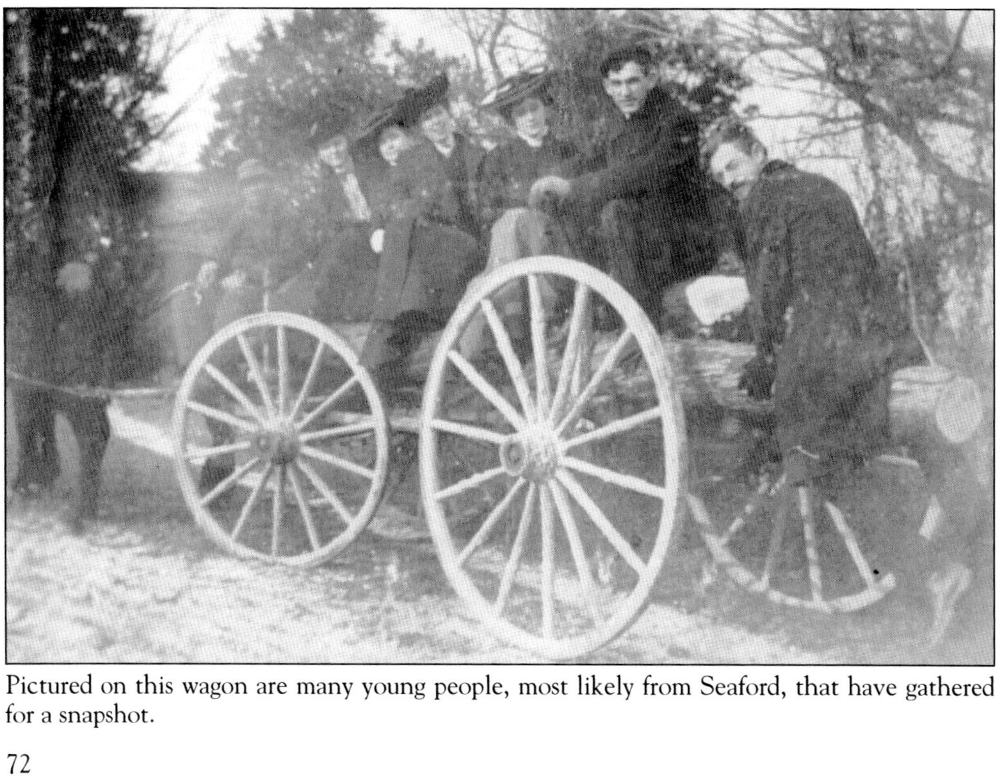

Pictured on this wagon are many young people, most likely from Seaford, that have gathered for a snapshot.

This was Martha Griffith Stewart, known affectionately as "Aunt Matt." She was born in 1861 and died in 1916. She was married to John D. Stewart, owner of an iron foundry on High Street. Aunt Matt owned and operated a confectionery store at the corner of Pearl and High Streets that sold candy fruit and baked goods made at Olrich's Bakery in Seaford.

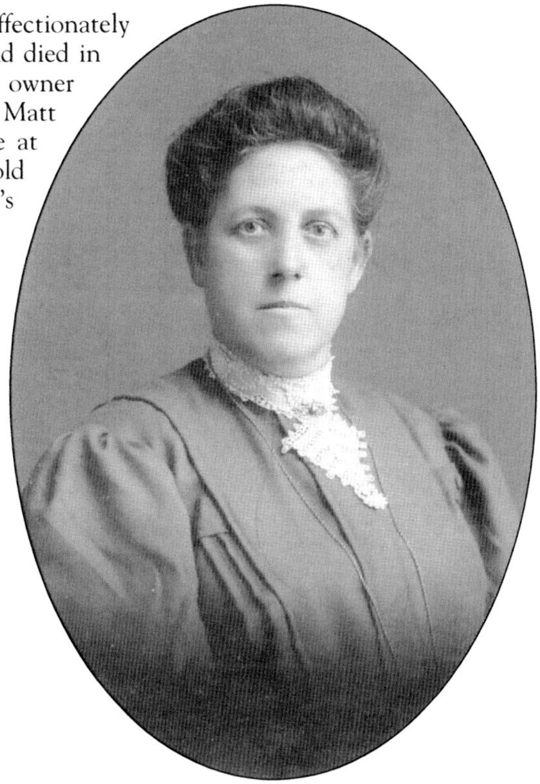

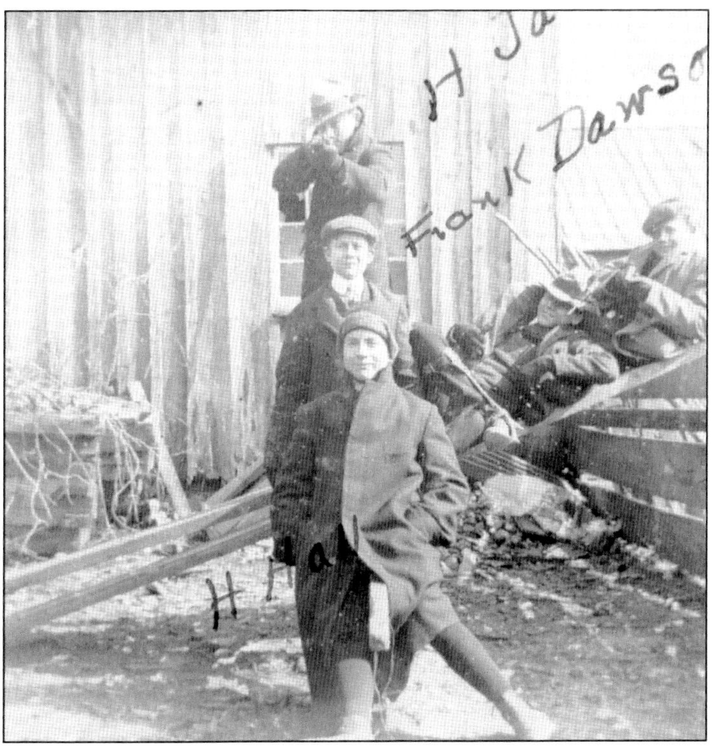

Taken in back of the Foundry that Mr. John Stewart owned on the corner of Pearl and High Streets, this picture shows Huey Jackson, Frank Dawson, and Avery Hobbs.

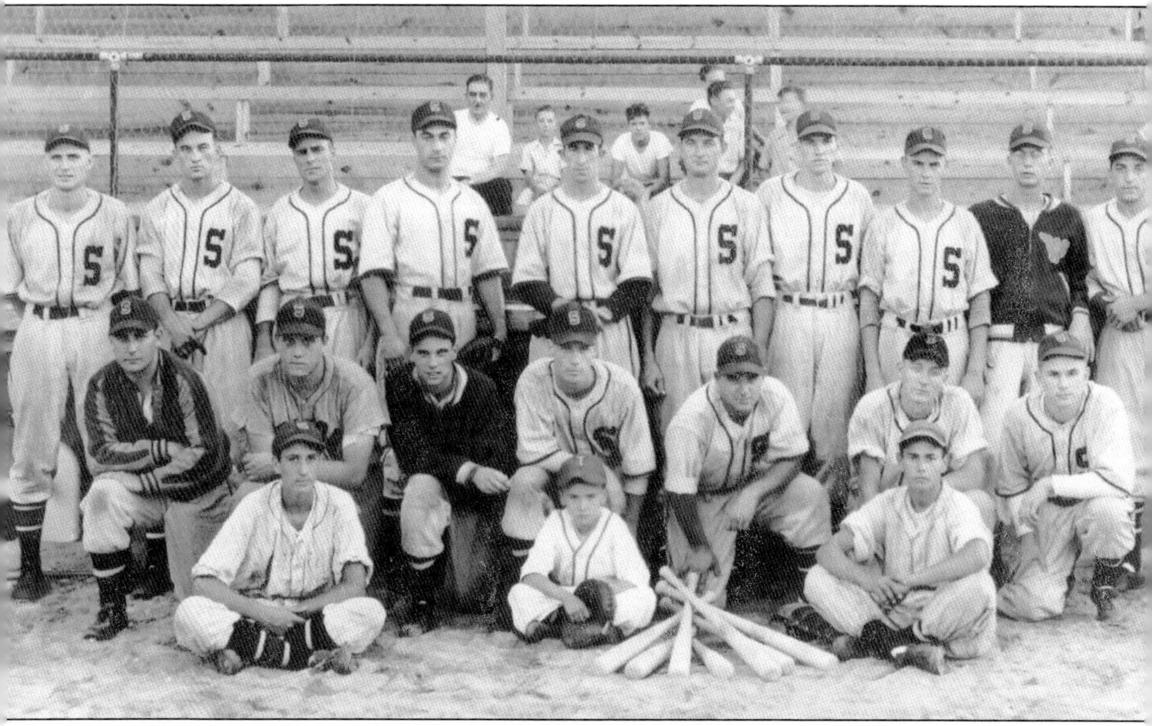

In the early middle part of the twentieth century, Seaford had a semiprofessional baseball team—the Seaford Eagles. Pictured here is the 1947 Seaford Eagles Team. Some of the players from the Eagles went on to the Major League years later. Prior to the Eagles, around 1918, Seaford had a semiprofessional baseball team. Two of the most famous players were Eddie Rommel, who pitched for the Philadelphia Athletics and was later a major league umpire, and Jimmy Dykes, who also played for the Athletics.

Pictured here is Nick Testa, the catcher for the Seaford Eagles in 1947.

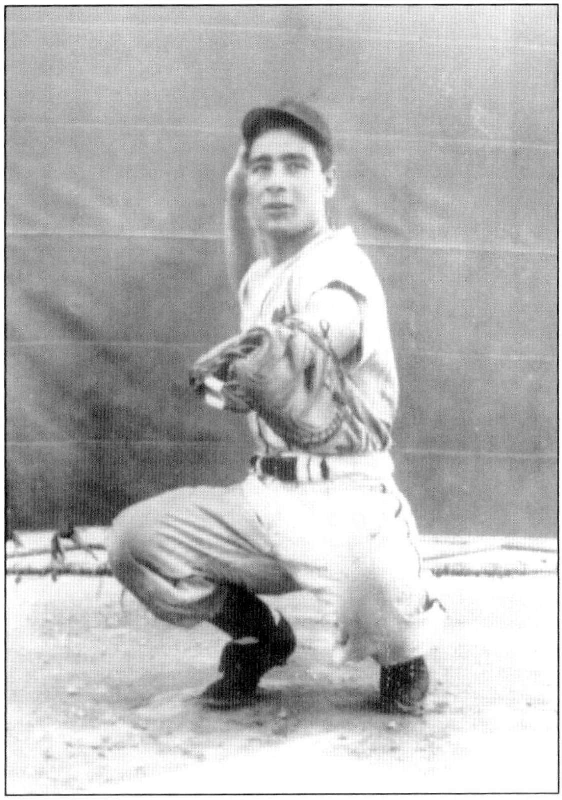

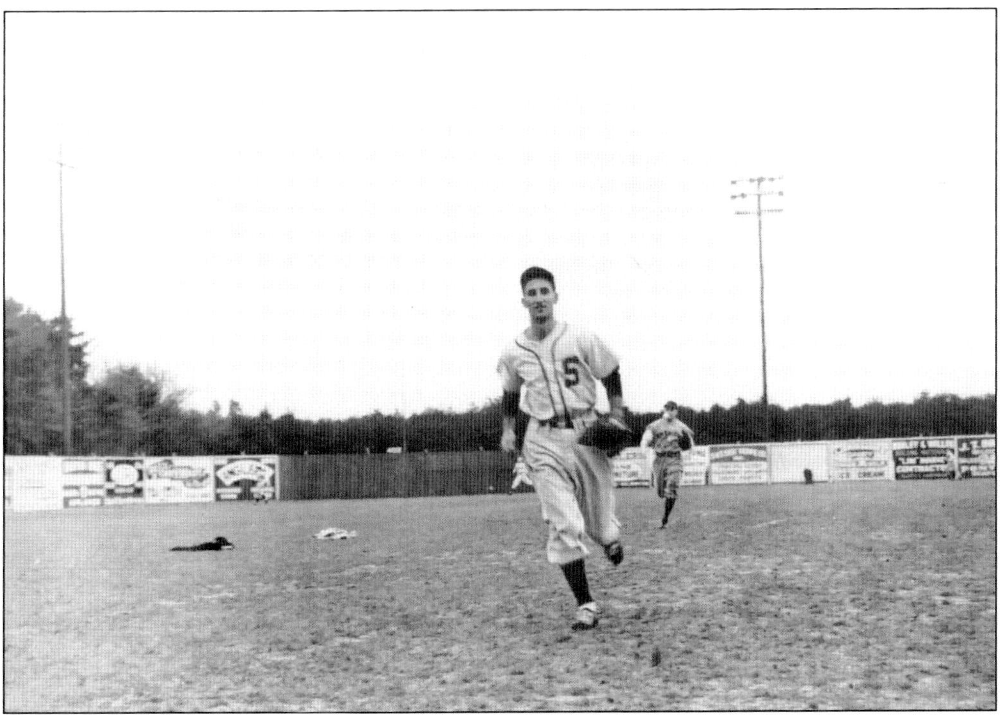

Seen running off of the field here is George McPhail, another player for the Seaford Eagles.

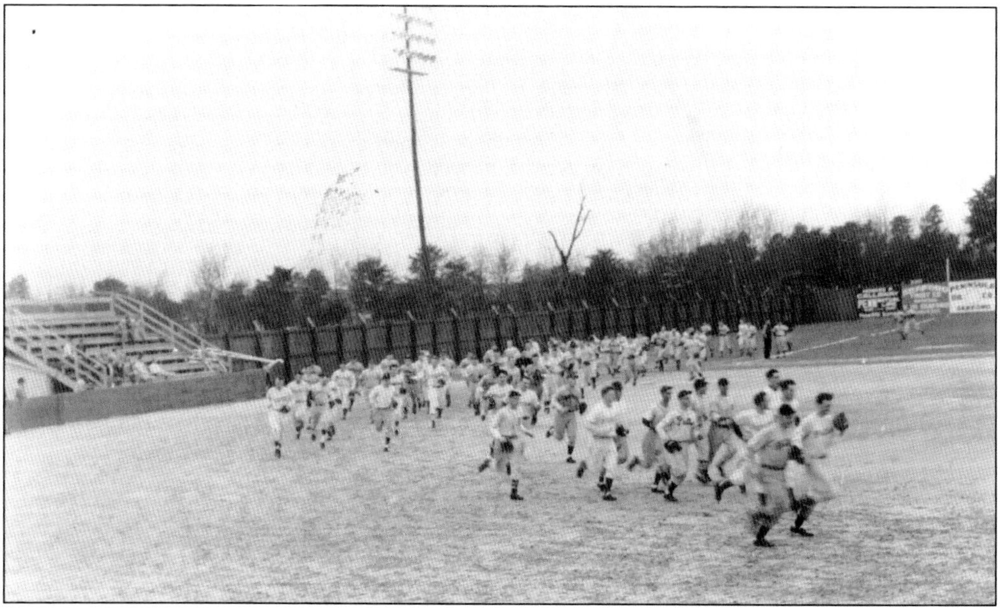

Seaford at one time was the training camp for many aspiring young baseball players. Around 180 boys would come to Seaford for tryouts for various farm teams of the Philadelphia Phillies. The boys would come from all over and stay in Seaford for a couple of weeks during the tryouts. Seaford residents would open their homes to these boys. This picture was taken during one such day of tryouts.

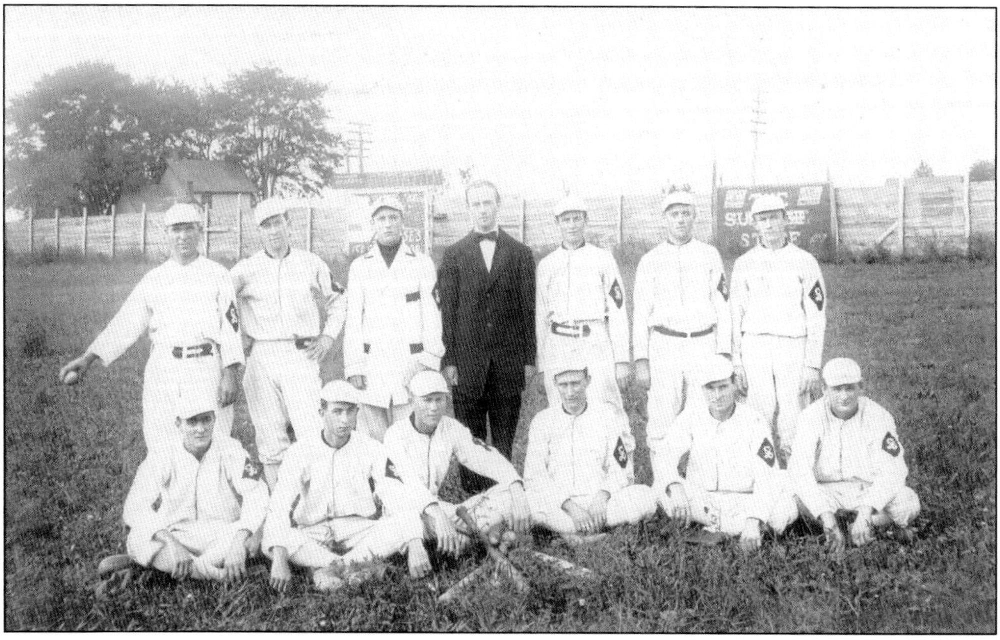

Seaford, like many communities, also had town baseball teams. Shown here is one such team posing for a picture at Seaford's own ballpark, which stood at Pine and Fifth Streets. Pictured from left to right are (bottom row) Jim Huston, Linwood Lloyd, Bill Parsons, Joe Cox, Marshall Hammond, and Olin Parsons; (top row) Jim Thompson, Ashby Shipley, ?, Manager Harlan Huston, Frank Dawson, Jake Moore, and Lindon Dawson.

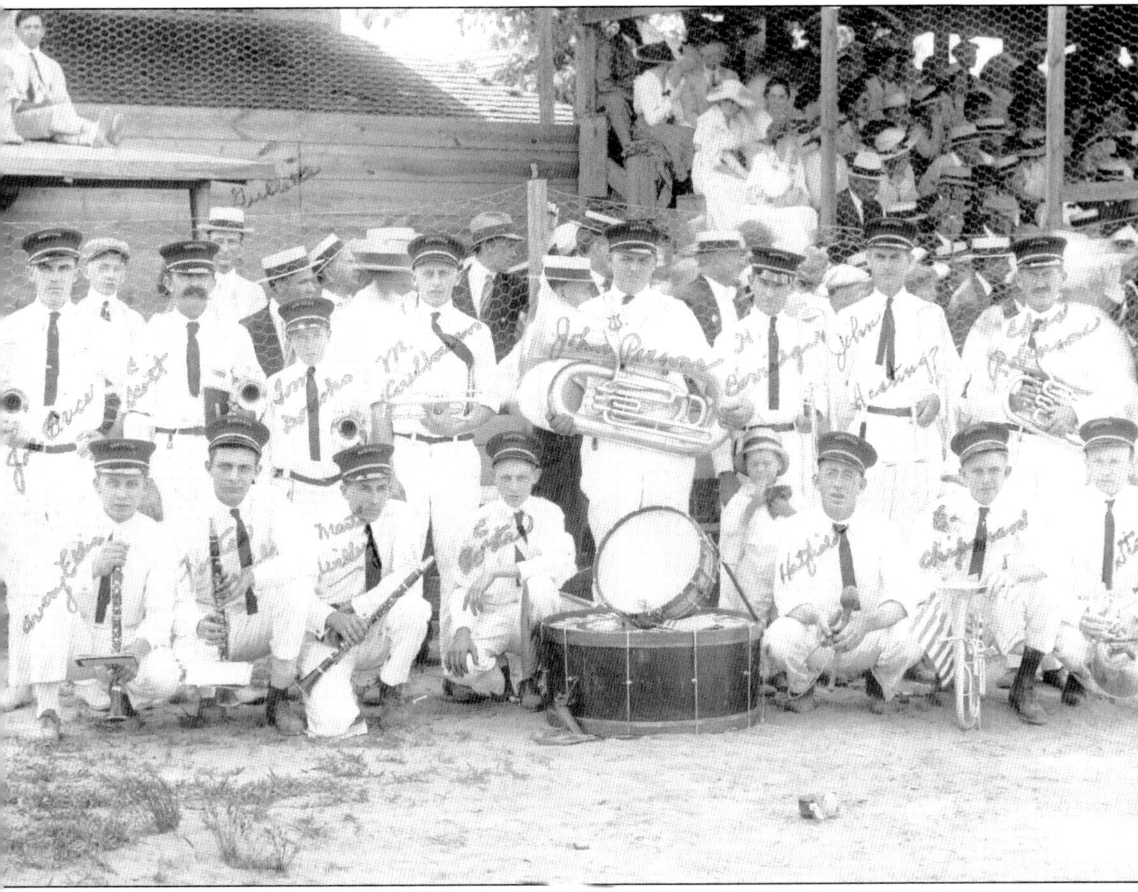

Seaford also had a town band. Taken at Seaford's Ball Park on the Fourth of July, this picture shows the Seaford Band in 1920. Pictured from left to right are (front row) Avery Ellis, Foster Tull, Martin Willey, Columbus Porter, Arthur Hatfield, Eddie Chipman, and Sam Stein; (back row) Joe Price, Clarence Scott, Tom Donaho, Milburn Coulbourn, John Parsons, Harry Berridge, John Hastings, and Charles Robinson.

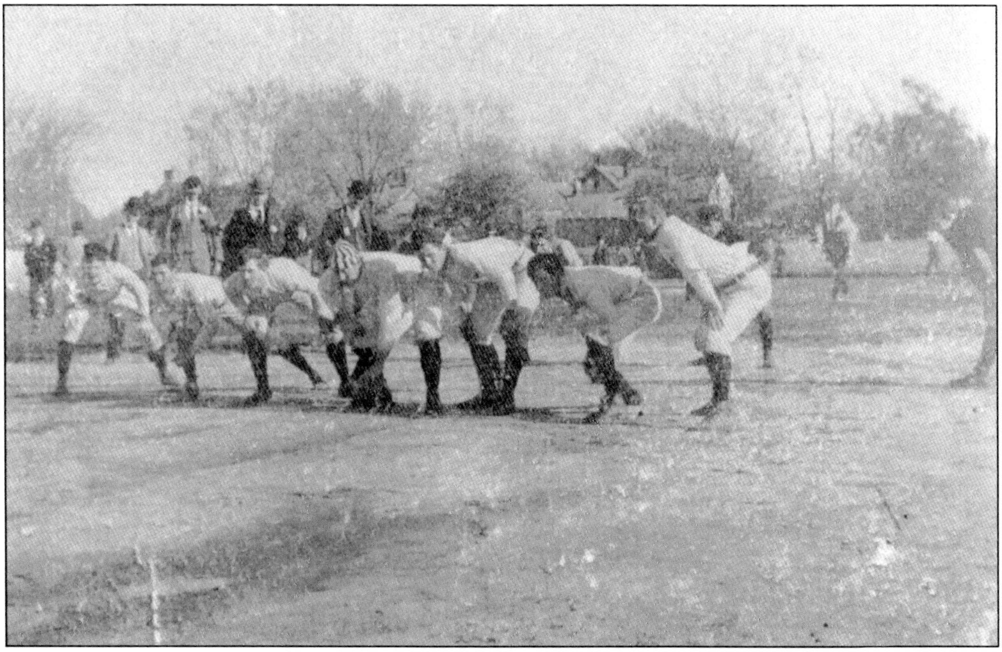

Baseball wasn't the only big sport in the community. This picture shows one of the famed football teams of Seaford in the early years of the game.

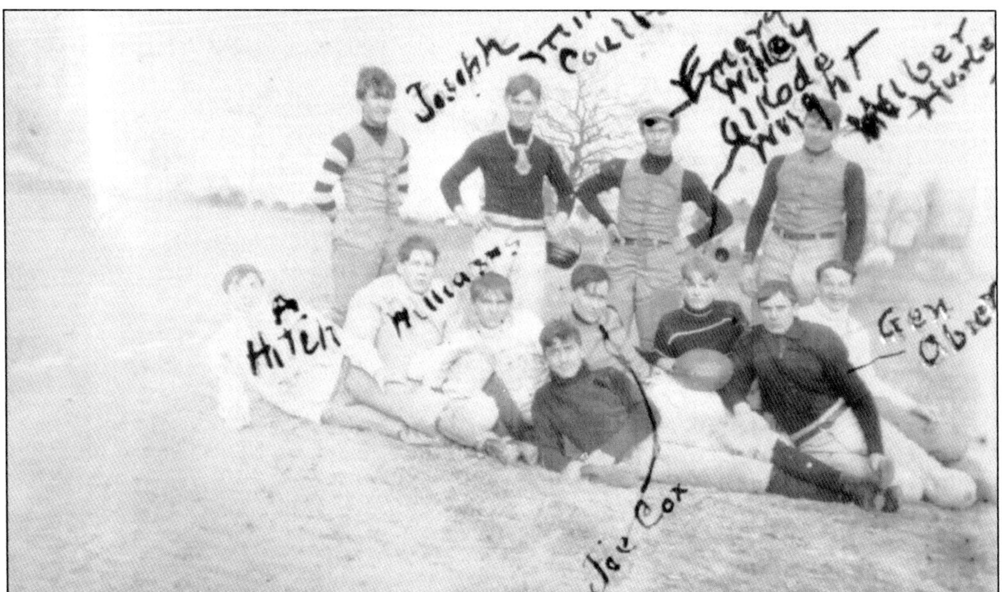

This is another picture of one of Seaford's early football teams. Some of the players are identified by the writing on the picture.

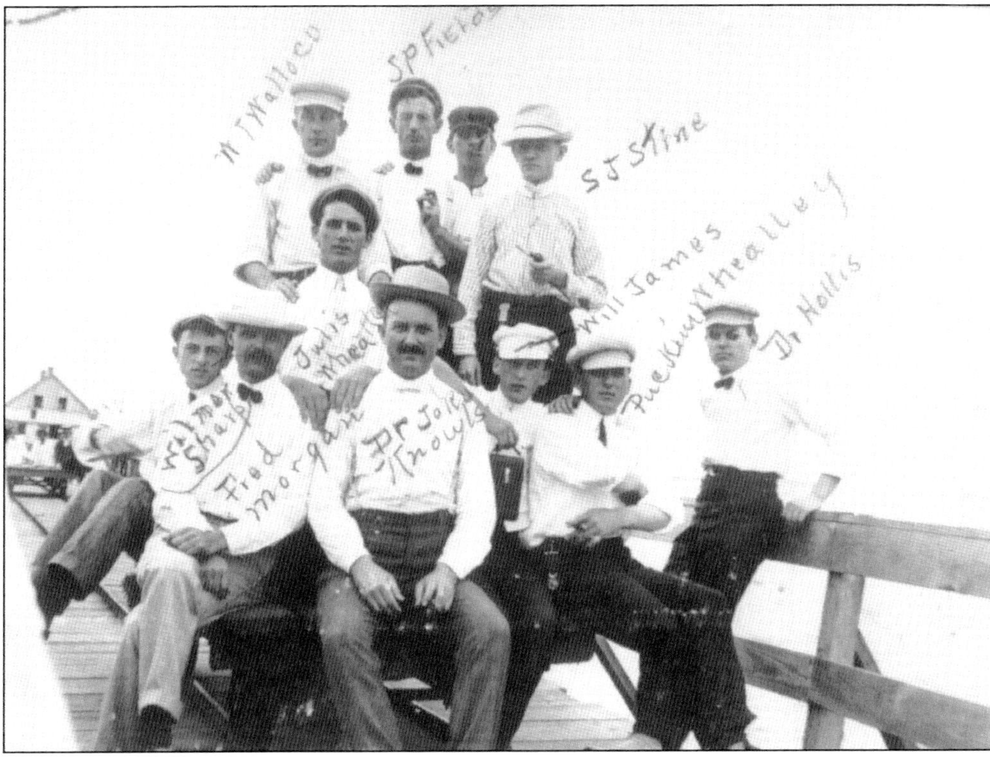

This is a picture of some of Seaford's citizens. It looks as if they are about to picnic, as that was a common occurrence along the river. Some of the individuals are identified in the picture.

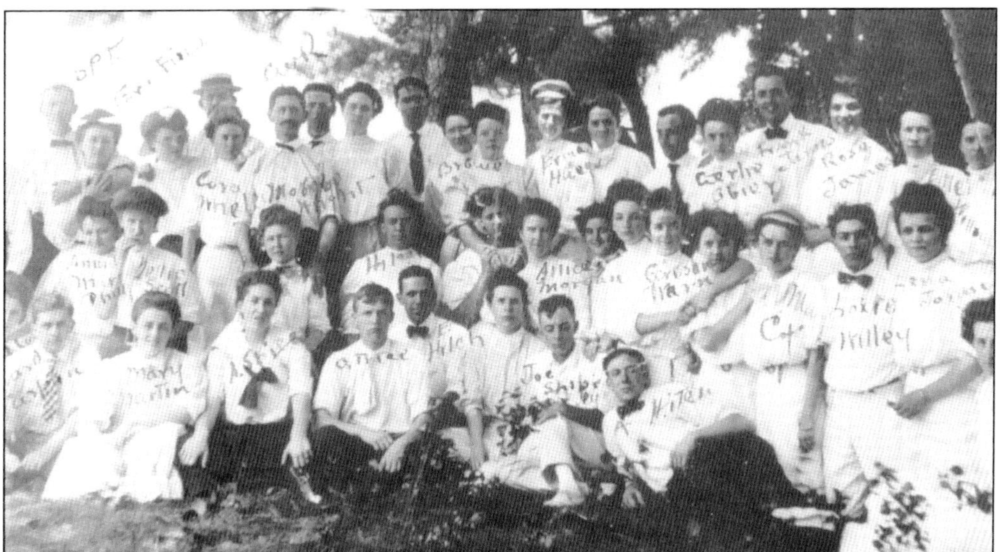

This picture symbolizes life in the Seaford community around the turn of the century. Social events included many people, and everyone enjoyed one another's friendship. This large group of people most likely assembled for some sort of social event. Some of the individuals can be identified by the writing on the picture.

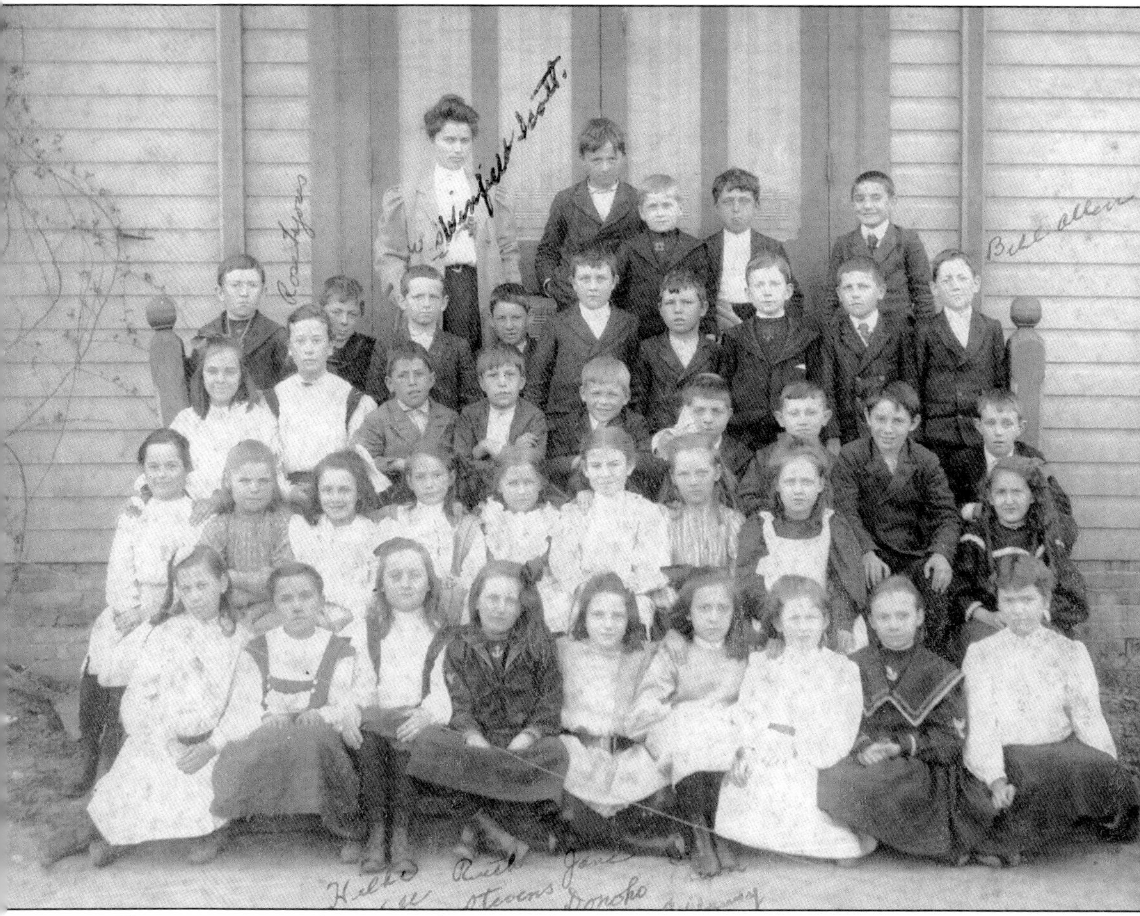

This picture was taken around 1908 and contains the future graduating class of 1915. The teacher, shown in the top left of the photo, was Winifred Scott. Some of the students have been identified as illustrated by the names written on the picture.

Five

Places & Things

This picture may very well be "Seaford's first house." It is believed that this was the home of Seaford's first settlers, the Hoopers.

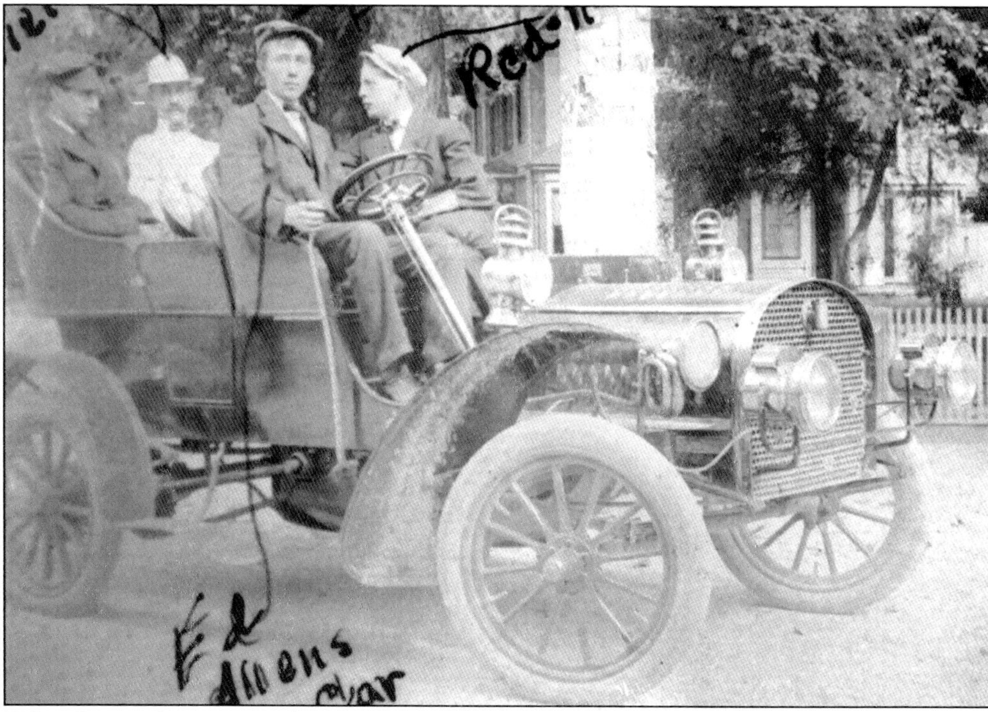

Taken late in the nineteenth century, this picture is believed to be of Seaford's first automobile. Ernest Fields and Arnold Greenabaum are in the back seat while Ed Allen is driving with Red Holt in the passenger seat. Mr. Allen had a bicycle repair shop and was very much interested in automobiles.

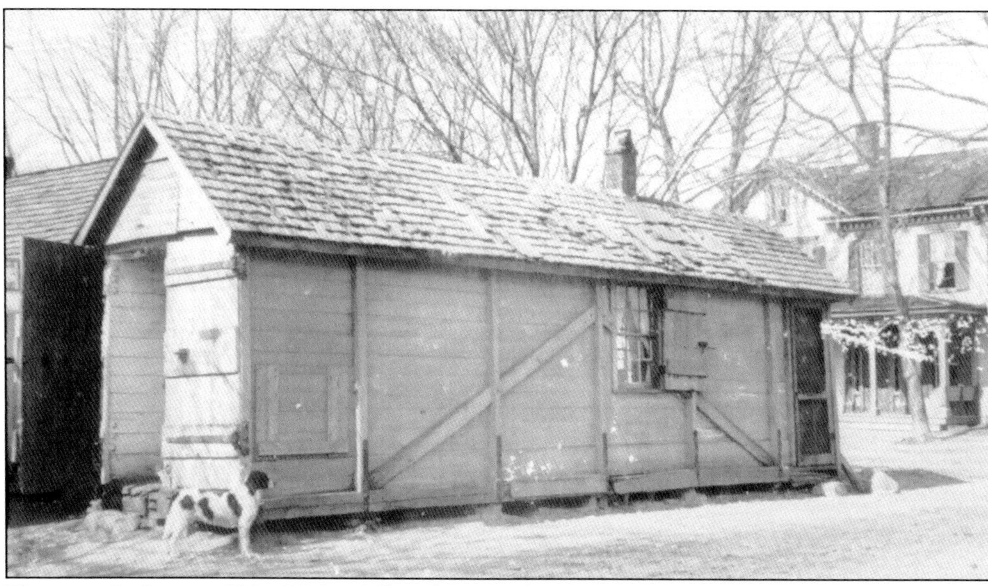

This was the home of "Car" John Allen that stood on Pennsylvania Avenue near the deep cut. The home was made out of a railroad car that had been transported up there. Mr. Allen lived and raised his children there, and for this reason, acquired the nickname "Car" John Allen. The house in the background was the Willey home, which still stands today.

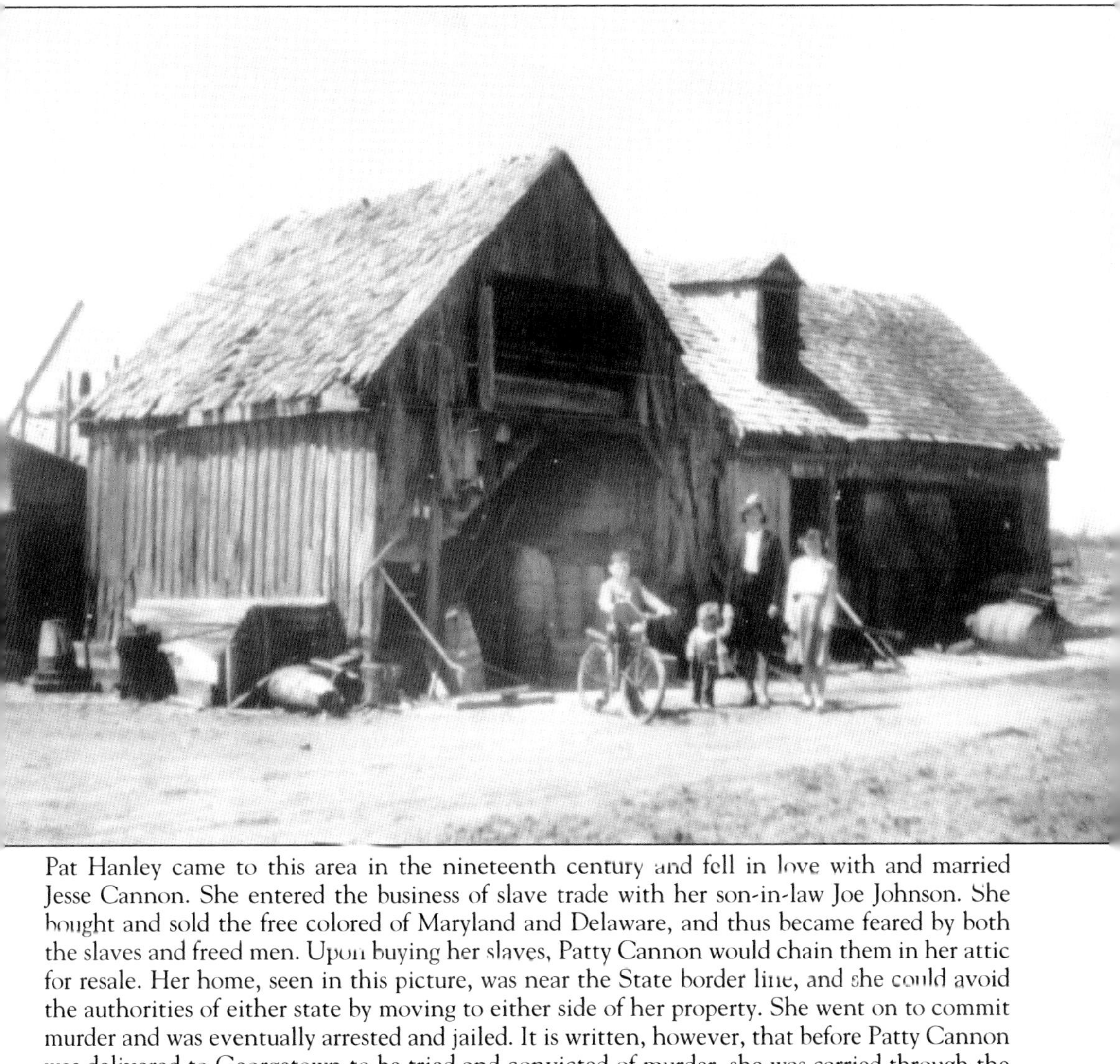

Pat Hanley came to this area in the nineteenth century and fell in love with and married Jesse Cannon. She entered the business of slave trade with her son-in-law Joe Johnson. She bought and sold the free colored of Maryland and Delaware, and thus became feared by both the slaves and freed men. Upon buying her slaves, Patty Cannon would chain them in her attic for resale. Her home, seen in this picture, was near the State border line, and she could avoid the authorities of either state by moving to either side of her property. She went on to commit murder and was eventually arrested and jailed. It is written, however, that before Patty Cannon was delivered to Georgetown to be tried and convicted of murder, she was carried through the town of Seaford chained in a cage-like compartment for public display. She wound up taking her life in prison before she was sentenced.

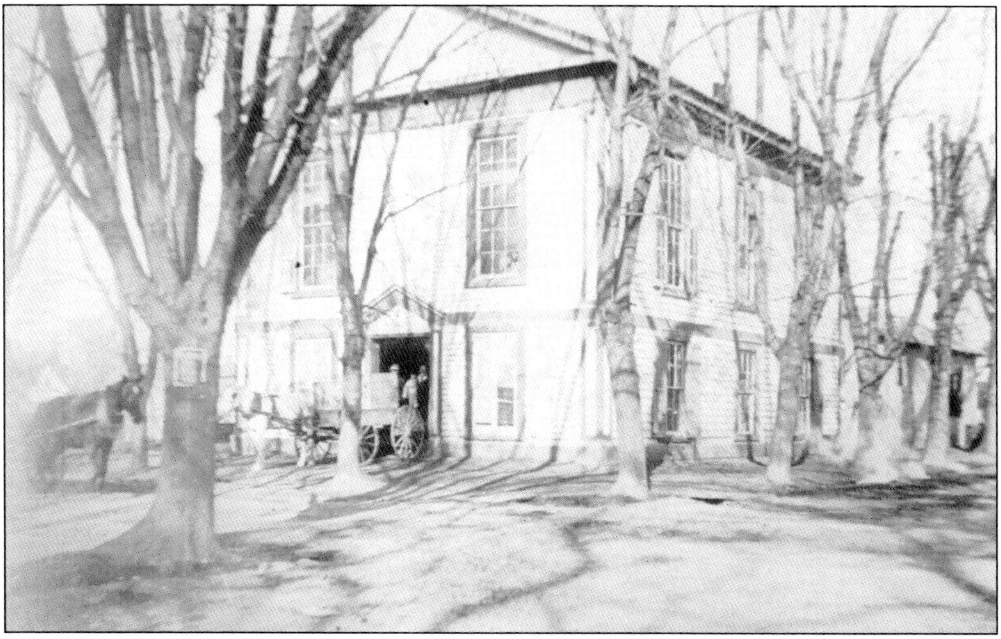

This is a picture of Bochim Temple, the first Methodist church in the community. The building, located at the present Legion site, was later converted into an ice house and then a moving picture palace. In its final transformation, it was a sewing plant, owned by Jesse Wright until it burned on Christmas night around 1910. When the Legion was built, it covered many graves that were part of the Bochim Temple Graveyard.

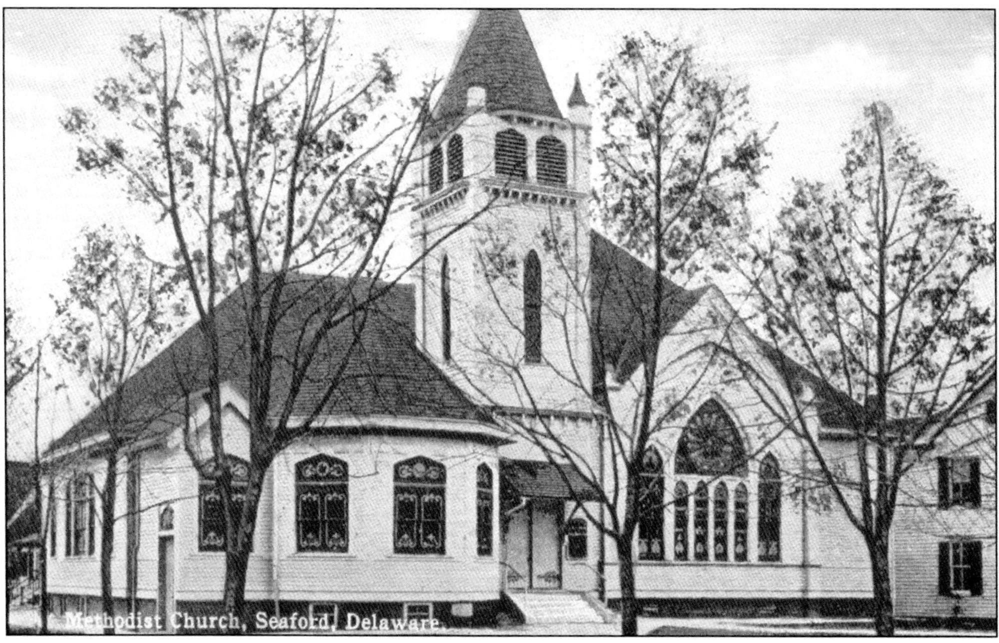

This is an early picture of what is now known as St. John's United Methodist Church (with some modifications). It was the second church in the area, but the original name was the Borhim Meeting House. It was finally changed to St. John's in 1870 in honor of the pastor, Reverend John Gaft. At one time, St. John's was the leading church in Seaford.

The earliest reference to an established church in Seaford was the branch of St. Luke's Protestant Episcopal Church. Plans for the building that now houses the church, shown in this picture, were discussed in 1827. The Church was constructed a short time after. This particular picture of St. Luke's was taken around 1900.

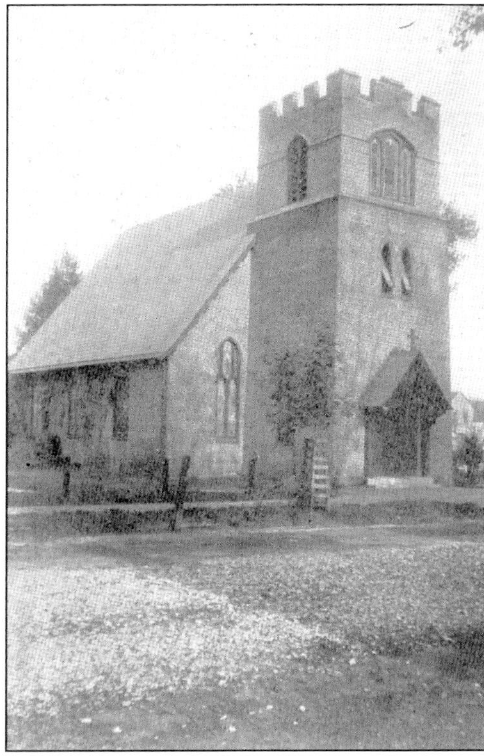

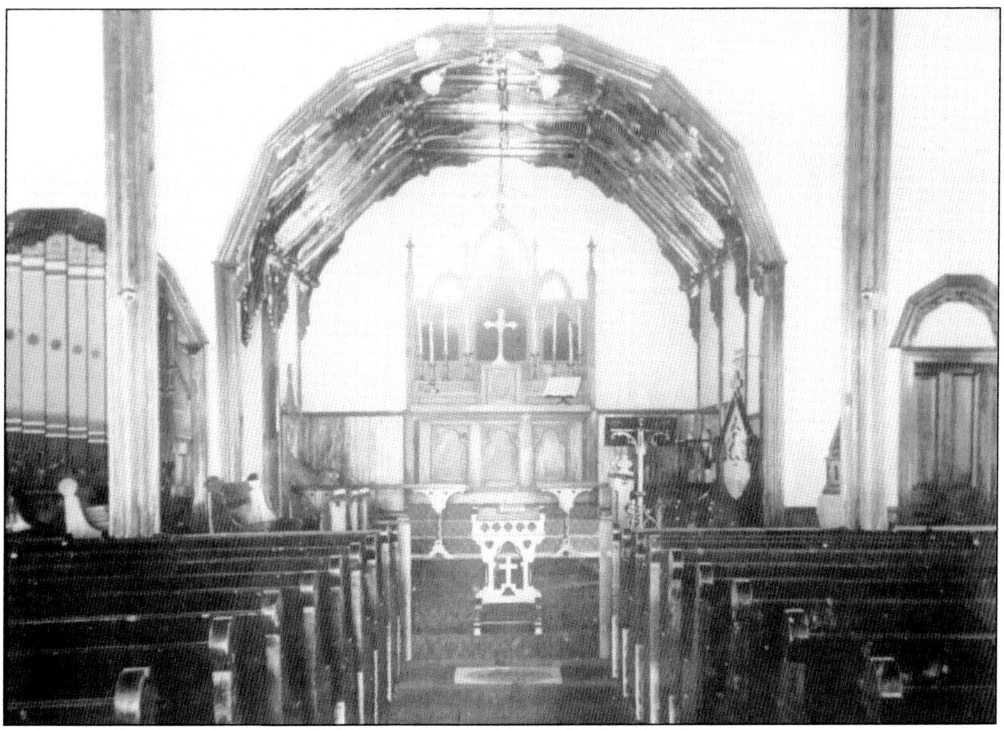

This is a picture of the inside of St. Luke's Church, taken in the early part of the twentieth century. The doorway shown on the right led to the director's study.

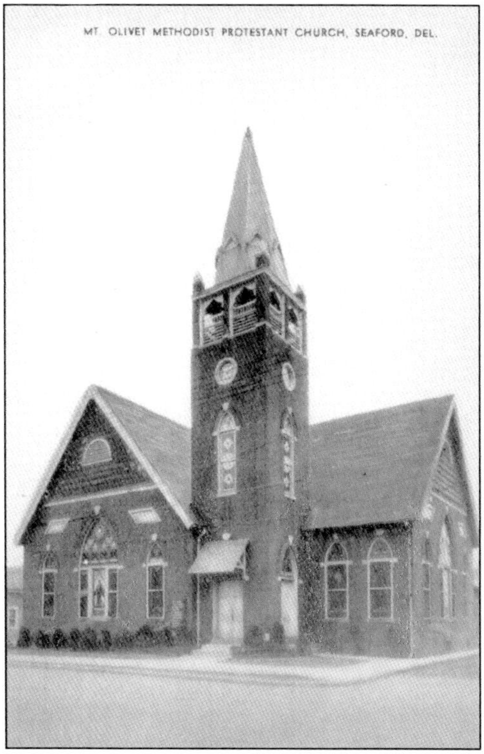

Mount Olivet Methodist Church was established in 1830. In 1850, a new church was needed due to the growth in membership. It was then that the building shown in this picture was constructed to house the church. Currently, Mount Olivet operates in this same location on High Street.

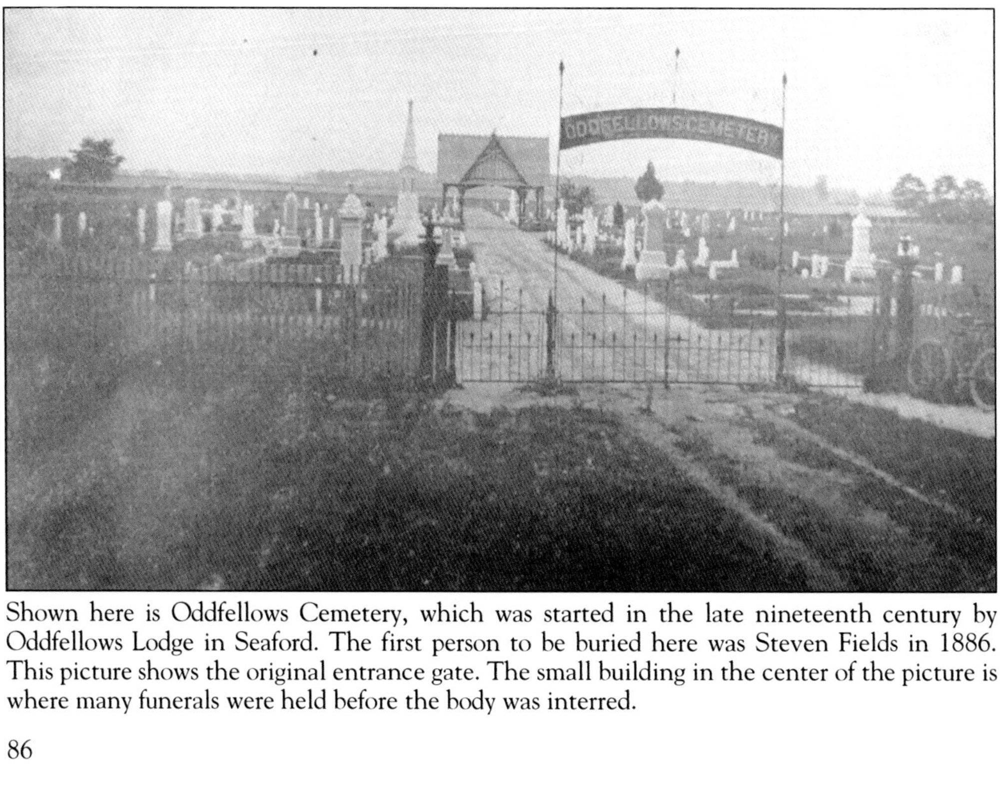

Shown here is Oddfellows Cemetery, which was started in the late nineteenth century by Oddfellows Lodge in Seaford. The first person to be buried here was Steven Fields in 1886. This picture shows the original entrance gate. The small building in the center of the picture is where many funerals were held before the body was interred.

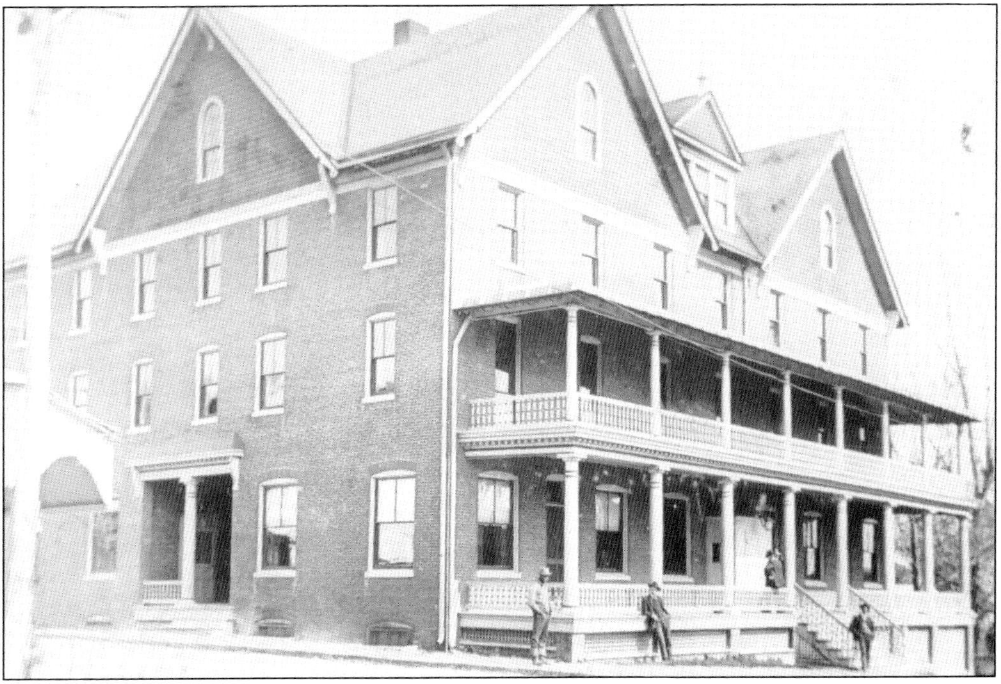

Taken around 1900, this is a picture of the famous Sussex Hotel, which was built in 1895 by Will Ross. In the left corner of the building, one of Seaford's most famous men had an apartment on the lower floor. Mr. Charles VanLeer was a Baltimorian who came to Seaford and became a well-known philanthropist, musician, and community leader in the early twentieth century.

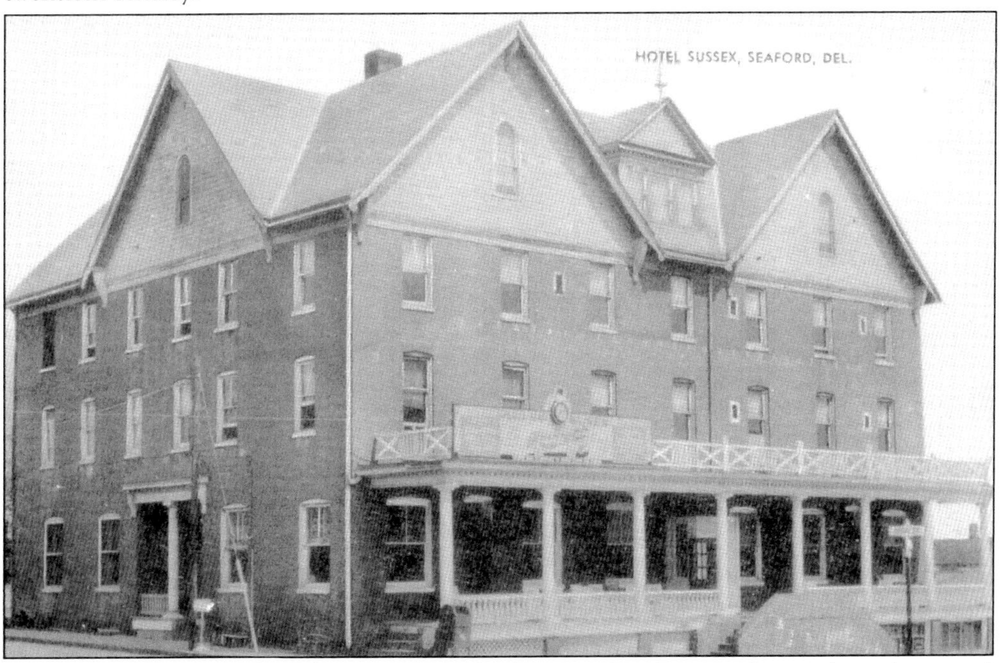

This is a later photograph of the Sussex Hotel. This is evident because the porch on the second story has been removed.

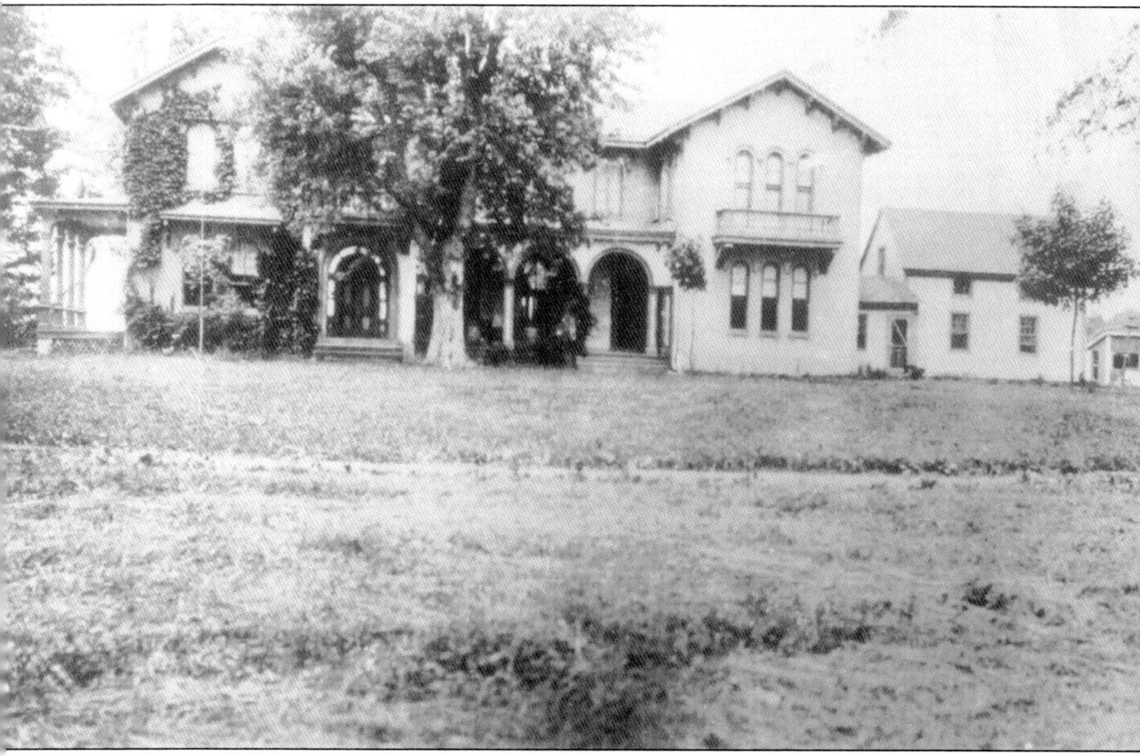

This Italian-style mansion, built in 1850, was the principal place of residence for William Henry Harrison Ross. Ross became the governor of Delaware in 1850 and was responsible for bringing innovation in agriculture and a railroad line to Seaford. This picture of the Mansion was taken around 1905. The home still stands in its original location in Seaford.

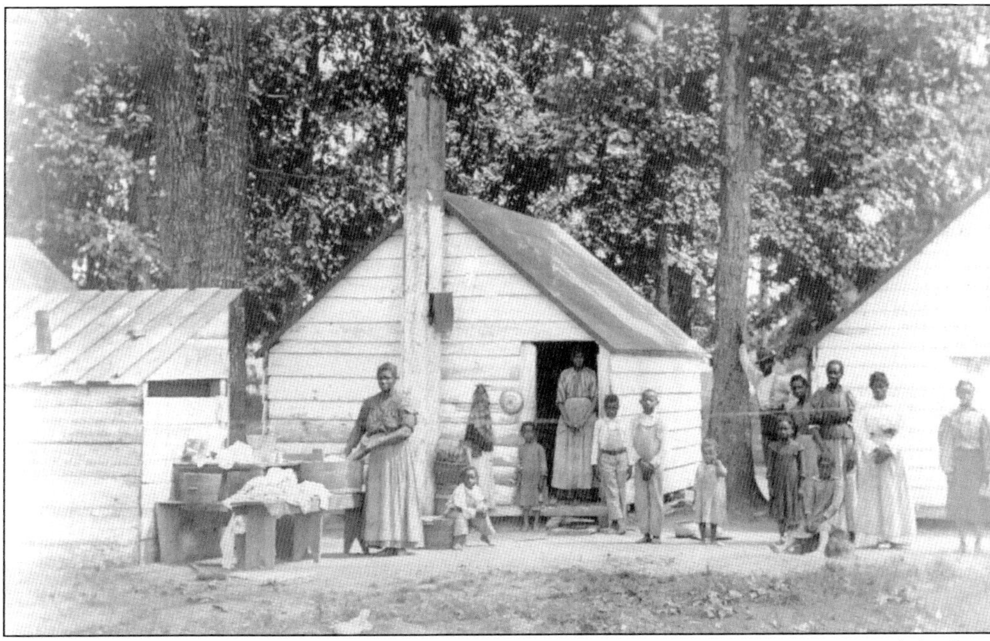

This picture was taken at "The Grove," an area between the Greenabaum Cannery and the Ross Cannery along the River. It was mostly occupied by blacks that worked in the two canneries or in the oyster houses.

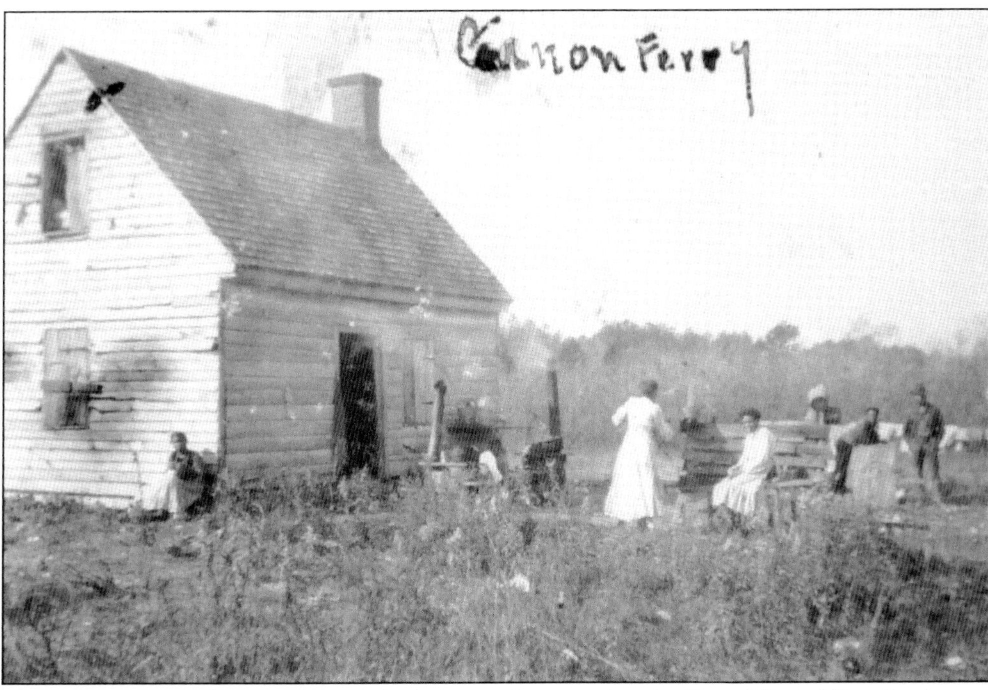

This is a picture of Cannon Ferry, a little home that stood at the Ferry Slip in Woodland.

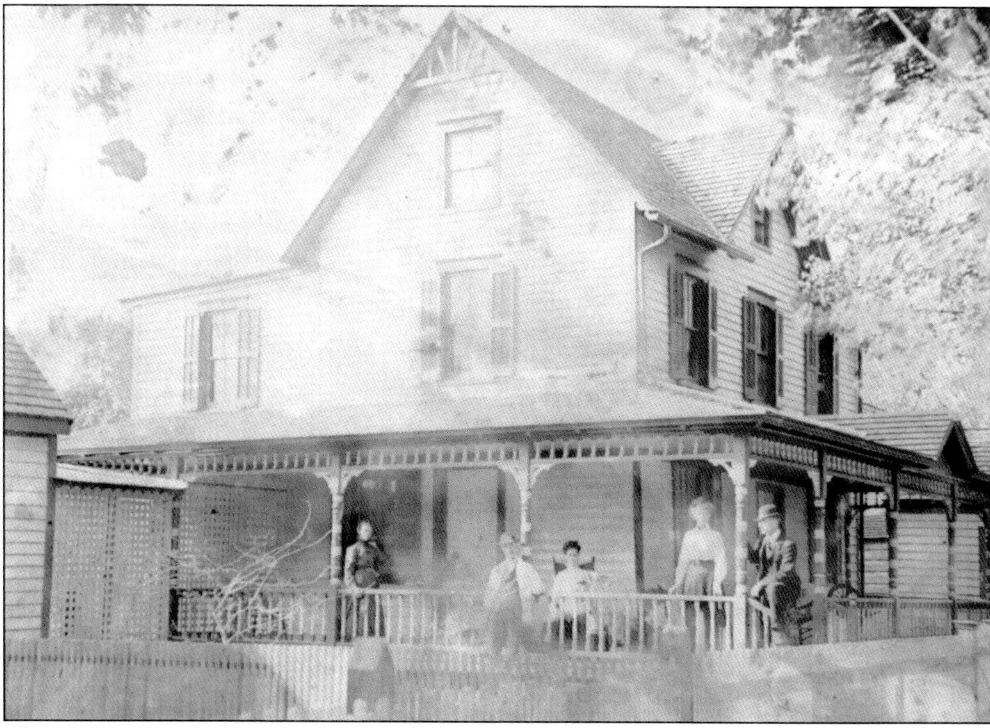

This picture shows what was the Fields' home on Market Street. The Fields were one of the pioneer families in the community.

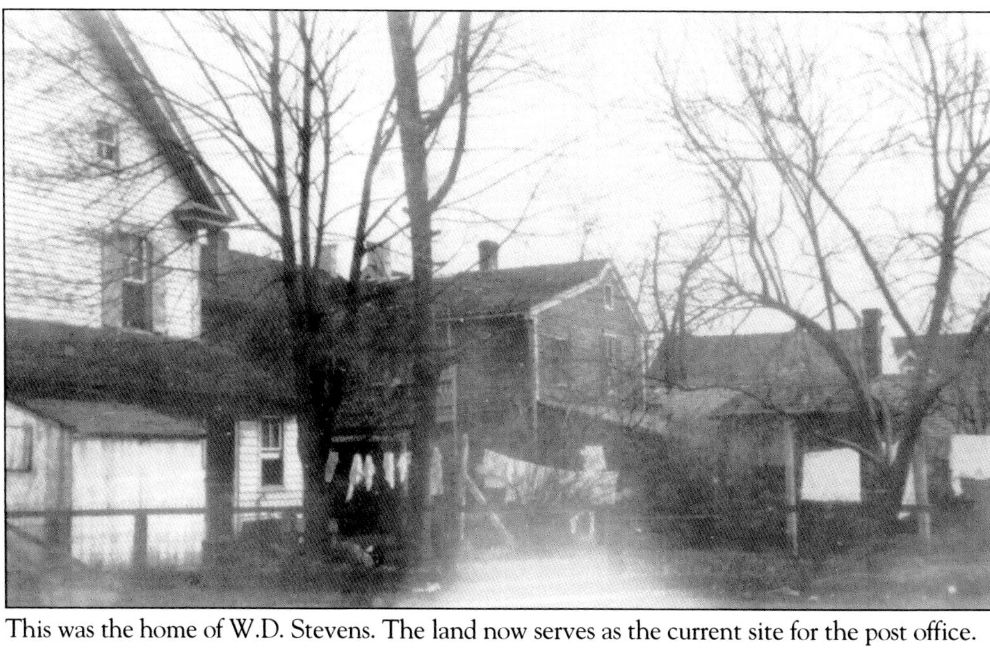

This was the home of W.D. Stevens. The land now serves as the current site for the post office.

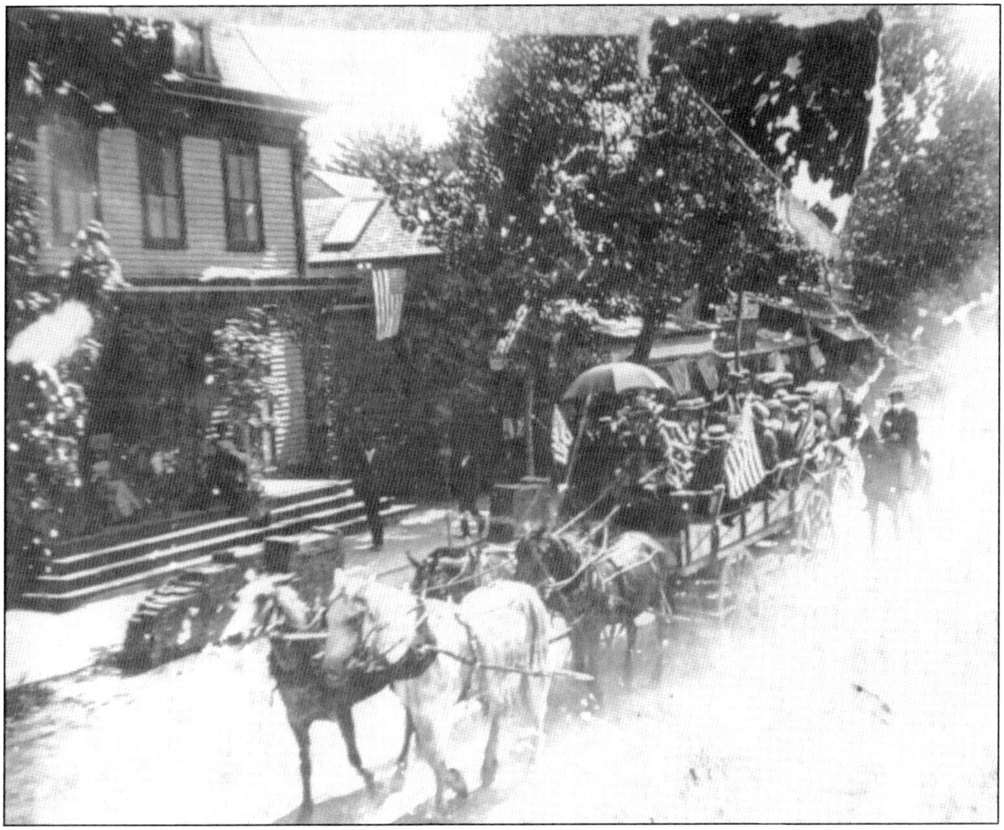

On the Fourth of July, Seaford would celebrate with a parade in the early twentieth century. Shown here is a float that took part in one of those parades.

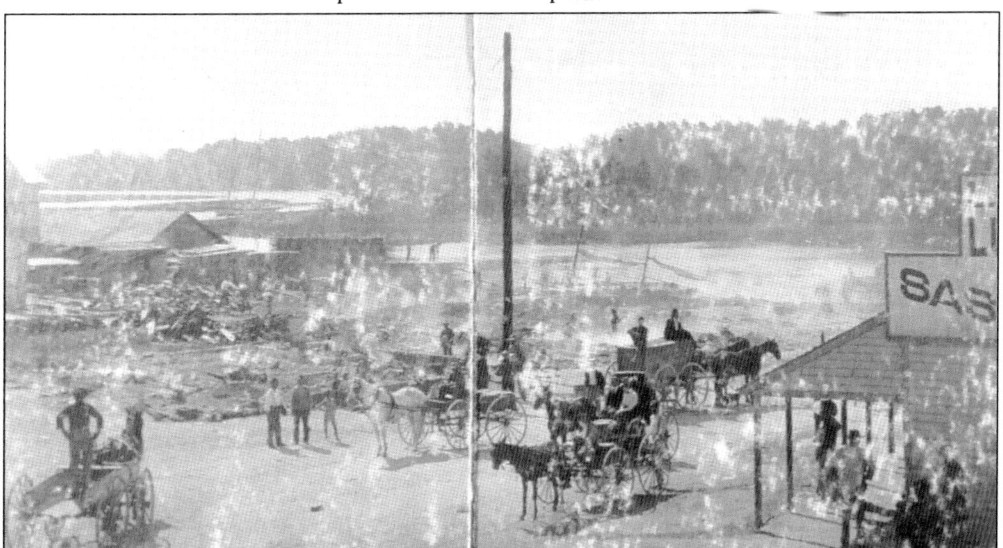

This was a fire drill near the bridge that was put on by the local firemen. Many would assemble to watch what the firemen were doing. It would actually turn into a fun-filled day along the river.

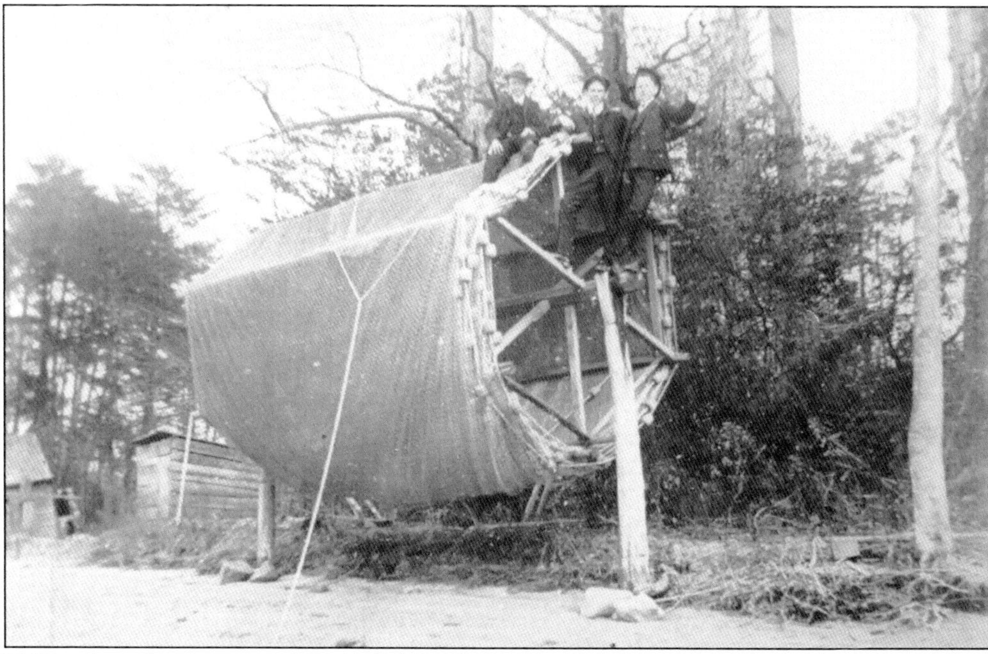

Taken about 3 miles west of Seaford along the Nanticoke, these pictures show seine nets being dried on a dryer. During Shad season, people would put these seine nets across the river and catch shad by the thousands. They would then ship them to the city markets. After the season, the nets were taken down and stored away.

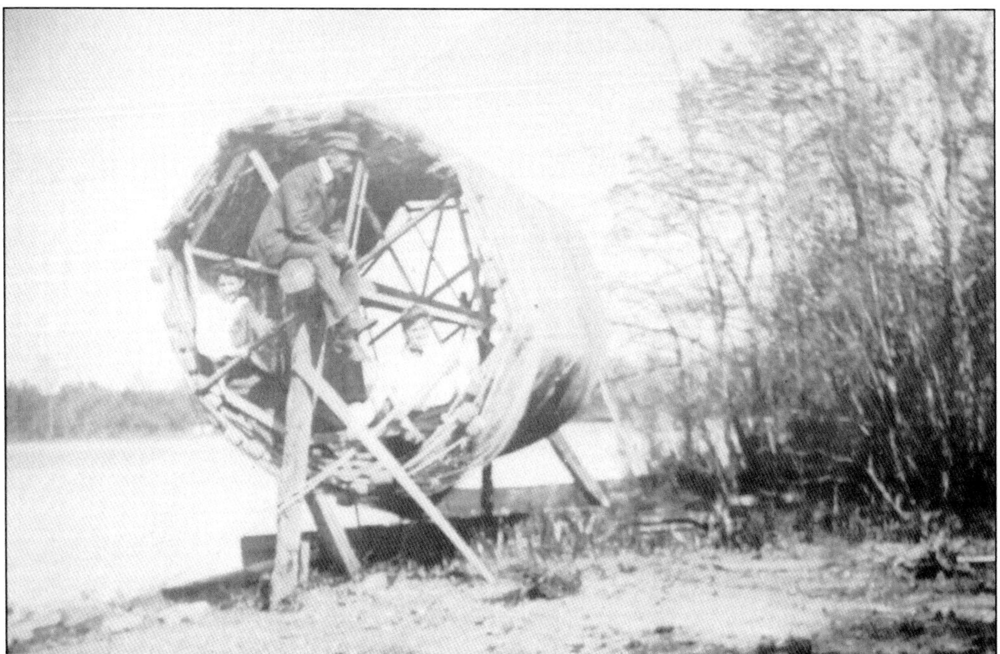

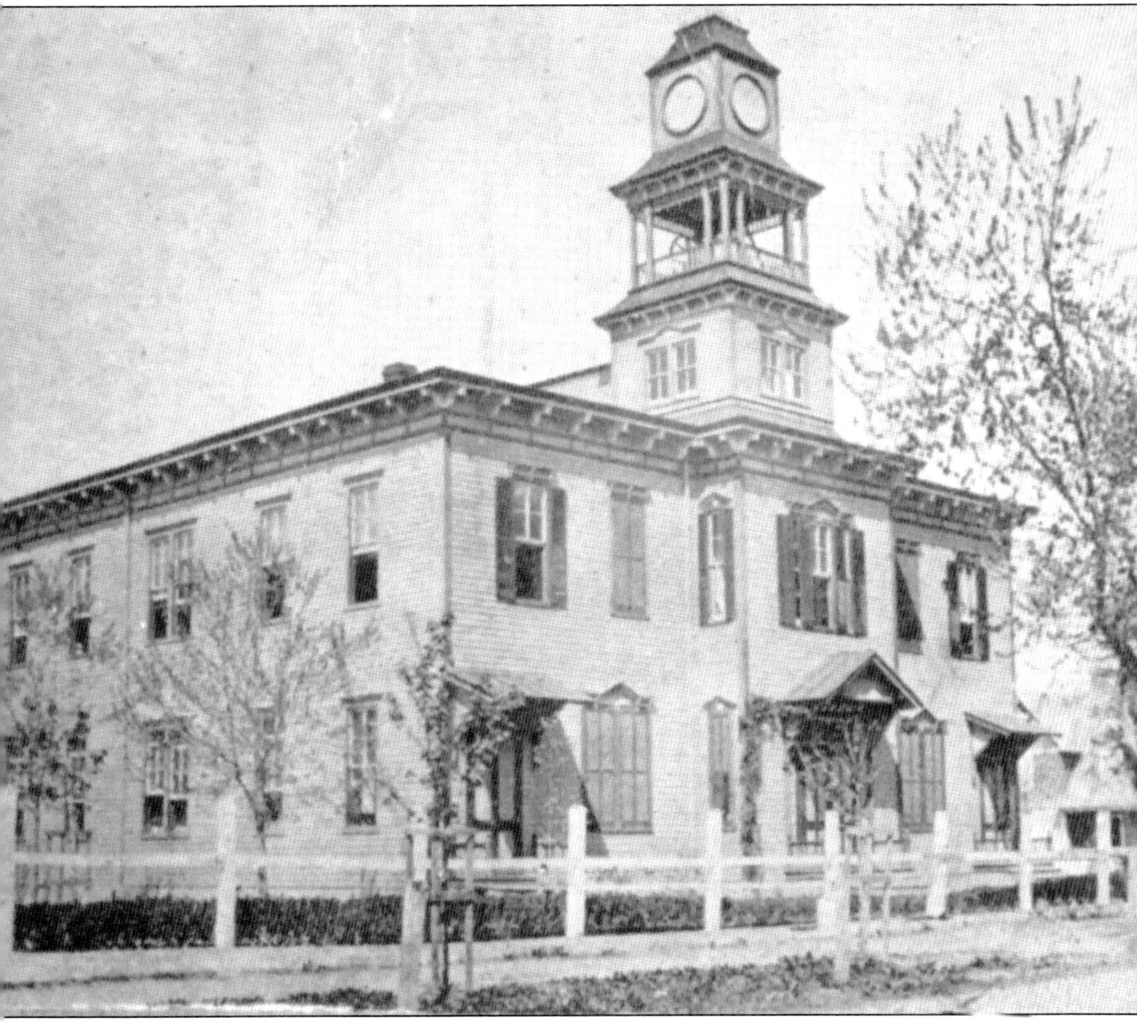

Taken around 1900, this picture shows the old Seaford School on Cannon Street. An addition was later added to the rear of the building, and toilets were added in the left and right wings. The building was completely destroyed in a fire, however, on April Fool's Day, 1928.

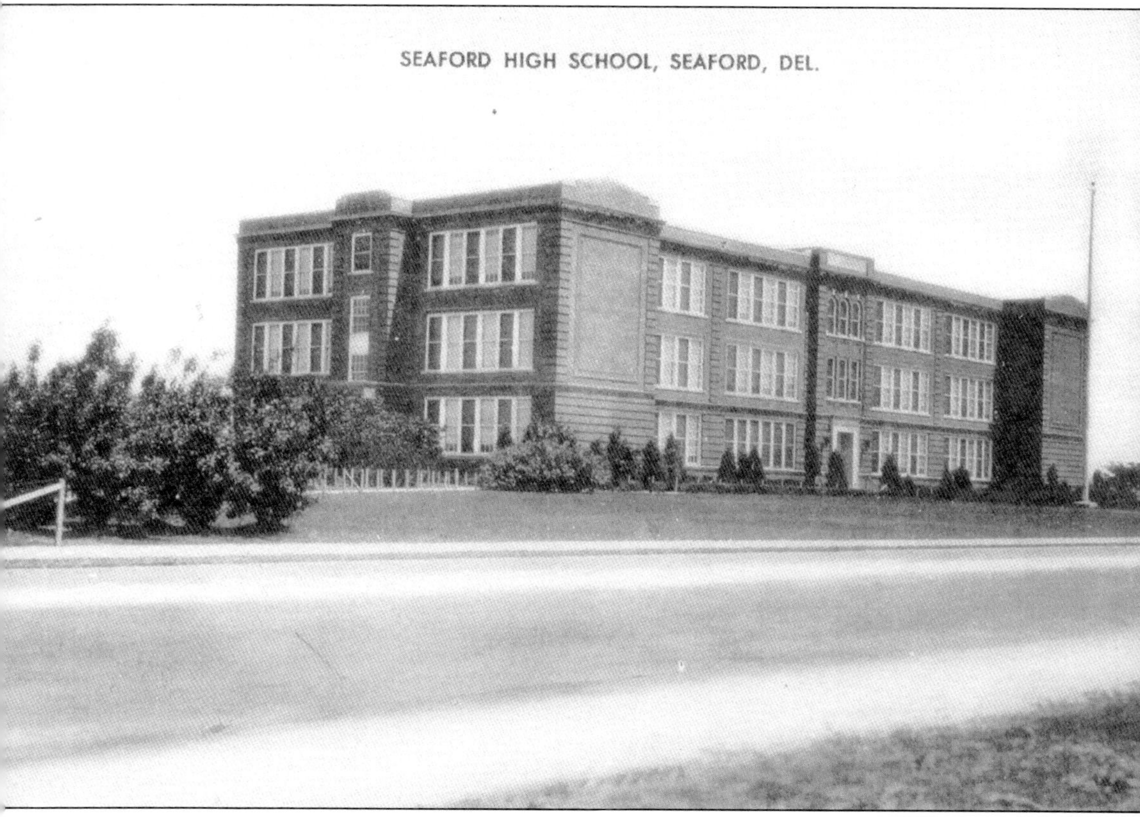

This school was constructed in 1929 at a cost of $310,000 to serve as the new high school. It was given as a gift to the Seaford School District by Pierre S. duPont. Wings were later added to the school, and it became the middle school when a new high school was built years later.

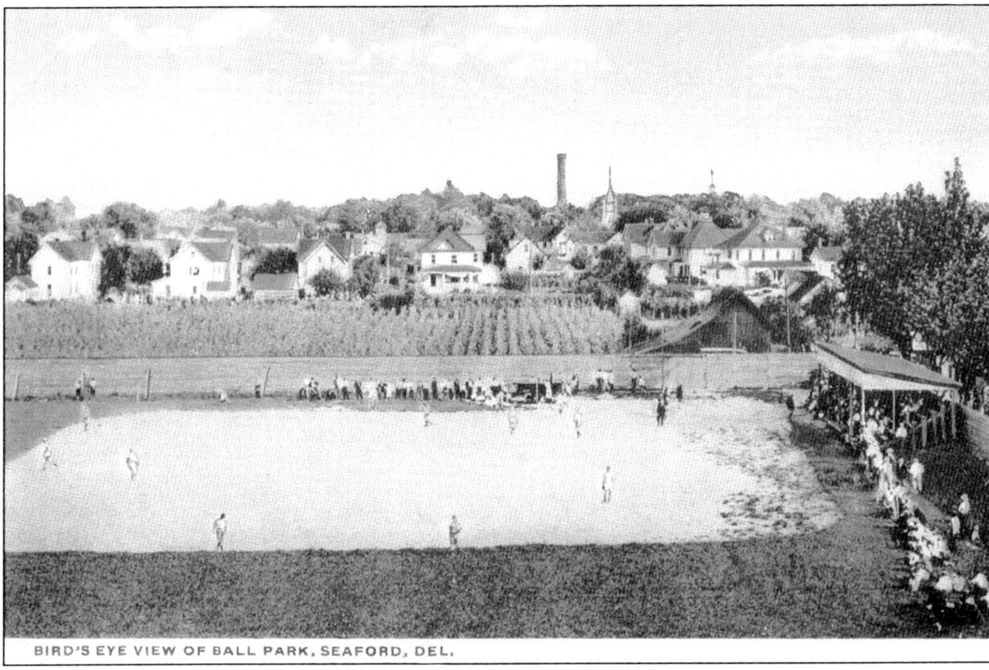

This field, located around where Fifth Street is now, was built for Seaford's first semiprofessional team. The field enabled many other teams to play games in Seaford as well.

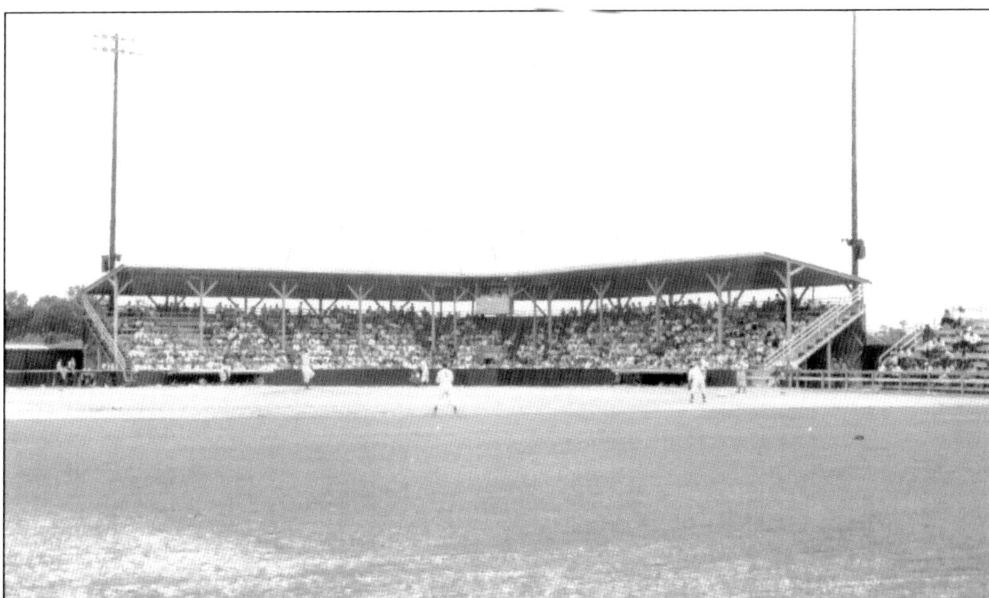

This is a shot of the ballpark on which the Seaford Eagles played. The stands are shown full, which was typical, as the games were a big draw from Seaford and neighboring communities.

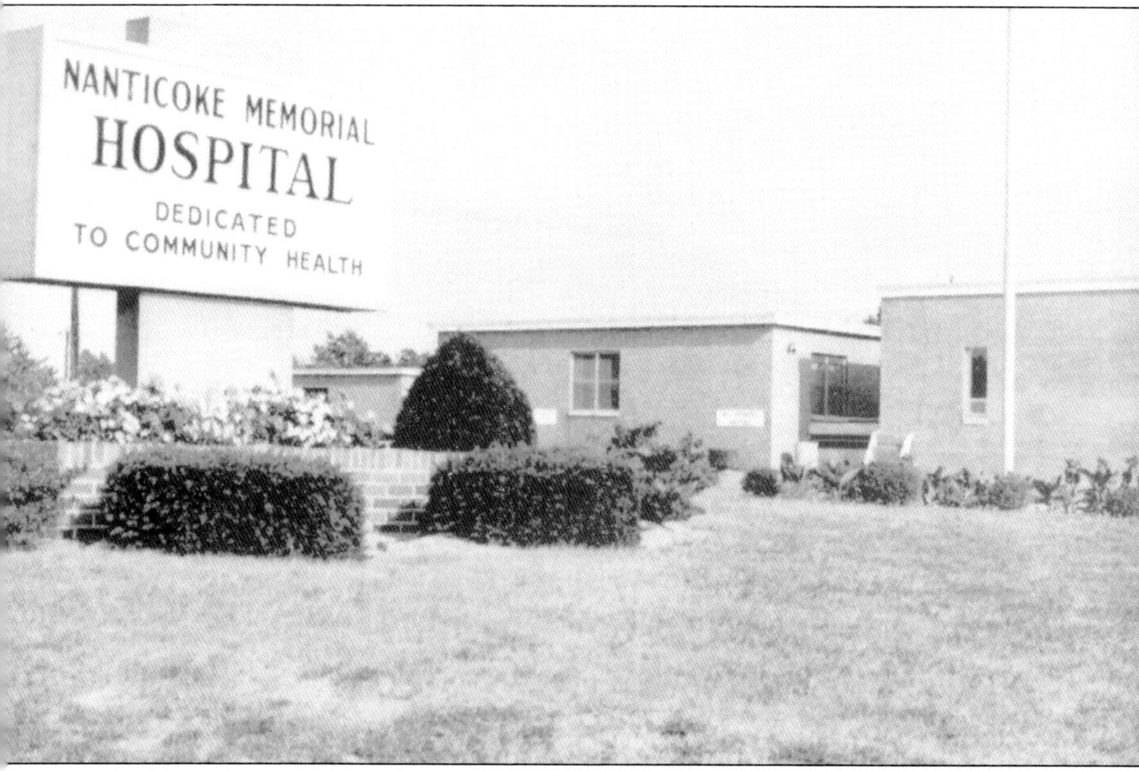

On November 27, 1945, delegates from Seaford, Laurel, Delmar, Bridgeville, Georgetown, and Sharptown met with W. Allen Hastings, president of the Seaford Lions Club, to discuss the needs for a hospital in the area. On July 4, 1950, groundbreaking ceremonies were held at the site of Nanticoke Memorial Hospital in Seaford. DuPont's contribution of $50,000 was announced by Plant Manager N.H. Winde. It was added to several other sizeable gifts from local citizens; the first of which was a $100,000 contribution from a Mr. Willin of Bridgeville. On January 28, 1952, the hospital, complete as shown in this picture, was opened for service.

Six

Nylon Capital of the World

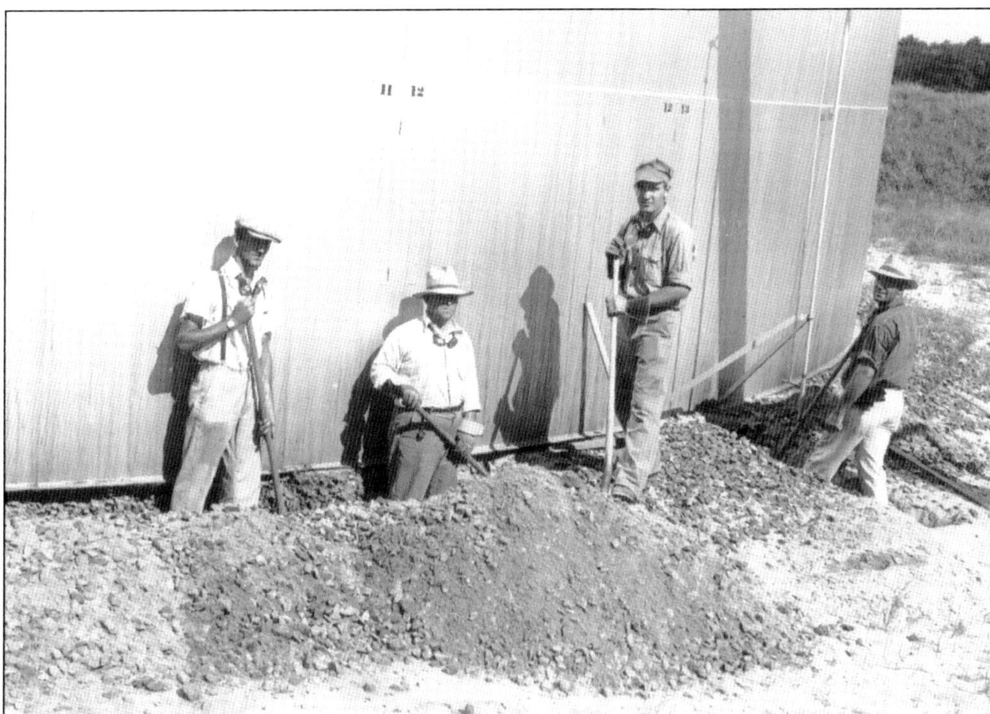

On October 19, 1938, a public announcement was made that E.I. DuPont de Nemours & Company, Inc. was going to purchase 340 acres of land on the Nanticoke River in Seaford for the purpose of constructing the world's first nylon plant. An impromptu parade took place immediately after this announcement. This picture shows the construction that took place in 1938 prior to the new plant construction in 1939.

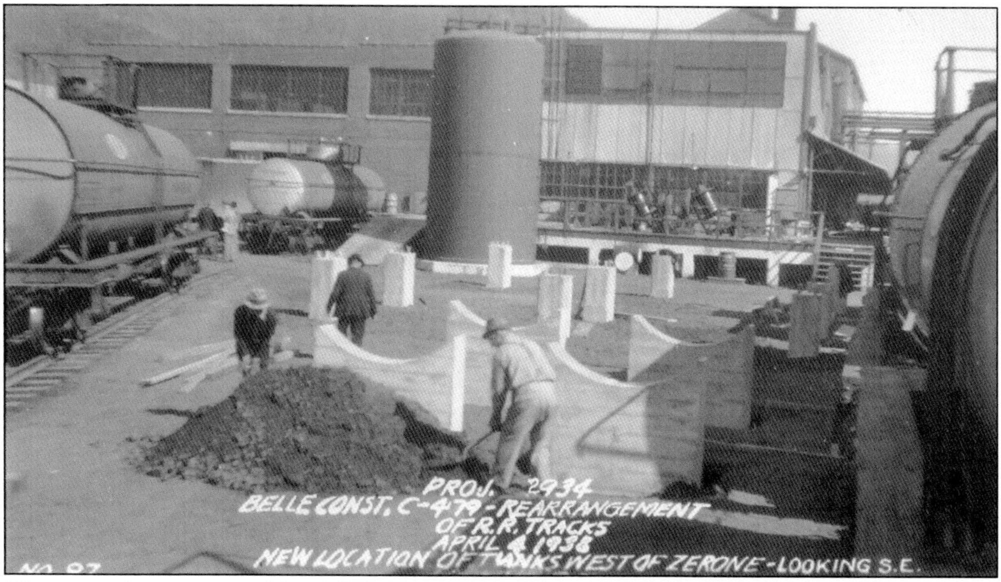

This is another picture of the 1938 construction. There was a farm owned by the Mears family on part of the property purchased by DuPont. It was moved to a new location, where it currently stands, on the corner of Sussex Avenue and Stein Highway.

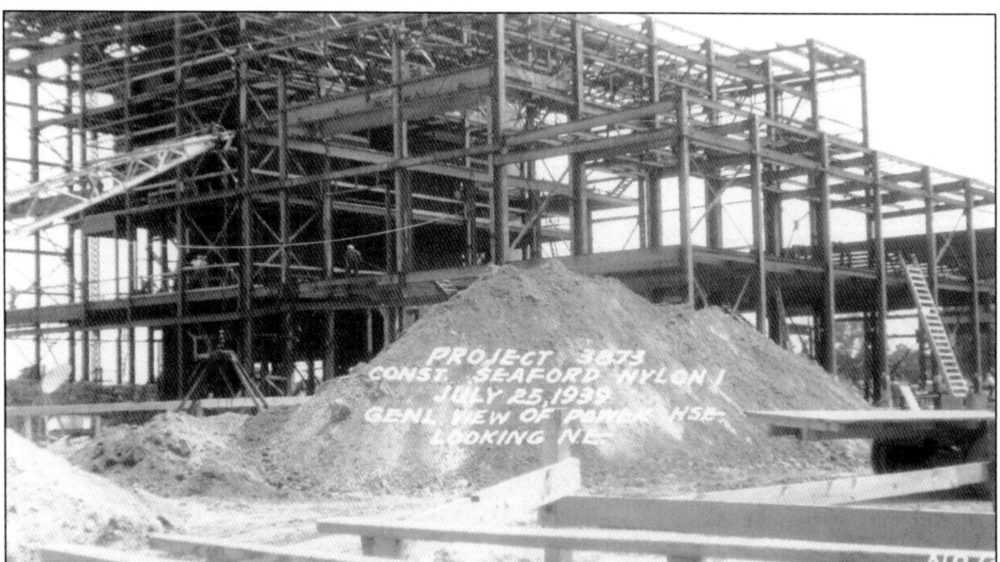

Construction engineers arrived at the site on January 16, 1939. On January 20, 1939, construction began on the plant, and by August of 1939, there were 900 construction employees and 400 workers of subcontractors at the plant site.

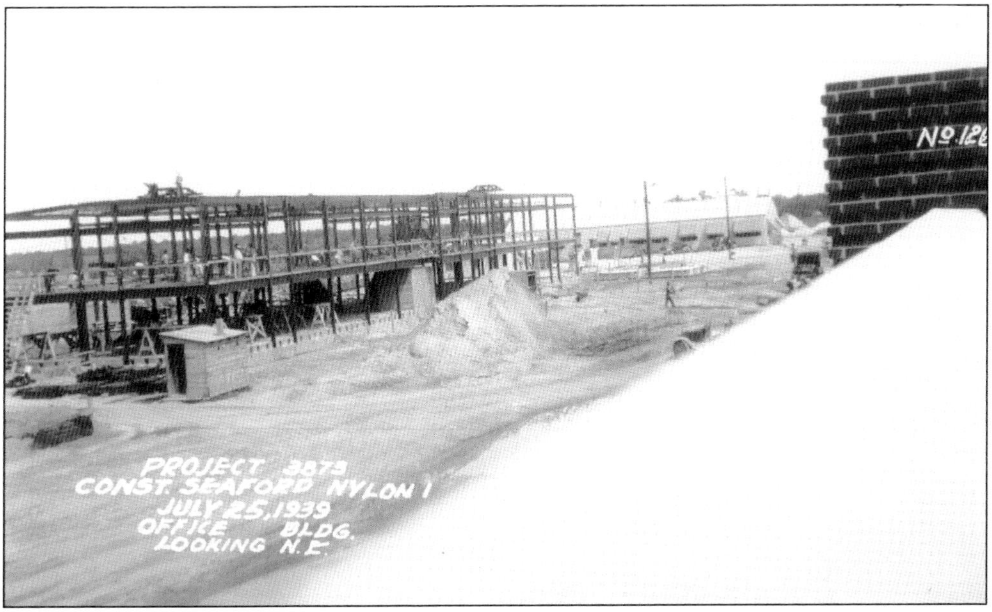

The addition of this new plant was a massive undertaking. To some, the new plant meant new jobs and opportunities, while to others, it meant a big change to Seaford's current way of life.

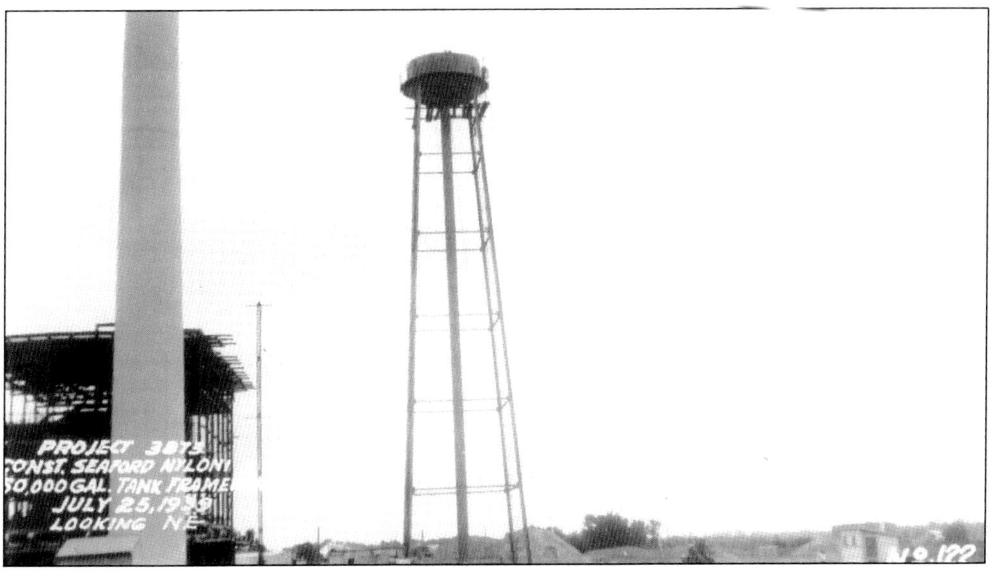

While DuPont was busy constructing the new nylon plant, the company was also assessing the need for housing in Seaford. On July 21, 1939, the company purchased 153 acres of land to build homes for supervisory and clerical workers.

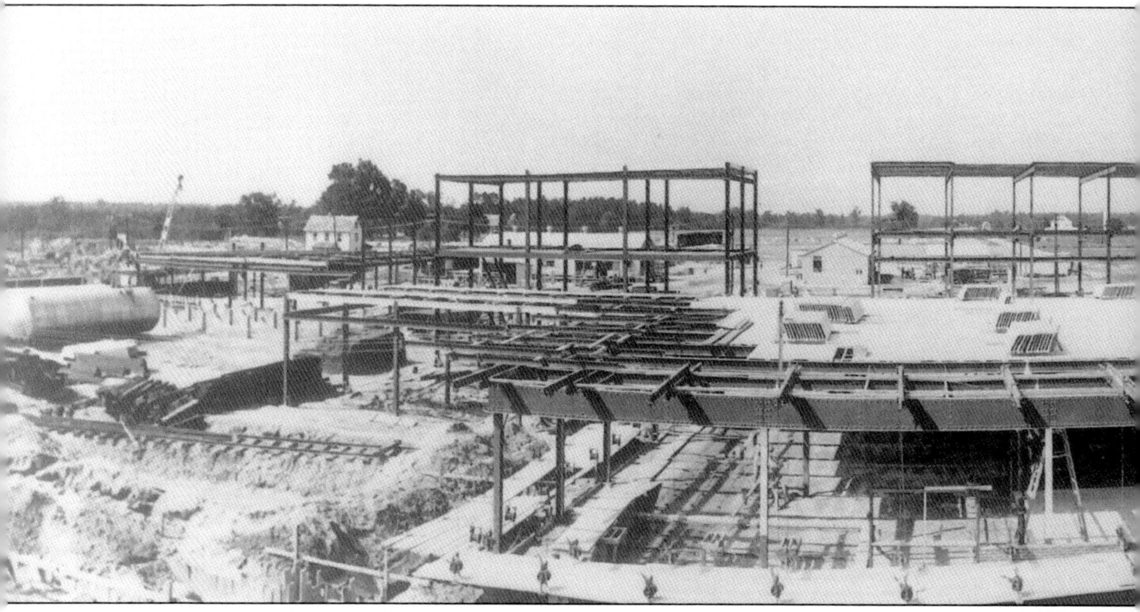

In this picture, taken in 1939 during the construction process, the layout of the entire plant can

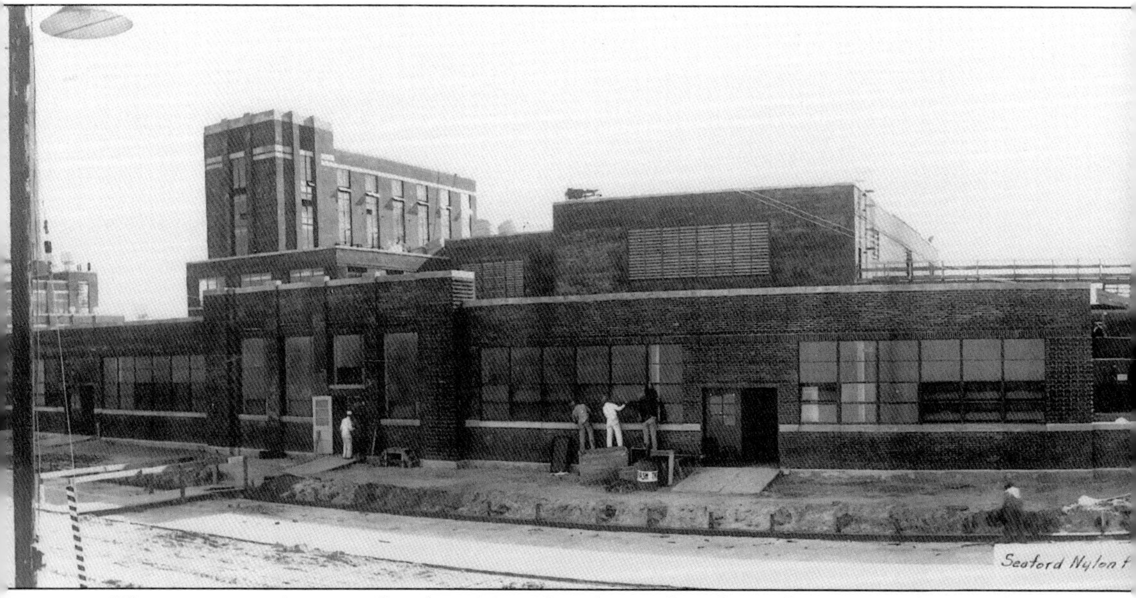

This picture, taken on October 16, 1939, shows the plant almost entirely complete. On December 12, 1939, at 12 midnight, the operators began and the first spin bobbin was produced.

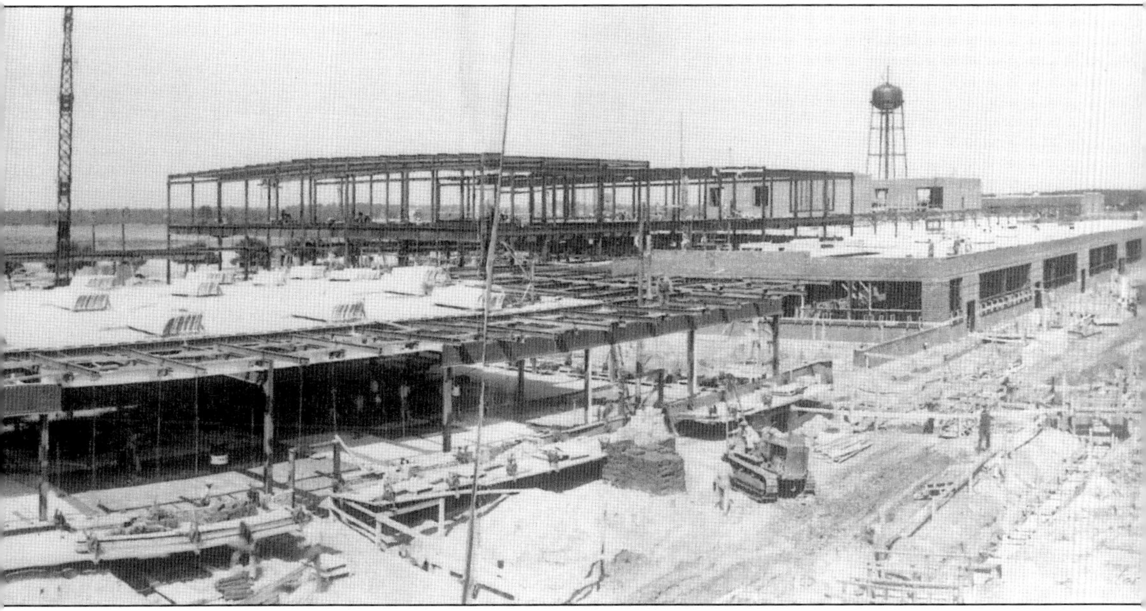

be seen. Finally, on October 2, 1939, the first operating personnel arrived at the new plant.

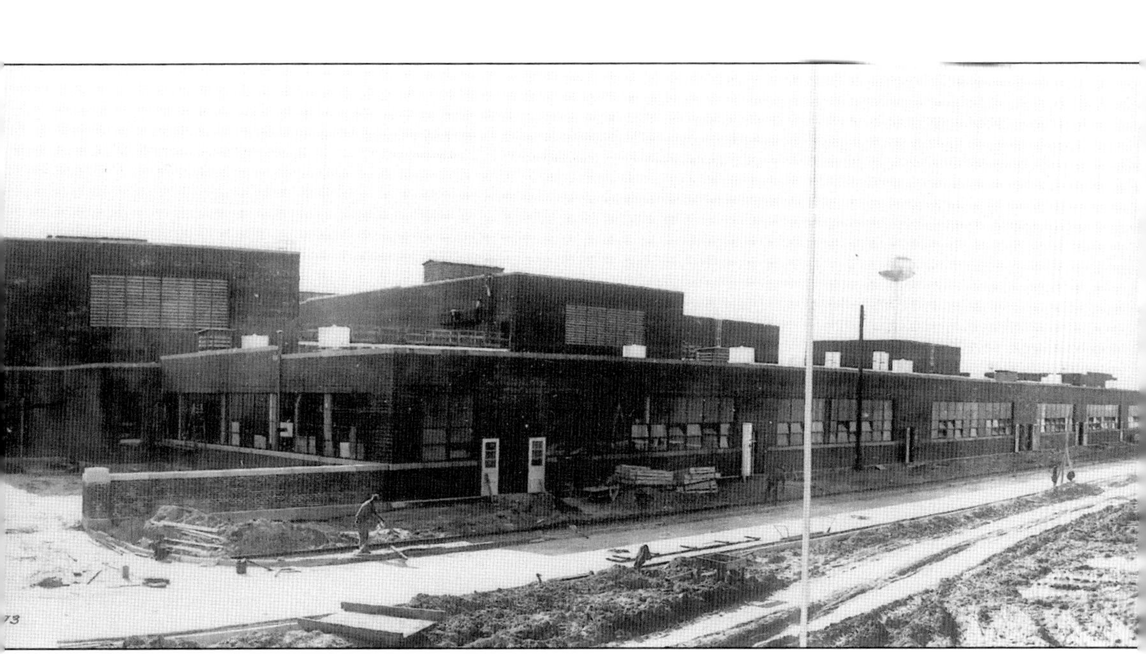

As the City would soon find out, DuPont would bring a great deal of growth and development for Seaford.

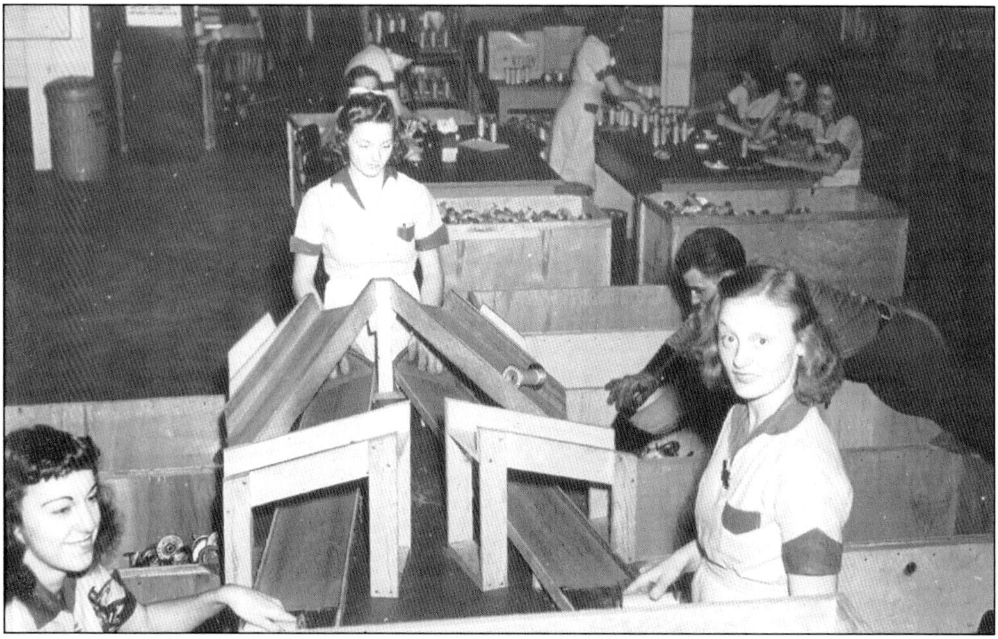

This picture, taken inside the Seaford plant in 1942, shows DuPont's spooling operation.

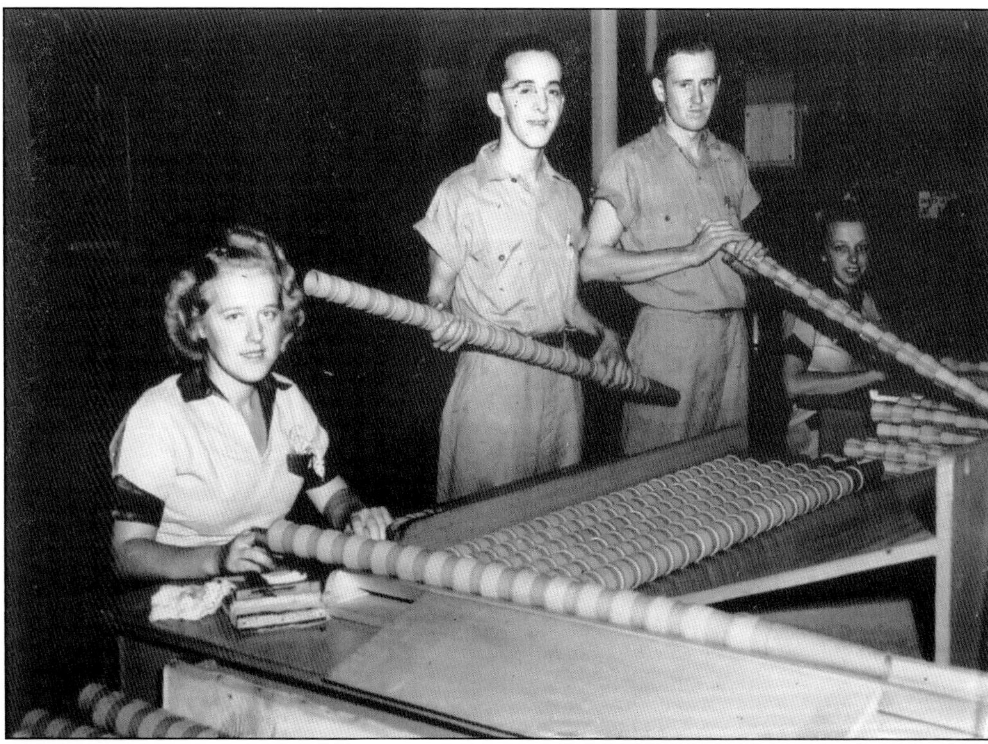

This is another photo of the spooling operation in the plant taken in 1942.

On December 15, 1938, E.F. DuPont, shown in this photo, was appointed as the new nylon plant's first plant manager.

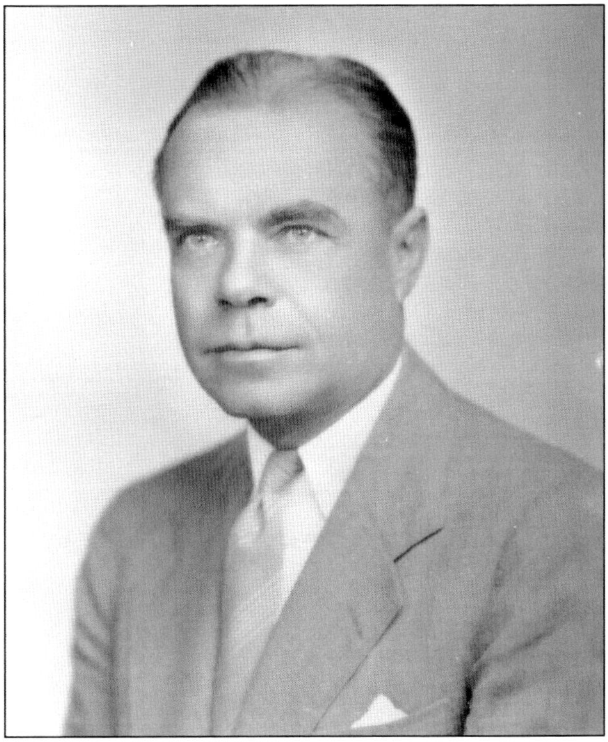

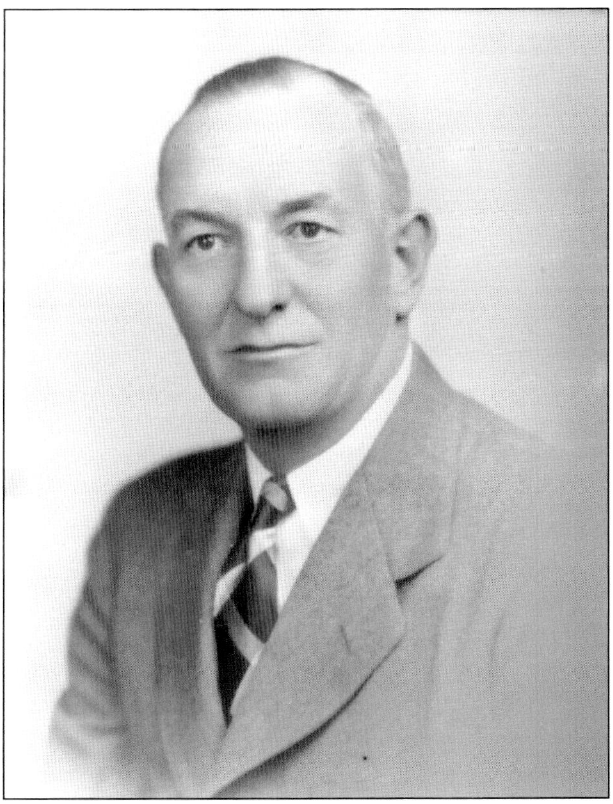

On January 1, 1941, W.L. Stabler, shown here, was appointed as the second plant manager of DuPont in Seaford.

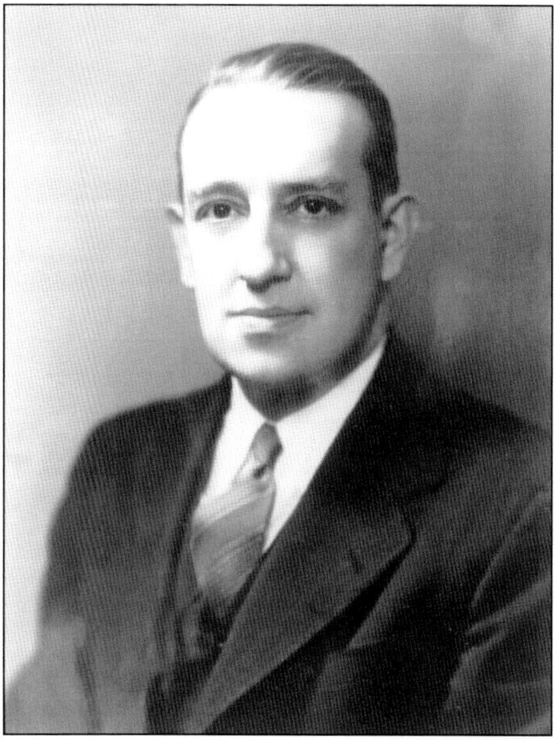

Seaford DuPont's third plant manager, W.E. Gladding, shown here, was appointed on October 1, 1945.

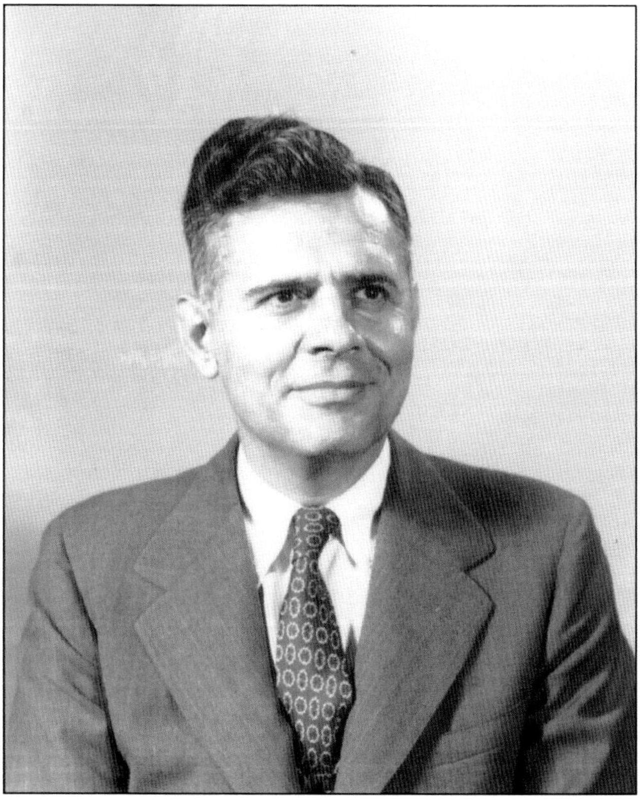

N.H. Winde, the fourth plant manager of DuPont in Seaford, was appointed on May 1, 1946.

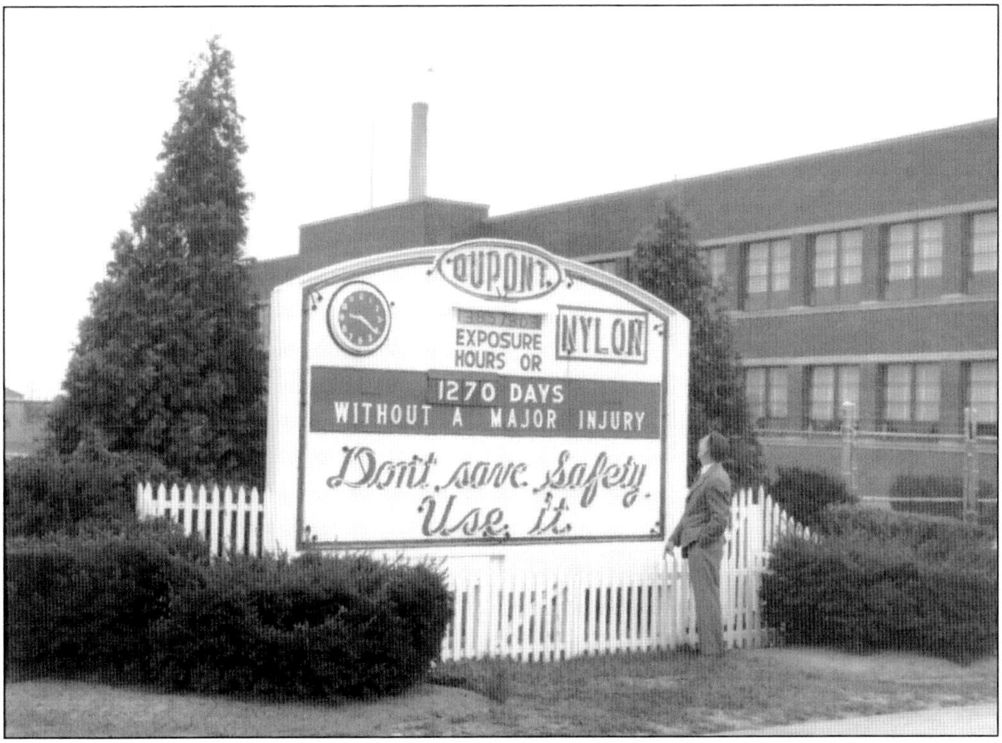

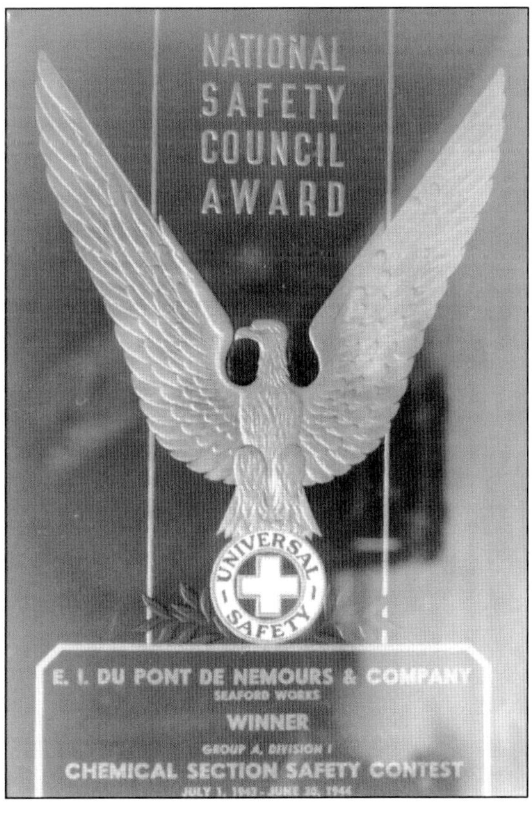

Safety was, and still is, one of the most important things to DuPont. This sign stood in front of DuPont noting that the company had operated for 1,270 days and 3,857,303 hours without a major injury at the time of this picture. The sign would keep a running count of the days and hours safely worked.

All of DuPont's hard work on keeping a safe workplace paid off. Shown here is an award that the company received from the National Safety Council in 1944. In 1945, the Seaford Plant went on to complete 18,871,795 exposure hours without a disabling injury, which was a new world's record.

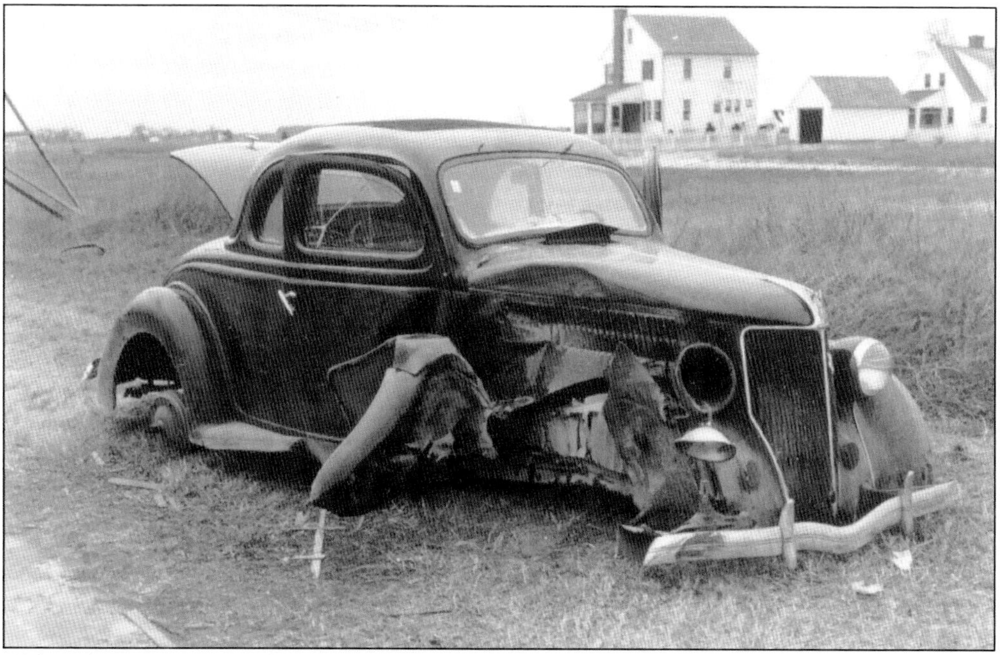

Although DuPont strived for an accident free workplace, they did experience the occasional mishap. This picture shows one such event. This automobile was involved in an accident in February of 1942 on the grounds of the DuPont plant.

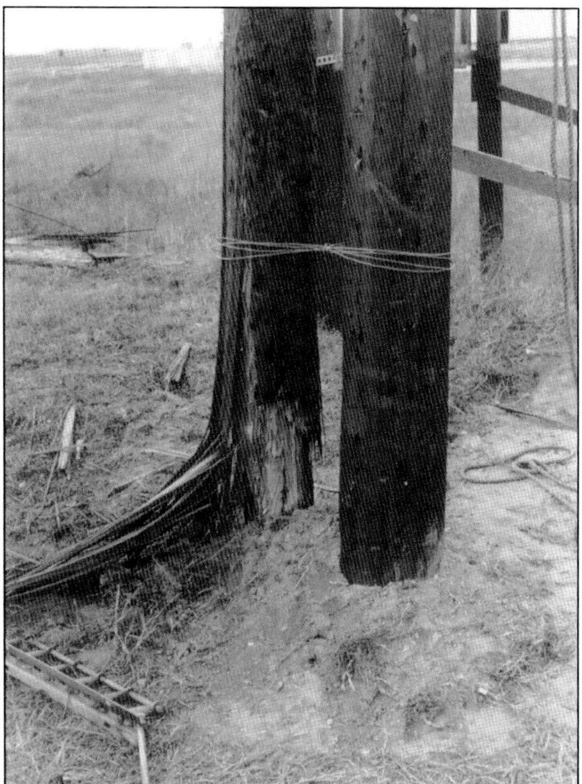

DuPont documented any accident that took place there very well. This picture shows the pole that the automobile above ran into.

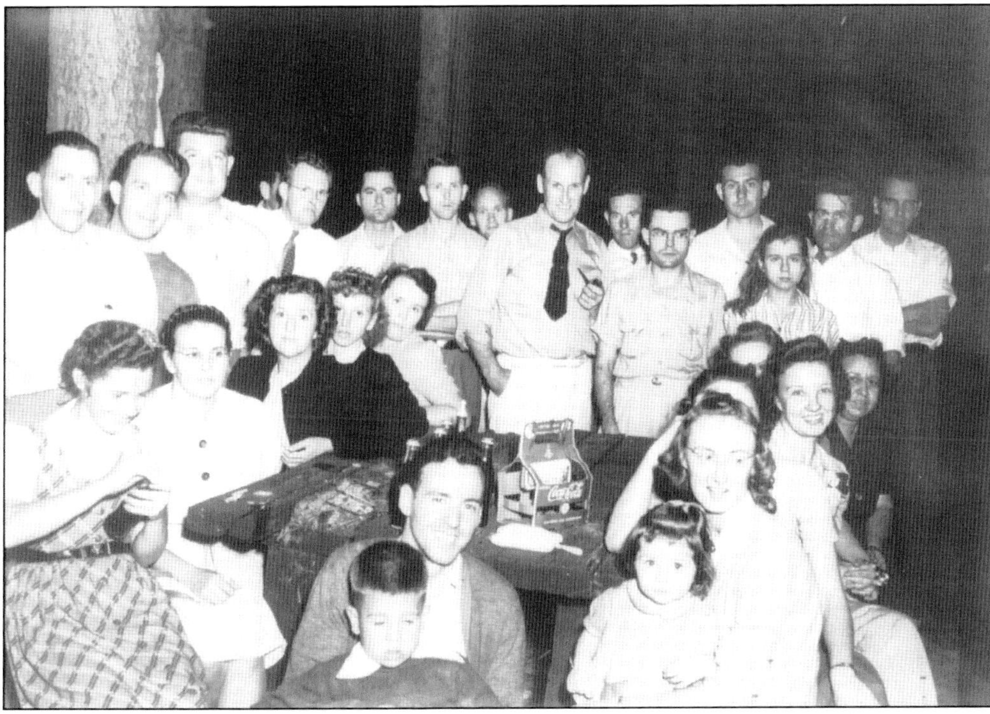

The employees of DuPont often got together outside of work for parties, special occasions, or sporting events. This picture was taken at a Stores Party in September of 1941.

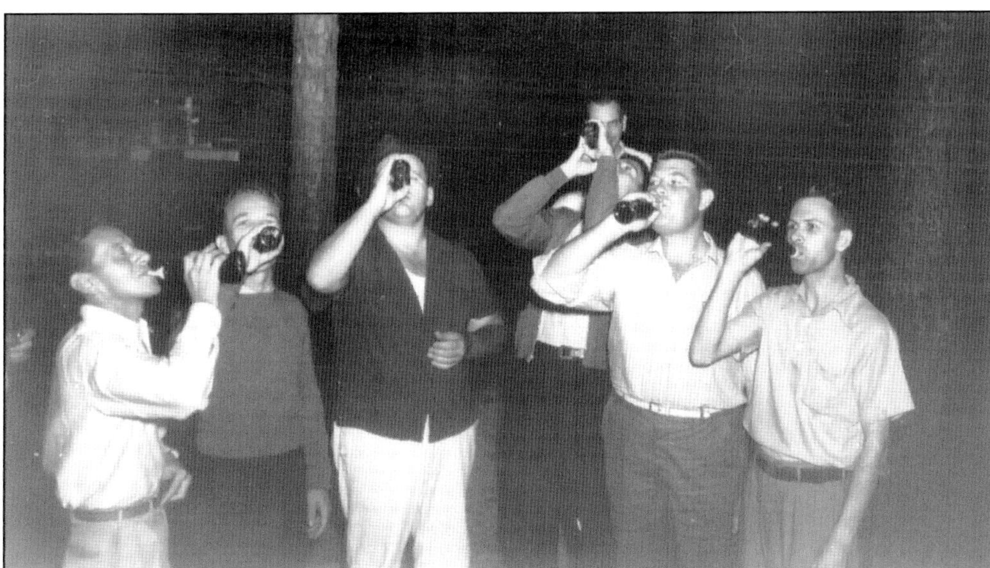

This picture was taken at the same DuPont party in 1941. The gentlemen have gathered for drinks out of baby bottles!

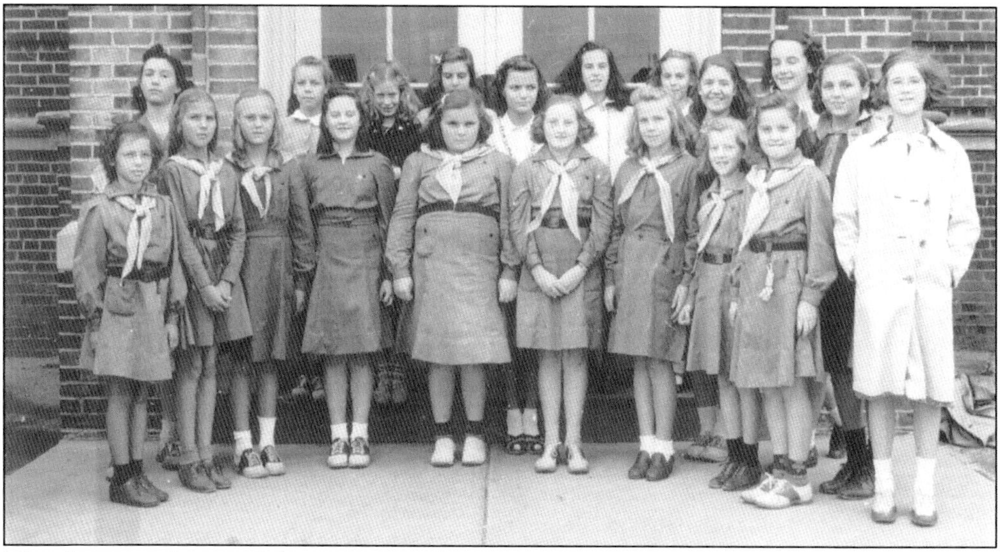

The diverse cultures of the many people who came to Seaford after the opening of the DuPont plant resulted in new organizations being formed. One such organization was the Girl Scouts, which were organized in 1941 in Seaford. Shown here is a picture of a troop from November of 1941.

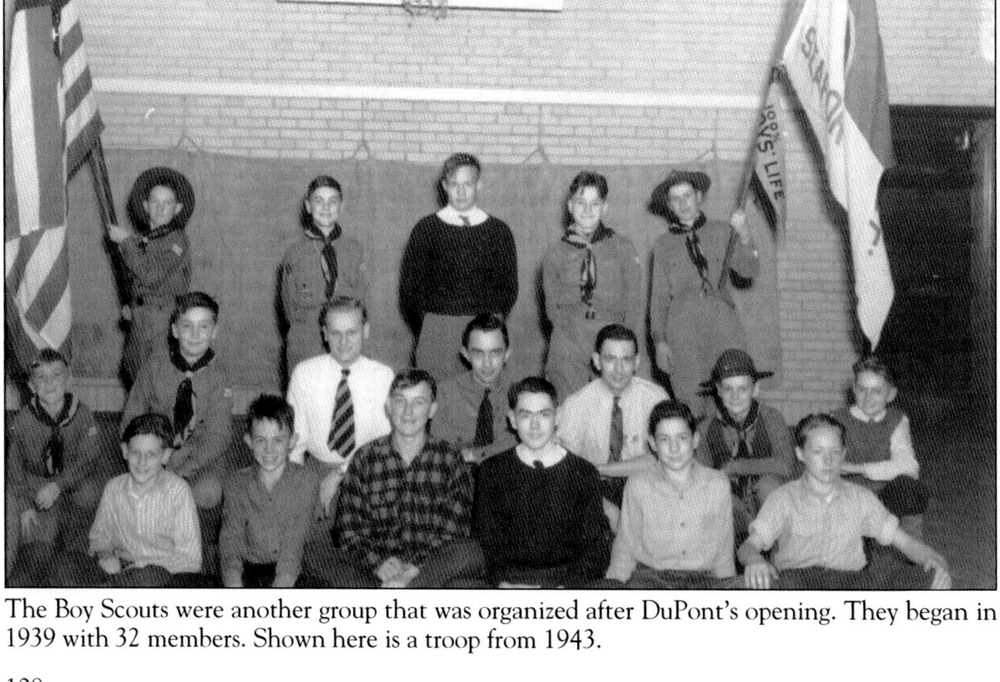

The Boy Scouts were another group that was organized after DuPont's opening. They began in 1939 with 32 members. Shown here is a troop from 1943.

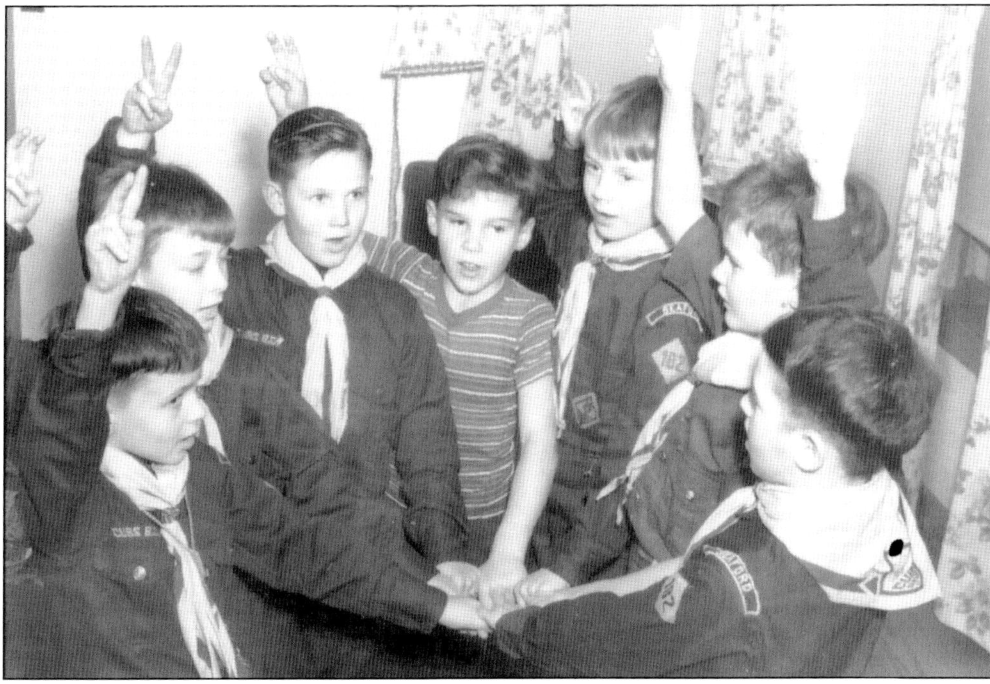

Also taken in 1943, this picture shows the local Boy Scouts chanting the "scouts honor."

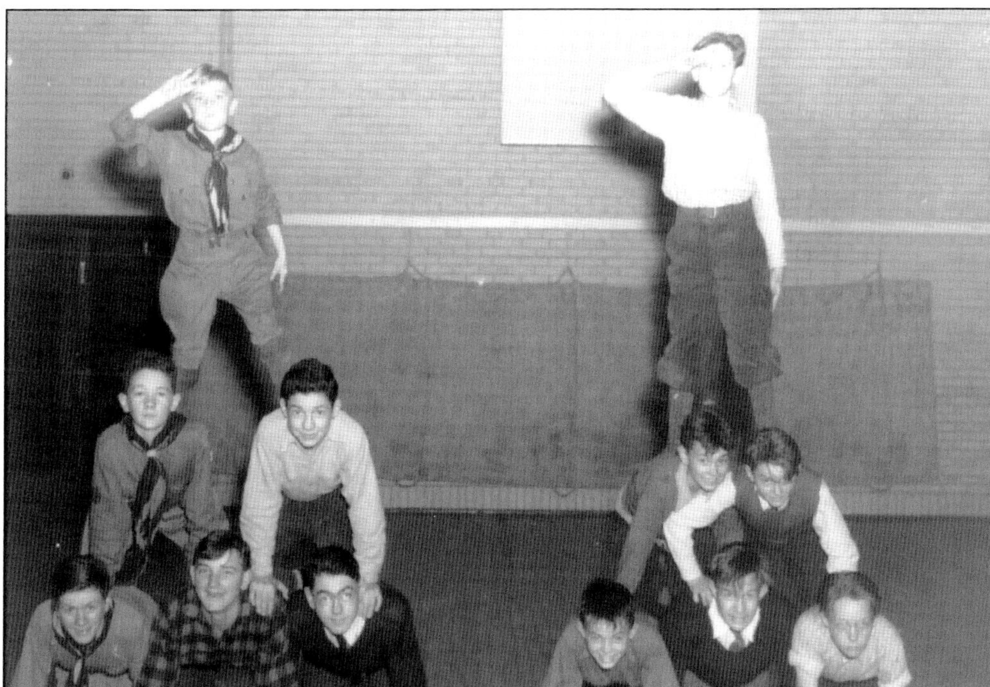

This picture, also of the 1943 Boy Scouts, shows the boys demonstrating their spirit in form of a pyramid!

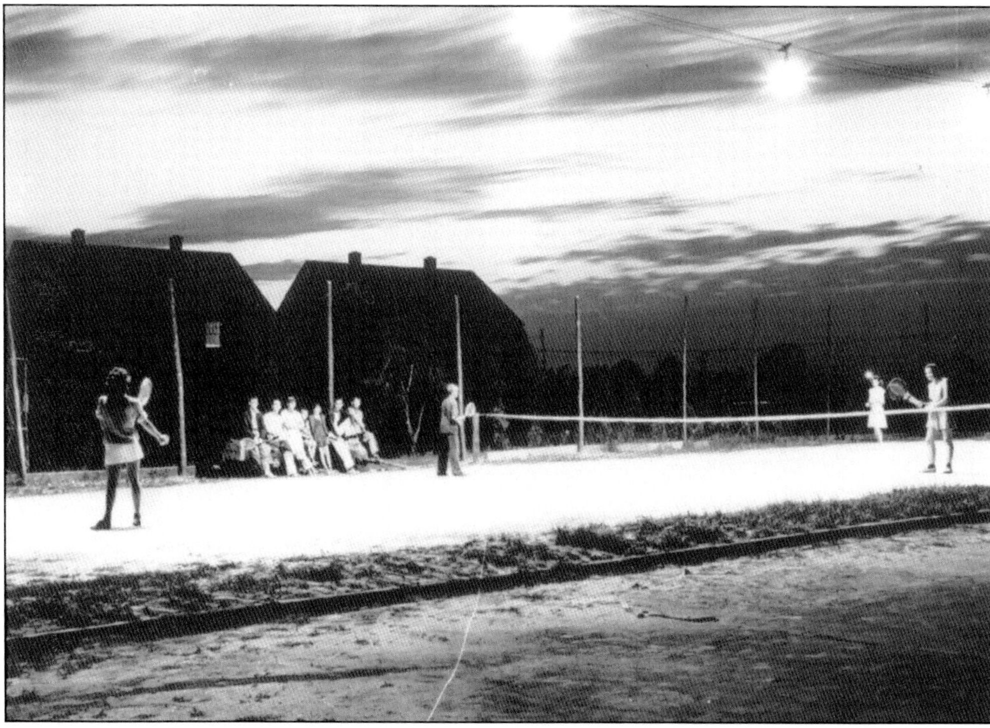

Other activities became popular with the increase in Seaford's population. This picture, taken in August of 1941, shows the Seaford Racquet Club and a game of night tennis.

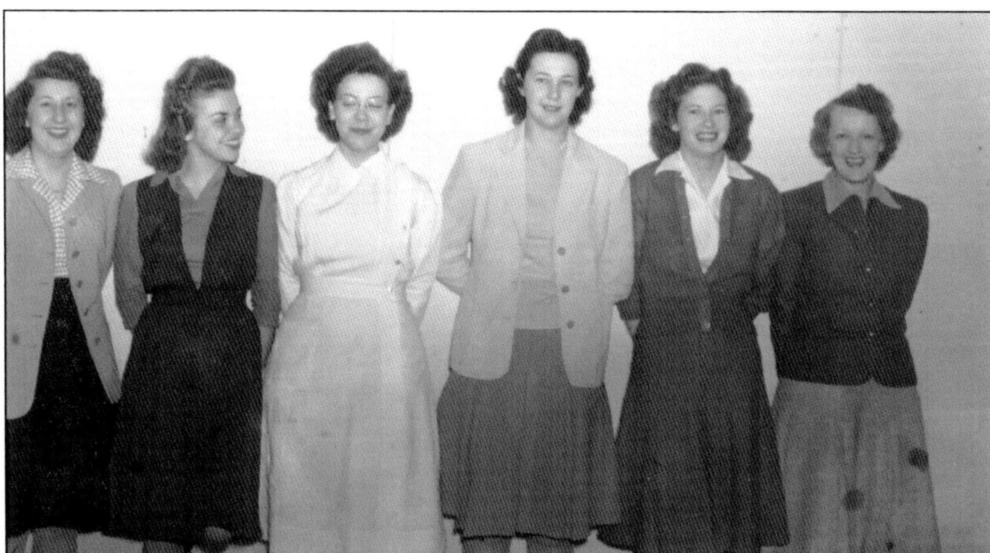

DuPont employees formed teams and competed against others from all over. The 1943 DuPont Office girls' bowling team can be seen in this picture.

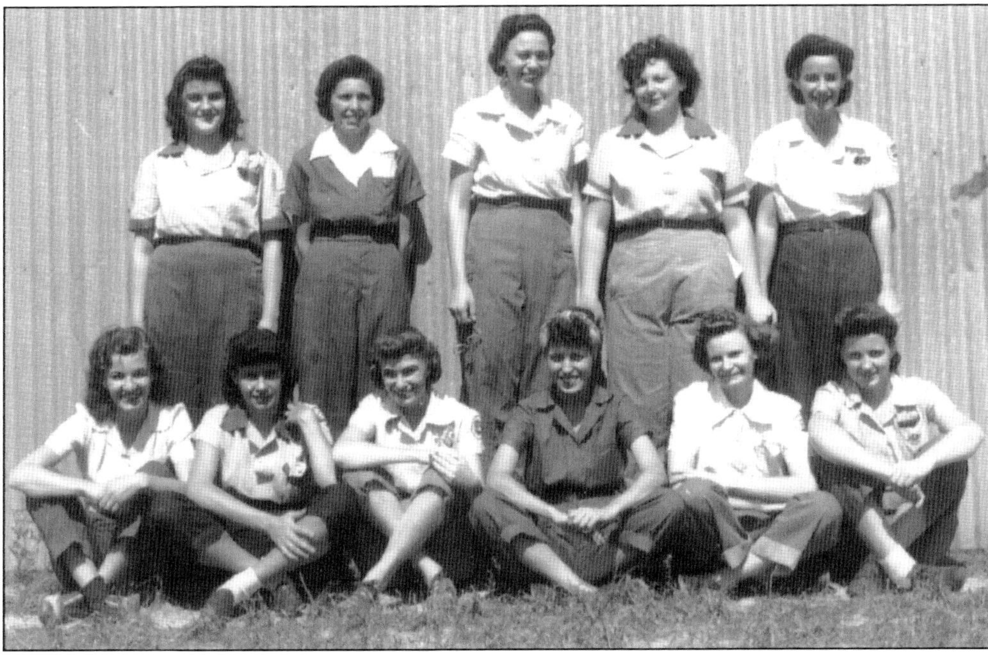

Softball teams were also formed by DuPont workers. This was the 1944 Girl's softball team.

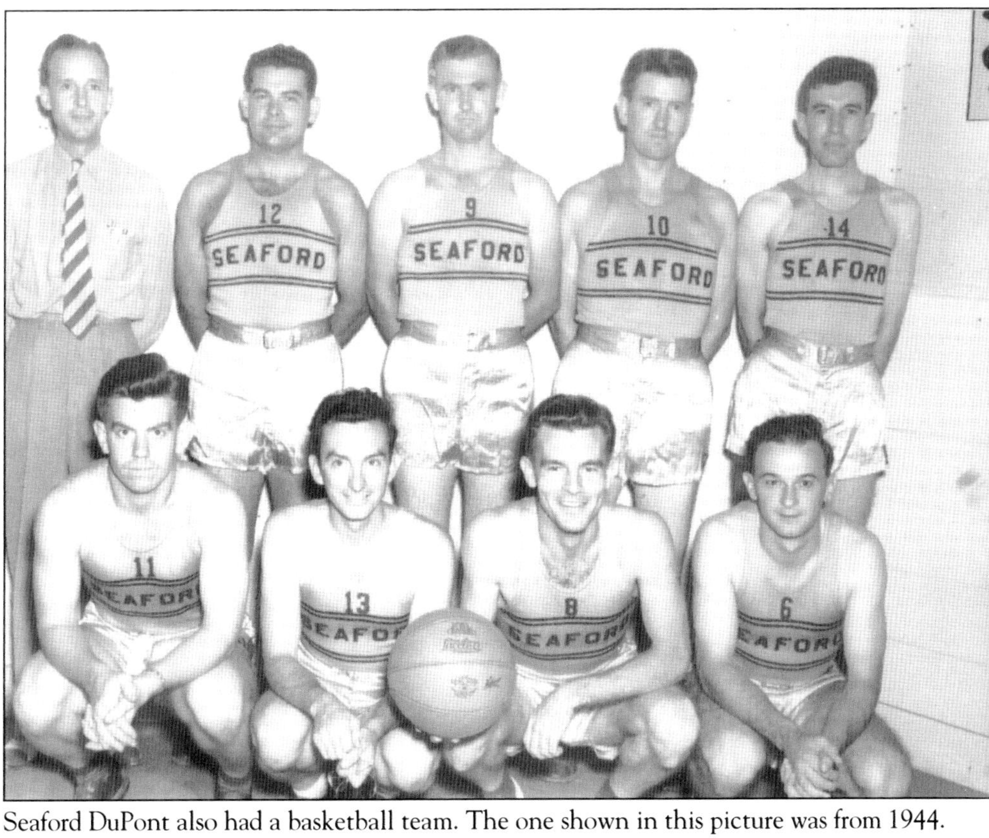

Seaford DuPont also had a basketball team. The one shown in this picture was from 1944.

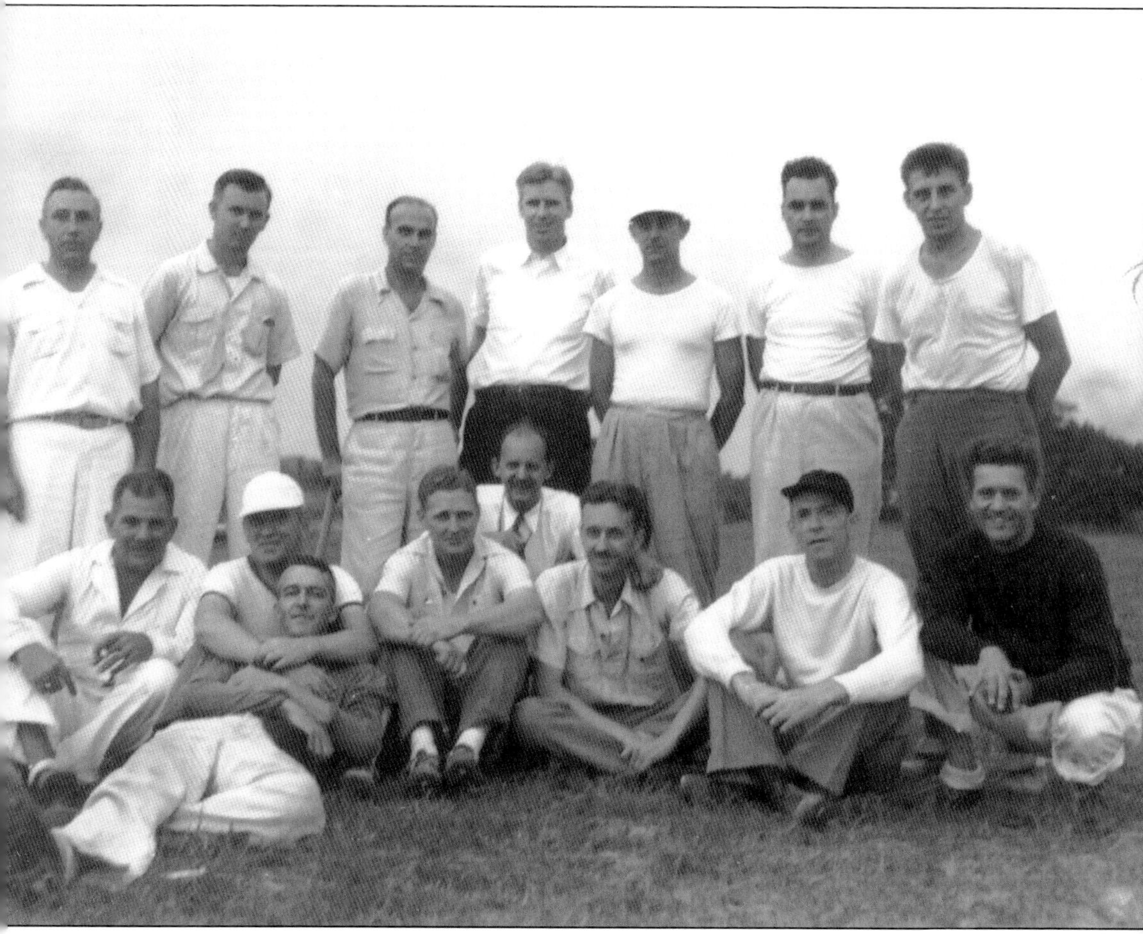

Baseball had always been a popular sport in Seaford. This group got together and formed the "Old Timers" baseball team in 1943.

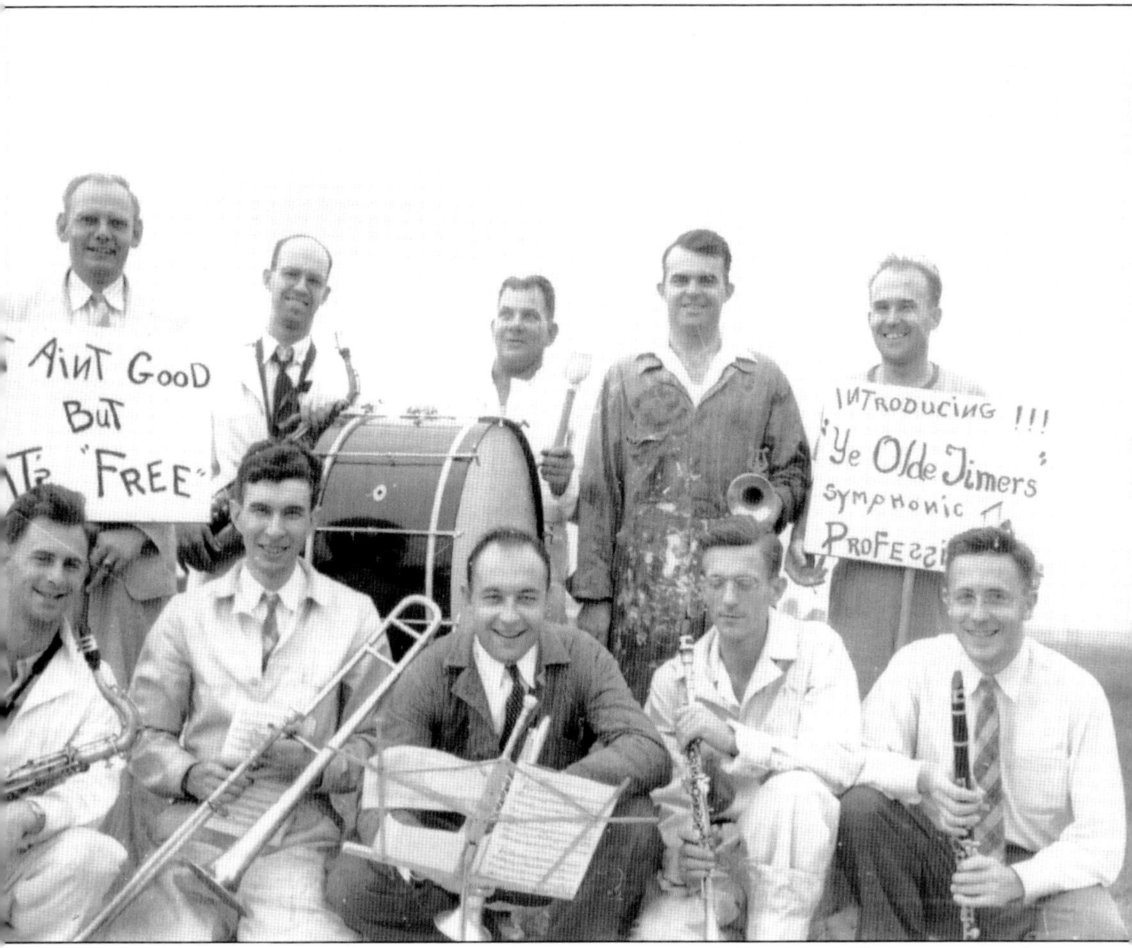

What team would be complete without a band? This bunch formed the "Ye Olde Timers" Band in October of 1943.

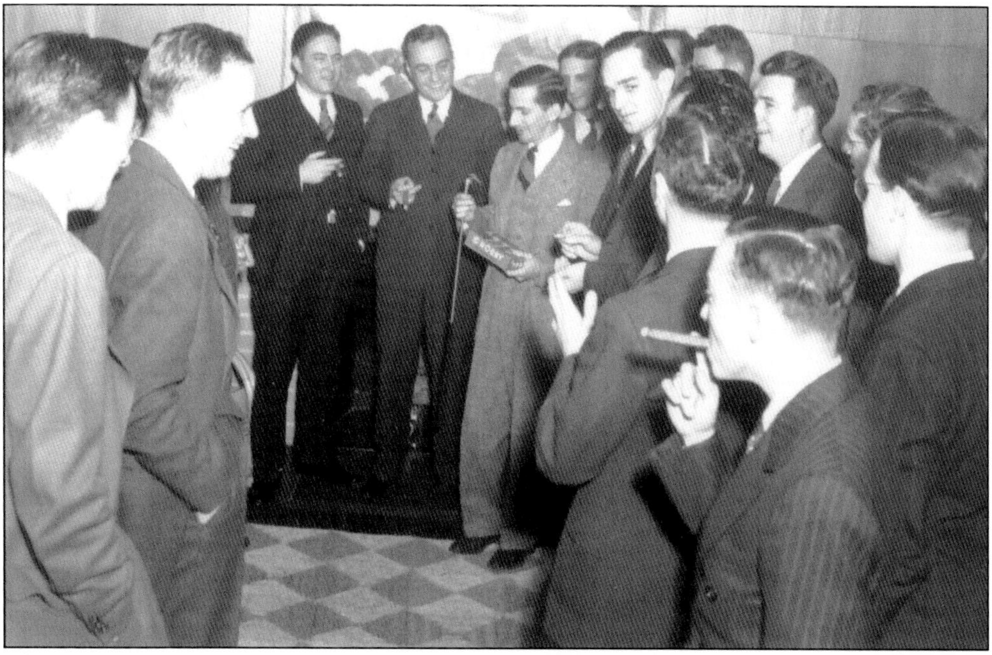

The DuPont company saw the need for recreational facilities for its employees and the local residents. For this reason, The Seaford Golf and Country Club was formed. On June 28, 1941, the golf course was opened, and on November 14, 1941, the Club House was opened. This picture was taken at that grand opening.

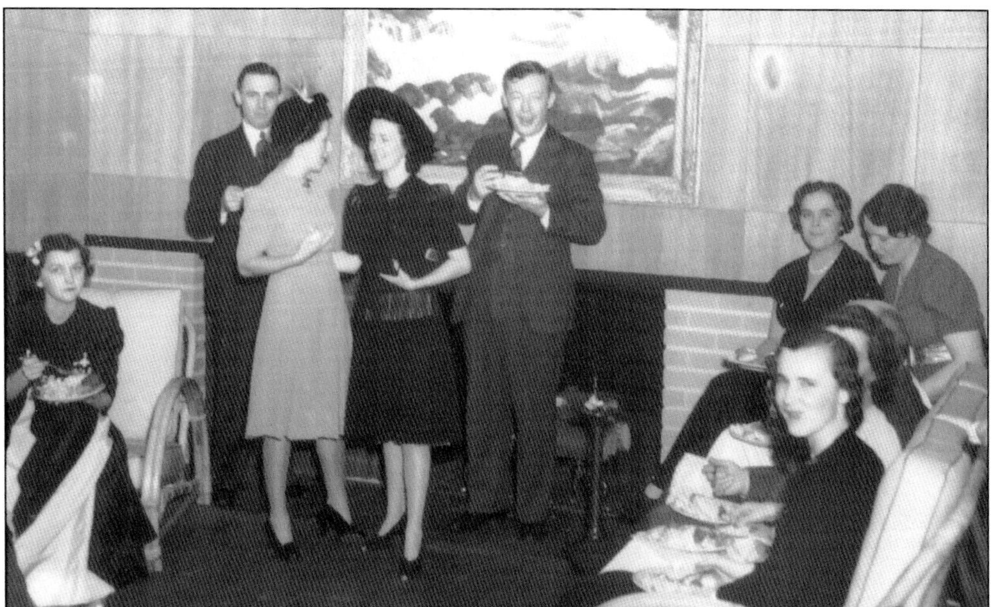

This is another picture that was taken at the grand opening of the Club House. When the Country Club was opened, there was no other facility of this type in the community. There were 35 community residents as members.

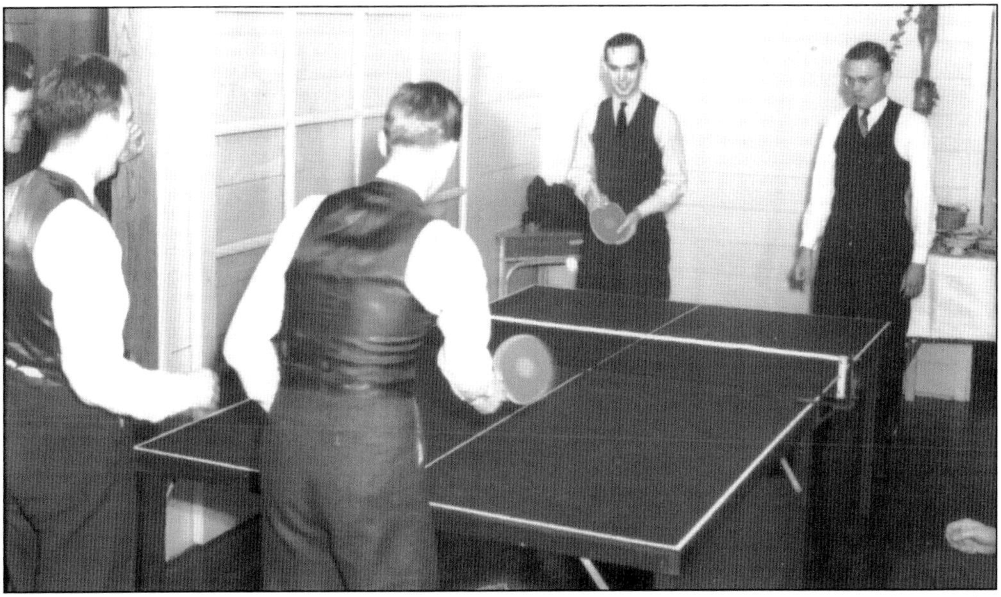

The new Club House offered many amenities. These gentlemen are enjoying one of them—the Ping-Pong table.

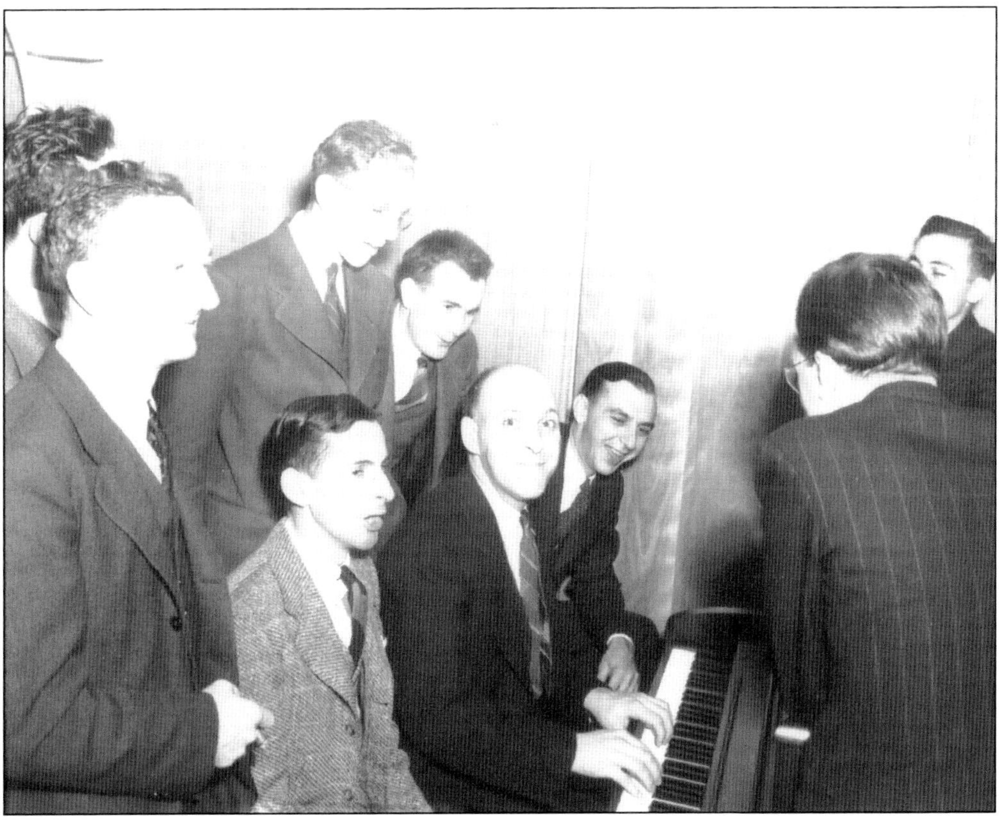

During the celebration, everyone joined around the piano for a little singing.

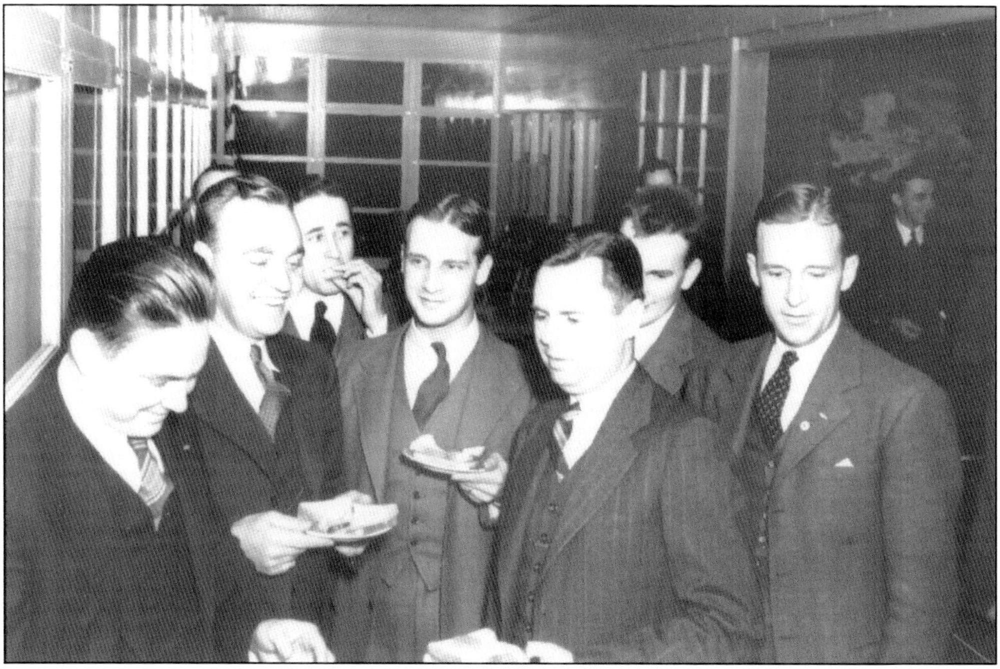

All great parties have great food. As shown in this picture, many enjoyed the great food prepared for this festivity.

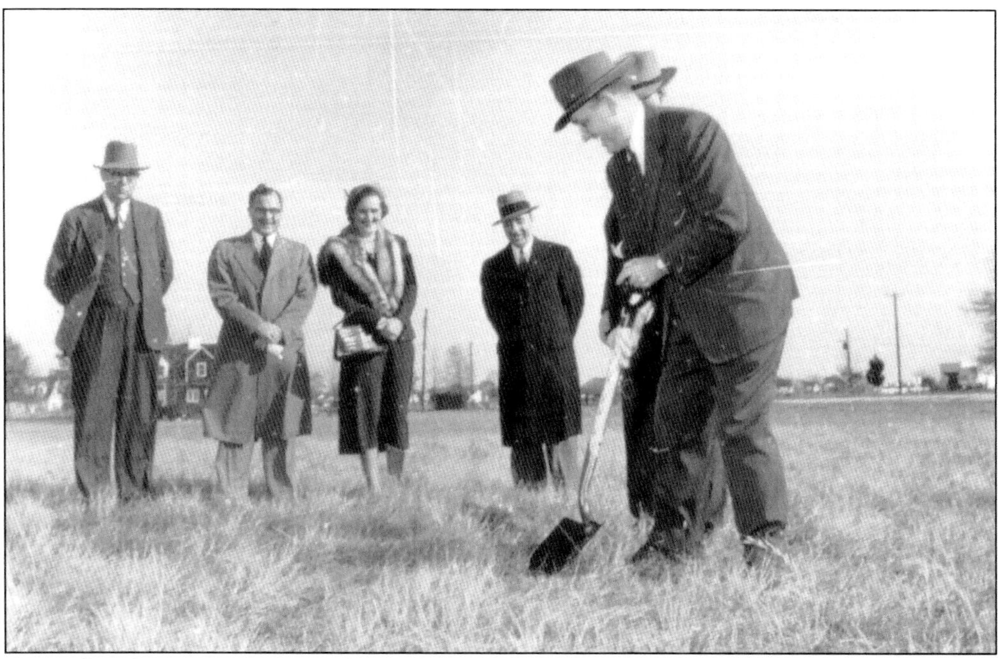

Groundbreaking ceremonies are being held in this picture on November 14, 1952, for a new elementary school, West Seaford.

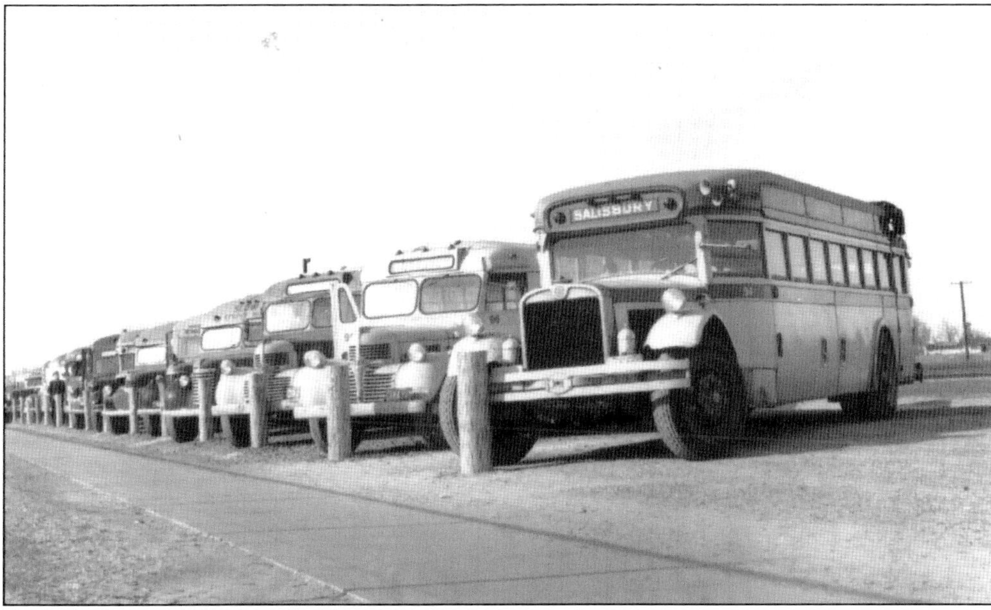

The buses in these two pictures are from 1944. During the War, DuPont arranged for buses to carry its' employees to and from work. This is because there was a shortage of gasoline, making it very expensive for others to purchase. The areas that the buses traveled to is denoted by a sign over the windshield.

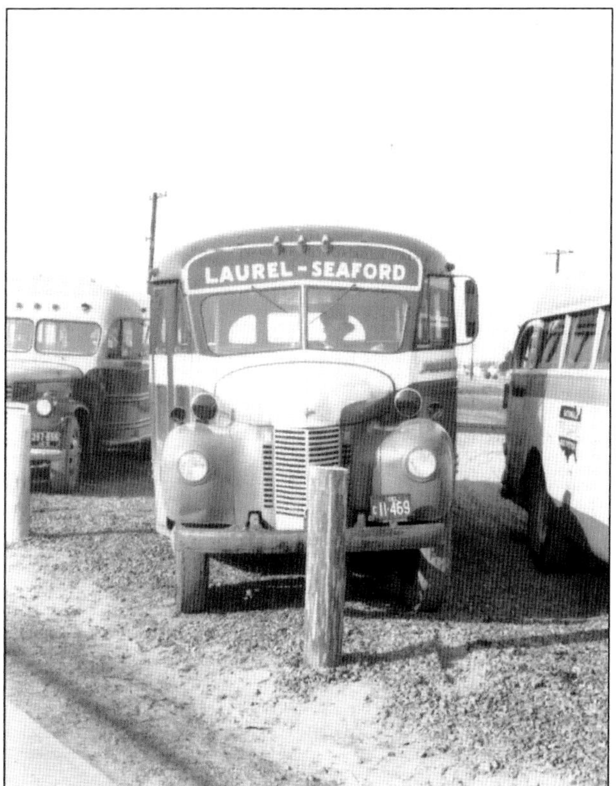

This particular bus provided transportation for those employees that lived in the Seaford and Laurel areas.

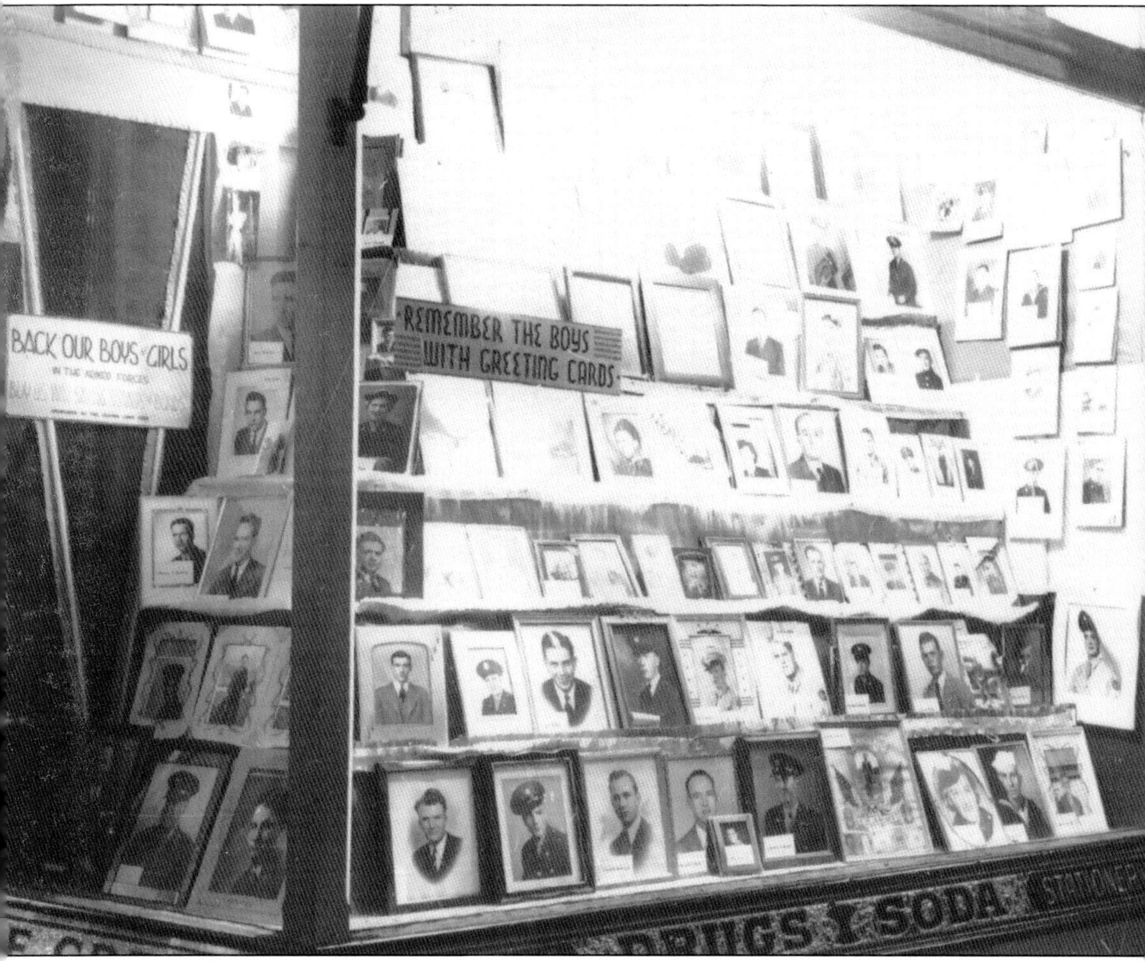

Displayed in Manning's Drugstore, these cards were for those in the Service during WW II. Seaford, like many other cities, was greatly affected by the War.

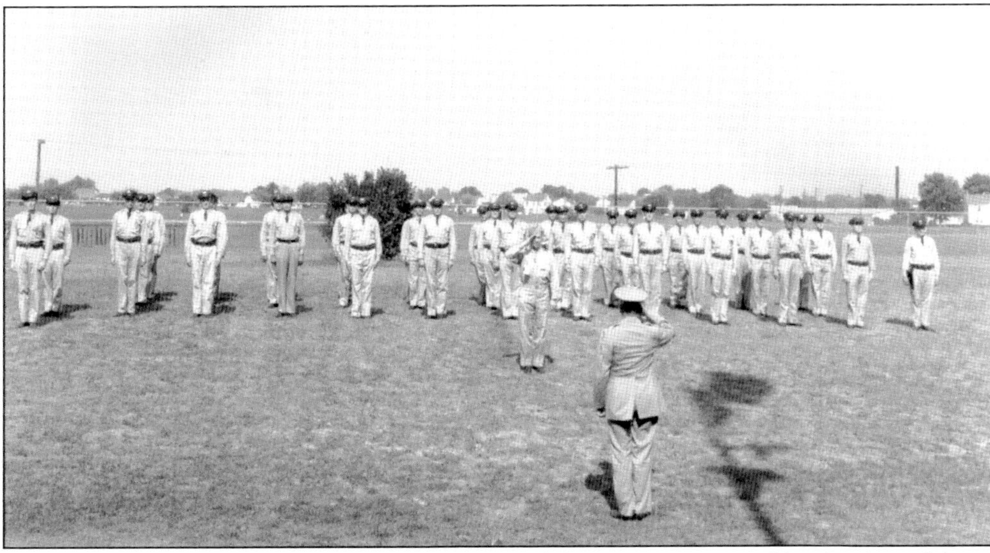

Seaford's nylon product was essential to National defense. Yarn was used by the Armed forces in parachutes, bomb slings, clothing, and many other applications. For this reason, steps were taken to protect the plant against enemy attack. Shown here is the Plant's Guard Force in 1943.

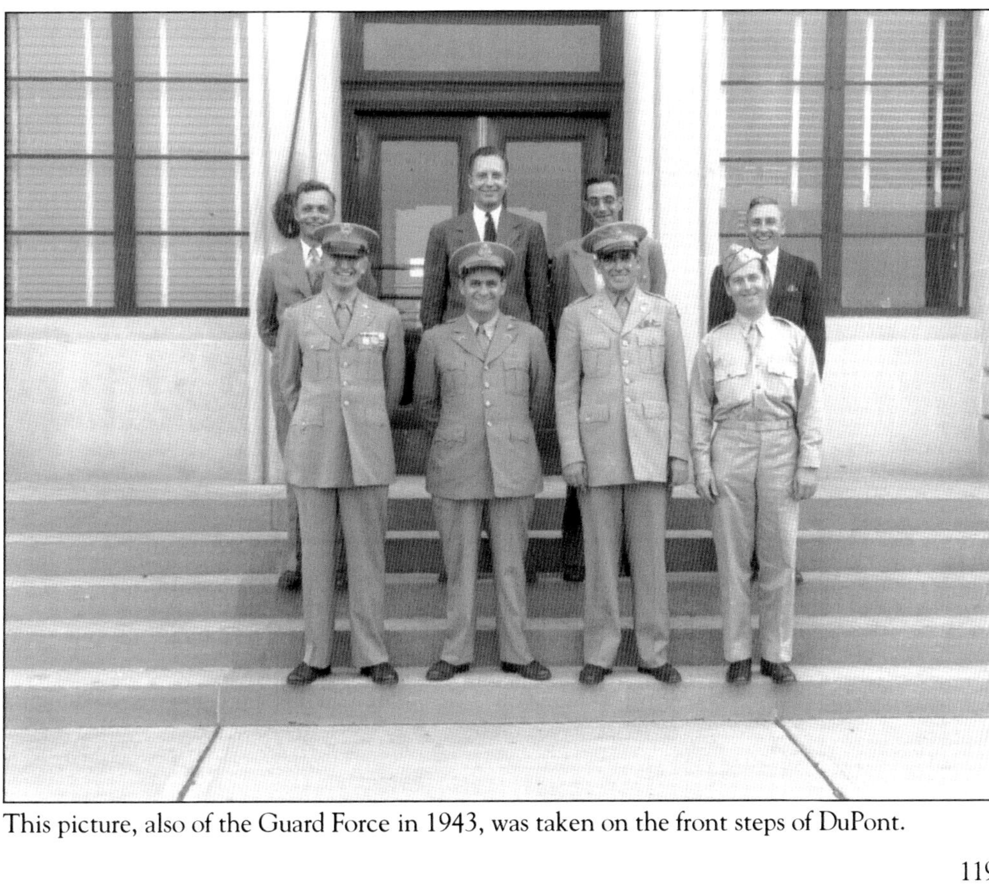

This picture, also of the Guard Force in 1943, was taken on the front steps of DuPont.

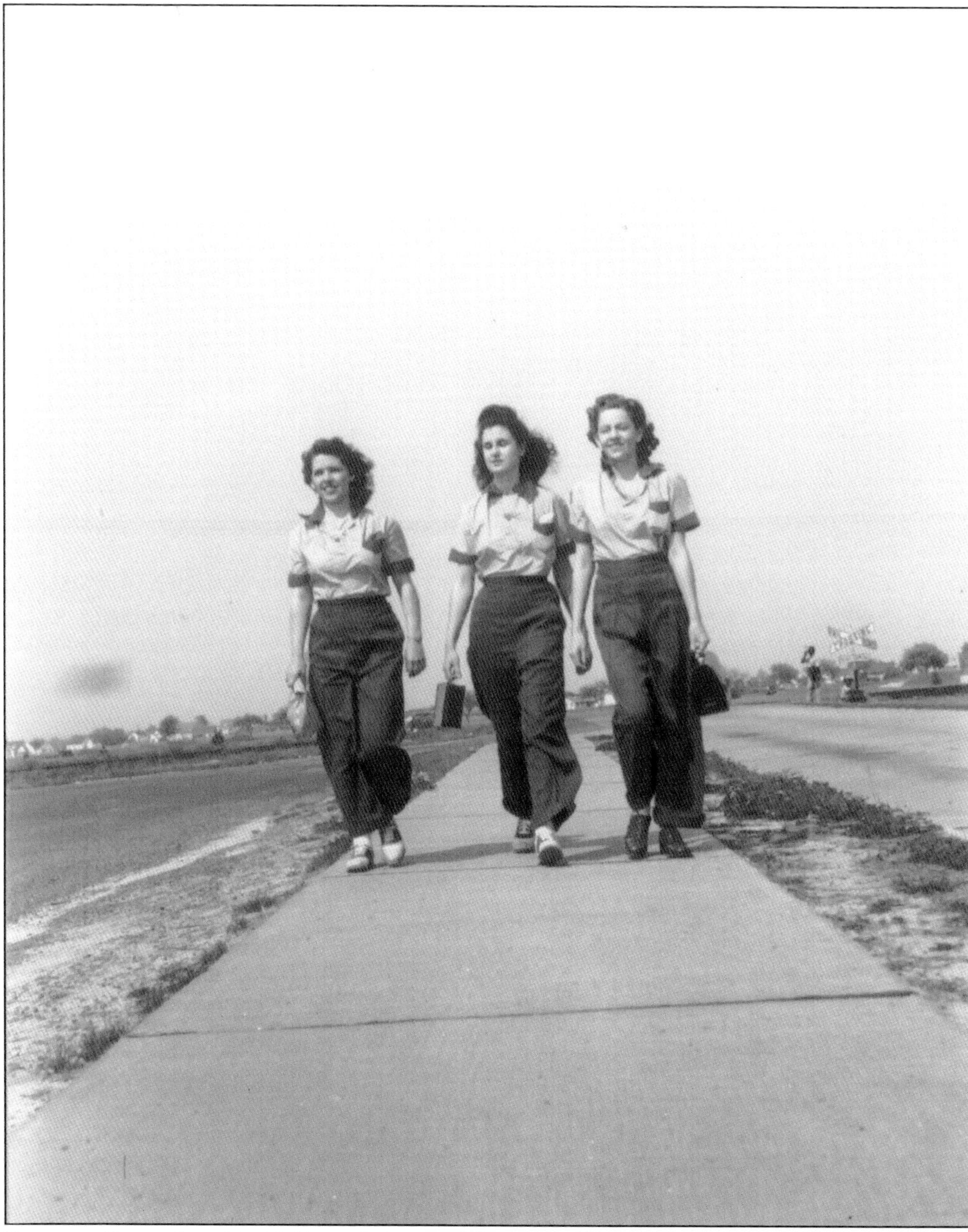

Between September 16, 1940, and August 14, 1945, nearly 1,100 employees of the Seaford Plant served in the Armed Forces, most of which were males. The loss of these males resulted in the hiring of young women to replace the men. The women lacked industrial experience and were not accustomed to working shifts six days per week. Despite such difficulties, the Plant continued to increase production and operate effectively. Shown here are three such working girls in 1942.

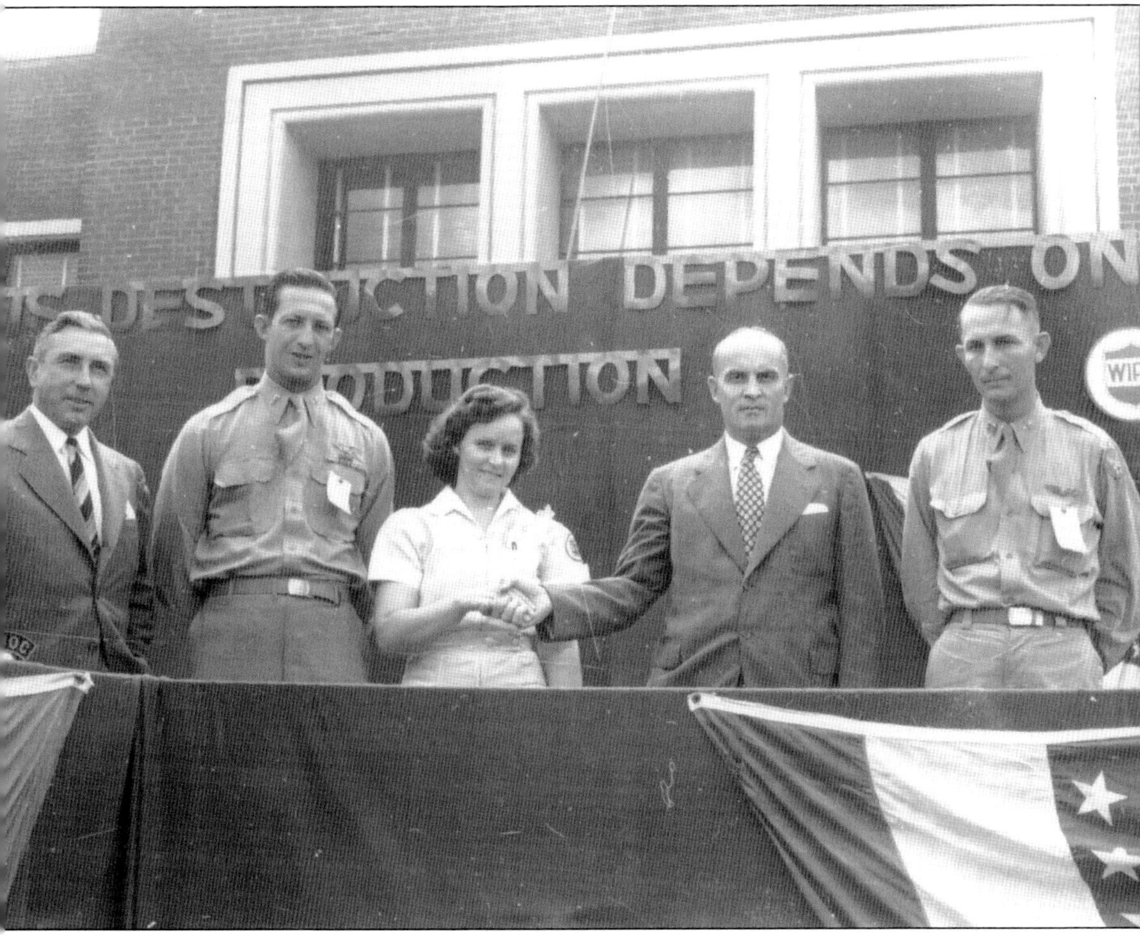

This is a photo of the inaugural ceremonies for Women in Production Service (WIPS) held on August 5, 1943. It was an organization set up to reward outstanding achievements in attendance, safety, production, war bond purchases, and civilian defense activities.

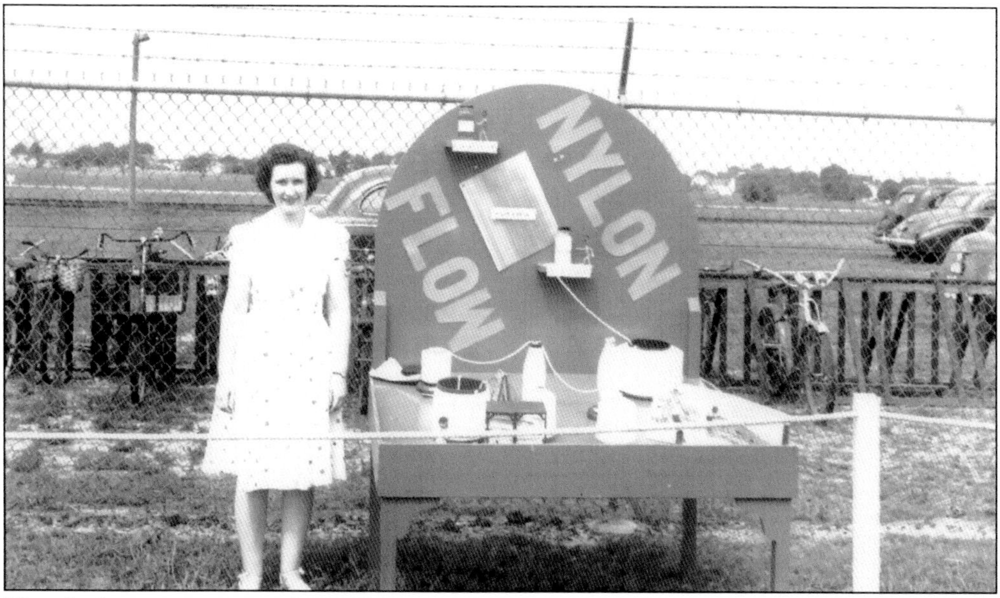

This display was set up at the WIPS ceremony. It most likely was to demonstrate the type of work that the women were accomplishing.

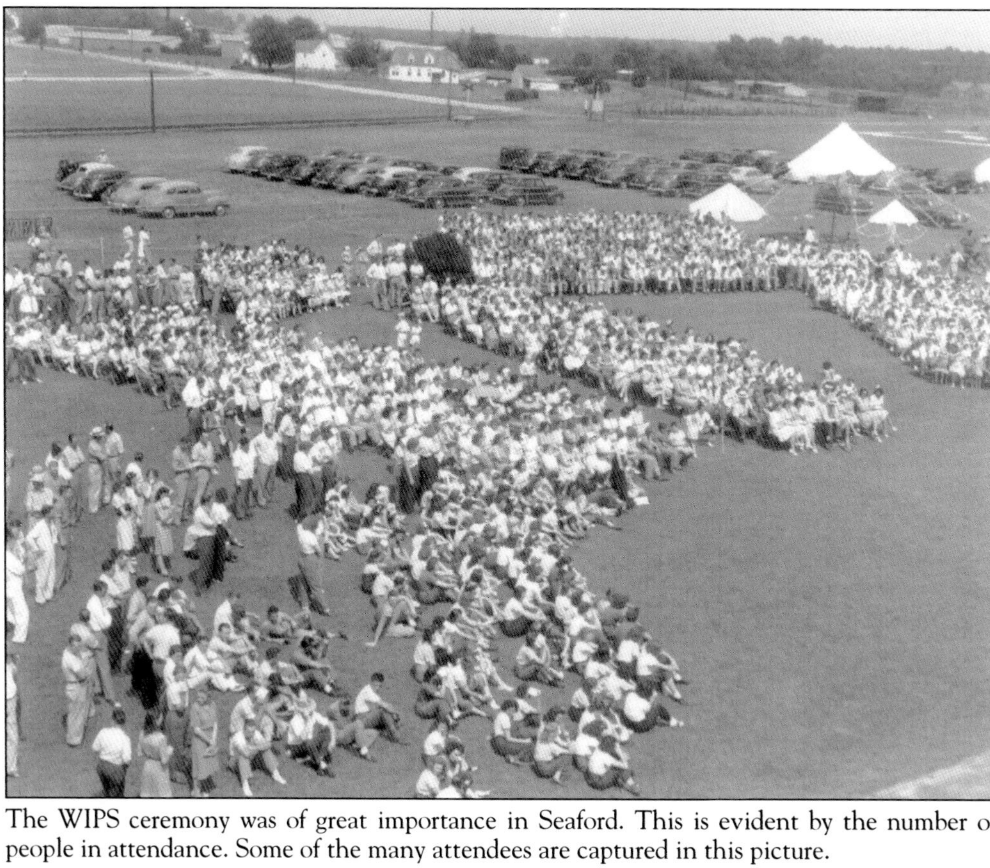

The WIPS ceremony was of great importance in Seaford. This is evident by the number of people in attendance. Some of the many attendees are captured in this picture.

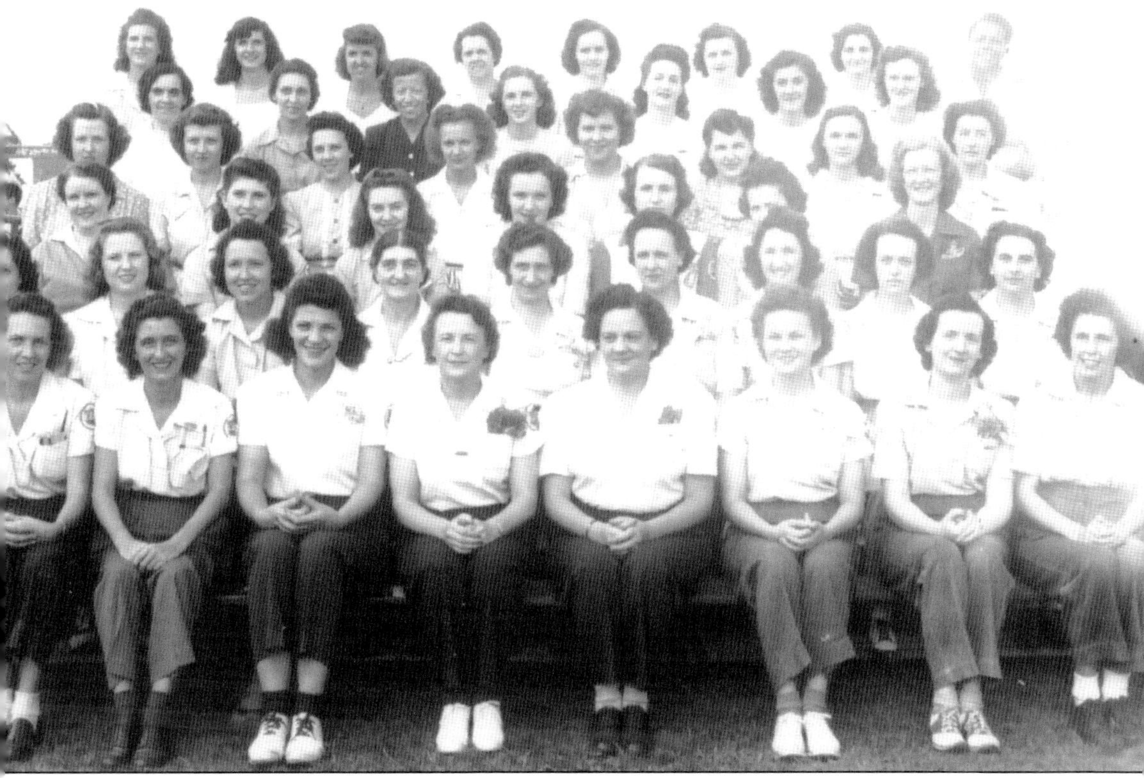

This picture, also taken at the WIPS ceremony, shows some of the many women that went to work while the men were defending the Country.

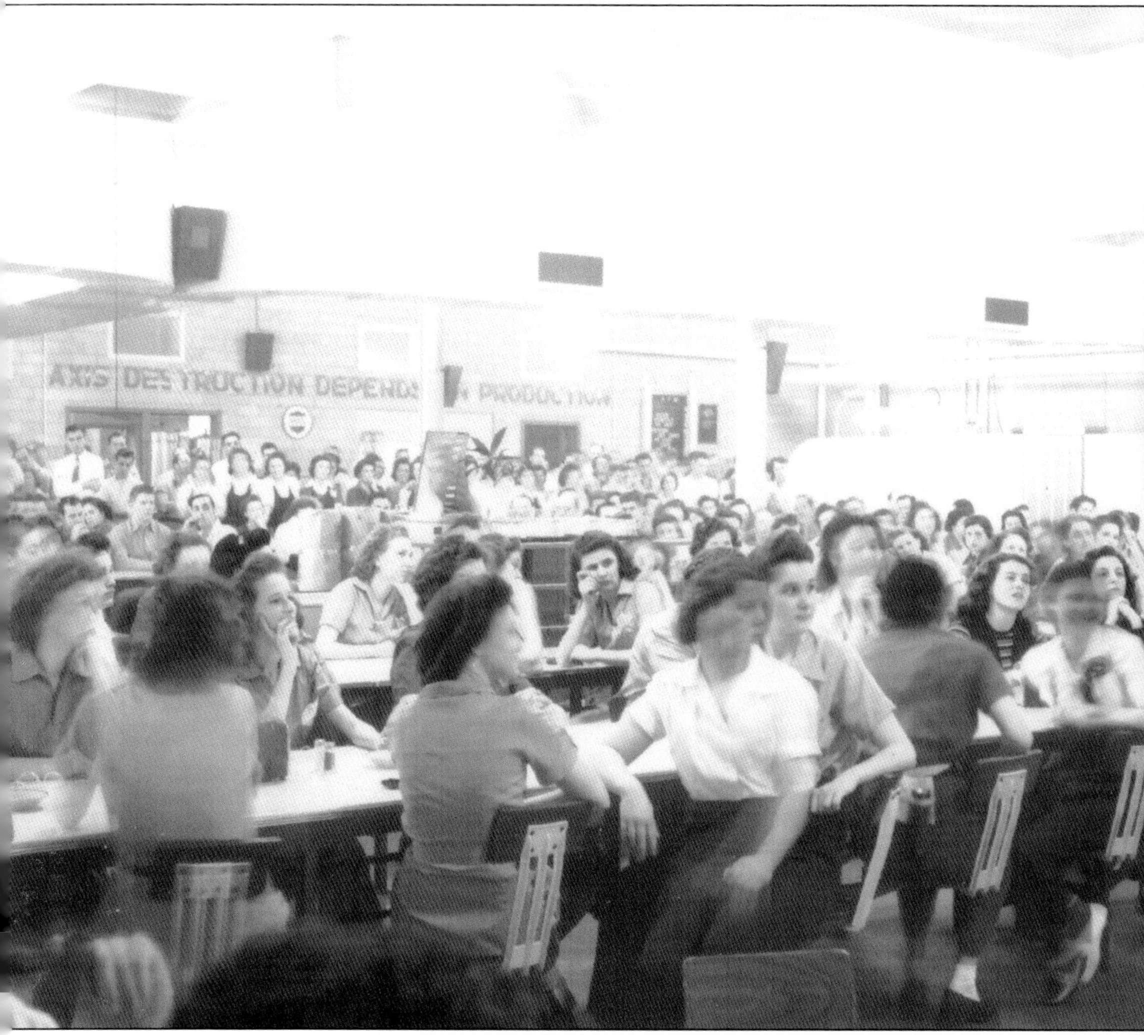

August 14, 1945, was VJ Day (Victory over Japan Day). The power house whistle in Seaford was blown when this was announced at 7:10 p.m., E.W.T. A War Production drive slogan contest had been held at DuPont. Harlan Cooper, a spinning operator, won the contest with the slogan "Axis Destruction Depends on Production." This slogan was used throughout the War and was proudly displayed at the VJ Day ceremonies held at DuPont on August 15, 1945 (on back wall). These pictures were taken at that ceremony.

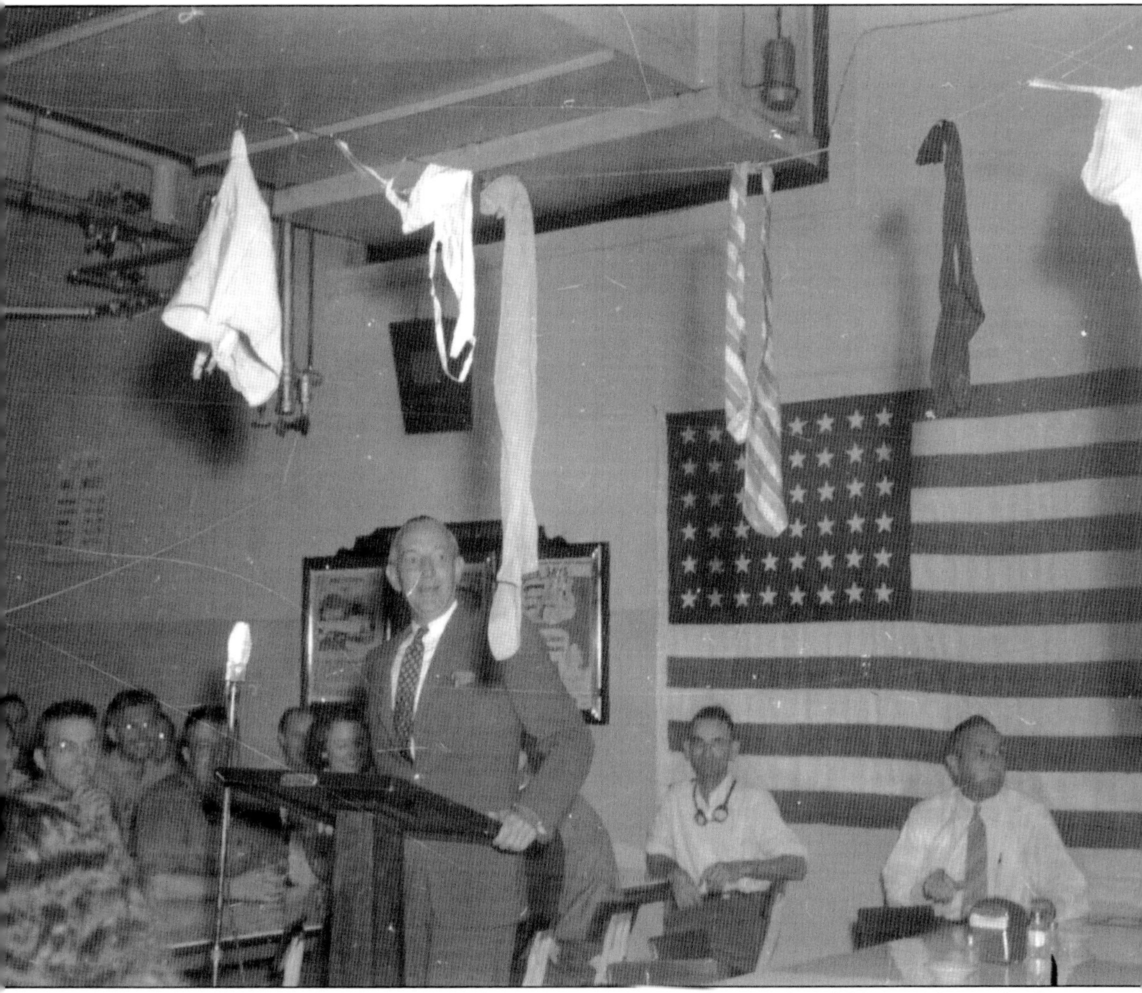

The ceremony took place in the Plant cafeteria at 9 a.m. One thousand and fifty employees had served in the armed forces, and 45 lost their lives fighting for the Country. Ceremonies were conducted by C.W. Setter, chairman of the War Production Drive Committee.

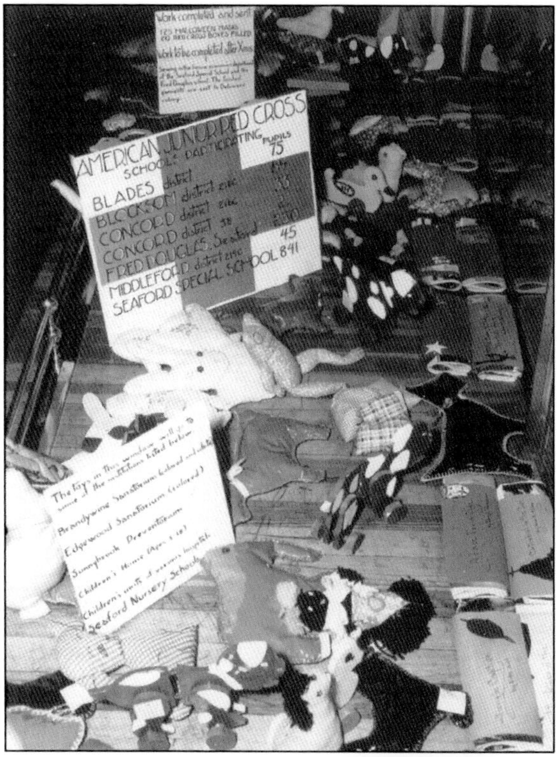

The Red Cross aided the community and the troops in many ways. Shown in these two pictures are displays that were set up by the Junior Red Cross in November of 1941. In 1944, the Red Cross drive in the Plant netted $8,058; in 1946, a drive netted $3,367.

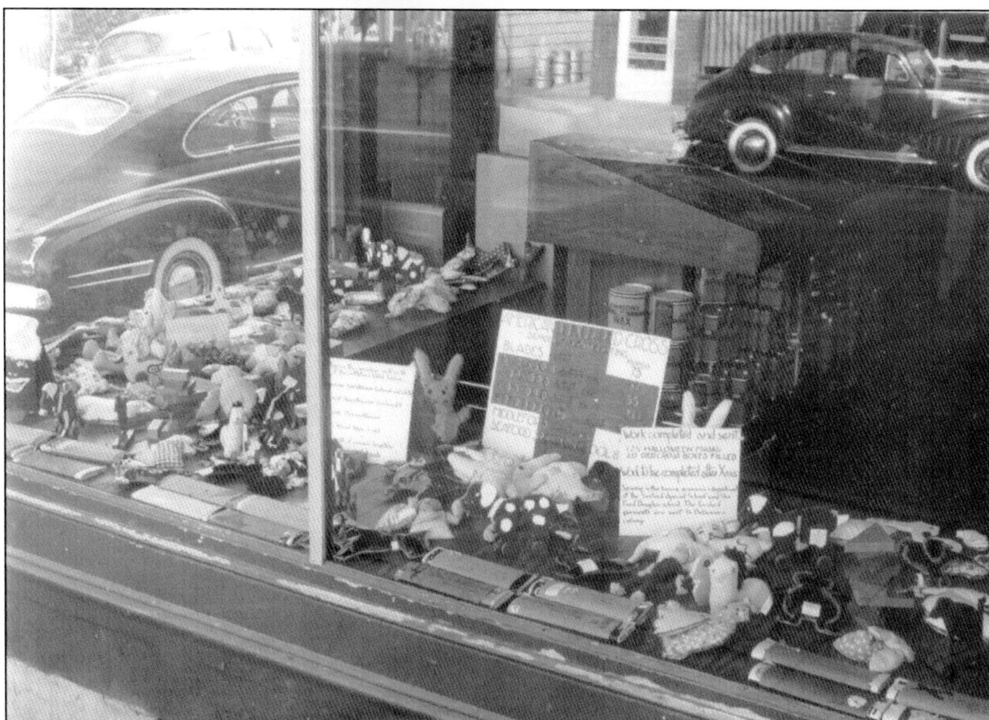

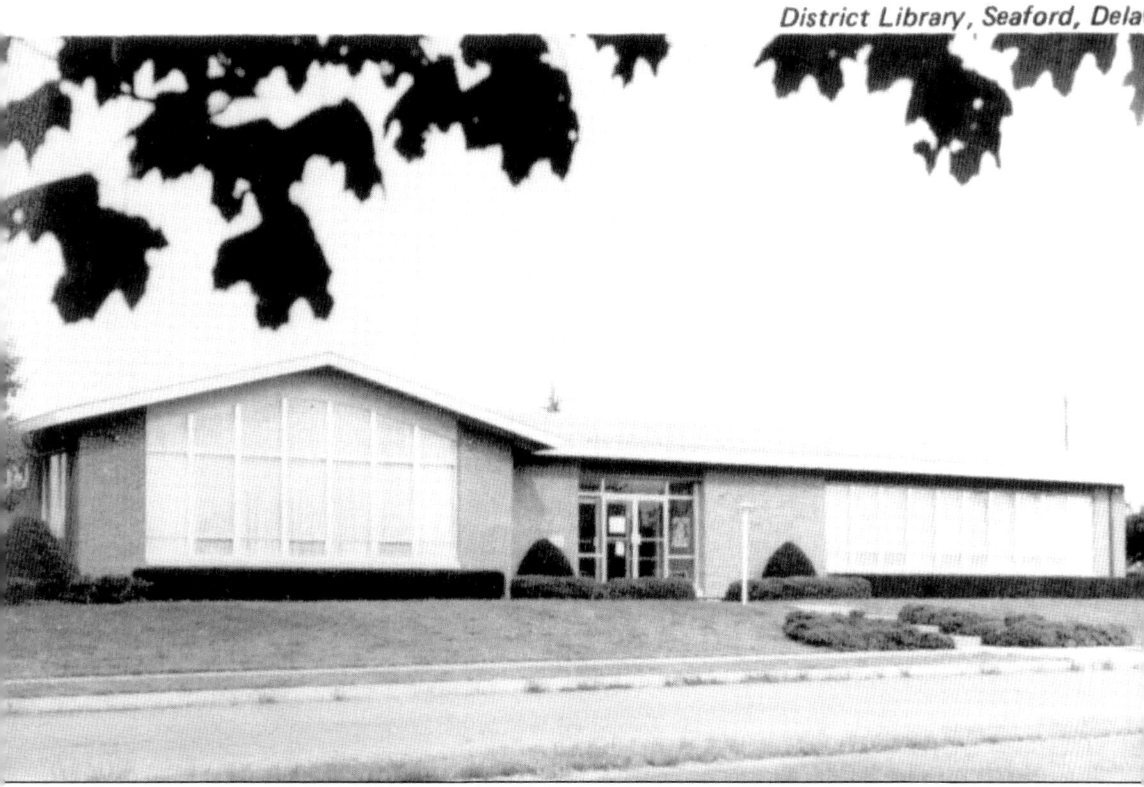

In 1902, the Acorn Club started the Public Library. In 1909, it was named the Seaford Public Library with 404 books in its selection. The library's first home was over what was known as Milligan's Store, and its second was the Henry White brick building on Pine Street. It is now in its current home, shown in the picture, on Porter Street.

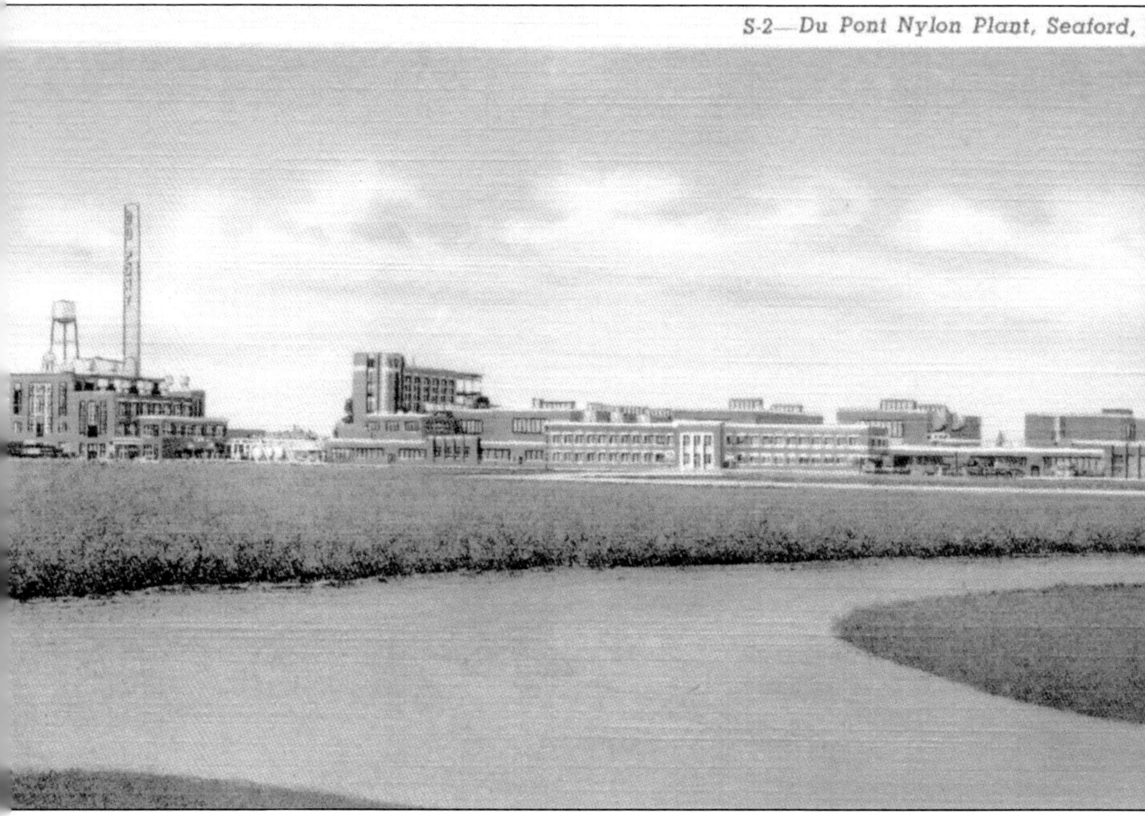

It is because of the decision by E.I. DuPont de Nemours & Co. Inc. to build the world's first nylon plant in Seaford, Delaware, shown in this photo, that the city acquired the name "Nylon Capital of the World."